MARK WAID | KWANZA OSAJYEFO | PHIL BRIONES

IGNITED

VOLUME TWO | FIGH

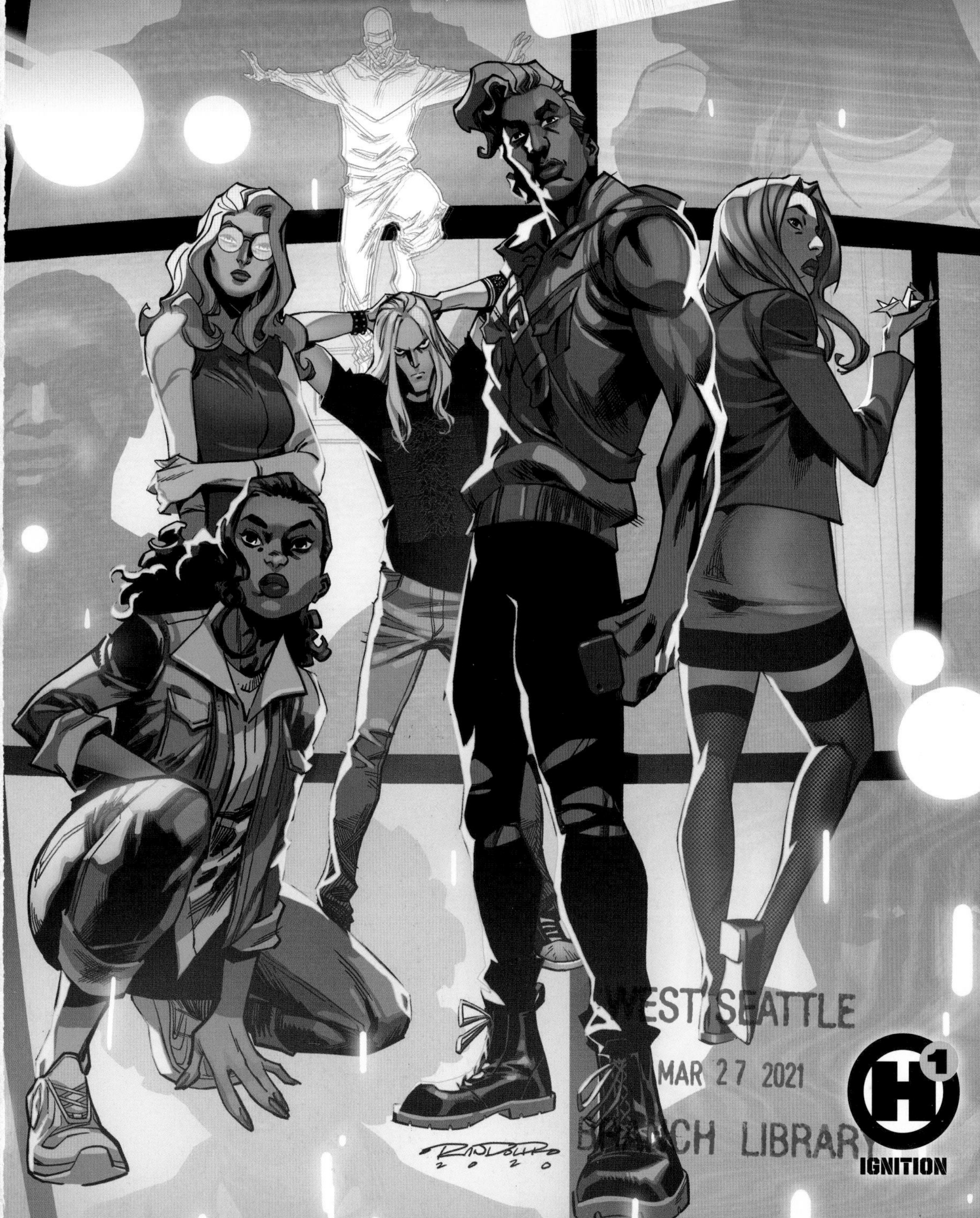
RANDOLPH
2020

IGNITION

IGNITED

WRITERS | **MARK WAID** (CH. 5-10) AND
KWANZA OSAJYEFO (CH. 5-8)
ARTIST | **PHIL BRIONES**
COLOR ARTISTS | **JEREMY LAWSON** (CH. 5-6),
ZAC ATKINSON (CH. 7-8) AND **JEROMY COX** (CH. 9-10)
LETTERS | **A LARGER WORLD STUDIOS**
COVER | **MIKE NORTON** AND **LEE LOUGHRIDGE**

TITLE PAGE ILLUSTRATION | **KHARY RANDOLPH** AND
MOHAMMED AGBADI
PAGES 2-3 ILLUSTRATION | **JOHN CASSADAY** AND **PAUL MOUNTS**
PAGE 4 ILLUSTRATION | **YANICK PAQUETTE** AND
LEONARDO PACIAROTTI

SHARED UNIVERSE BASED ON CONCEPTS CREATED WITH
KWANZA OSAJYEFO, CARLA SPEED MCNEIL, YANICK PAQUETTE

PUBLISHER | **MARK WAID**
CHIEF CREATIVE OFFICER | **JOHN CASSADAY**
SENIOR EDITOR | **ROB LEVIN**
ASSISTANT EDITOR | **AMANDA LUCIDO**
LOGO DESIGN | **RIAN HUGHES**
SENIOR ART DIRECTOR | **JERRY FRISSEN**
JUNIOR DESIGNER | **RYAN LEWIS**

CEO | **FABRICE GIGER**
COO | **ALEX DONOGHUE**
CFO | **GUILLAUME NOUGARET**
SALES MANAGER | **PEDRO HERNANDEZ**
SALES REPRESENTATIVE | **HARLEY SALBACKA**
DIRECTOR, LICENSING | **EDMOND LEE**
CTO | **BRUNO BARBERI**
RIGHTS AND LICENSING | **LICENSING@HUMANOIDS.COM**
PRESS AND SOCIAL MEDIA | **PR@HUMANOIDS.COM**

Library of Congress Control Number: 2019909800

This volume collects IGNITED issues 5-10.

H1 is an imprint of Humanoids, Inc.

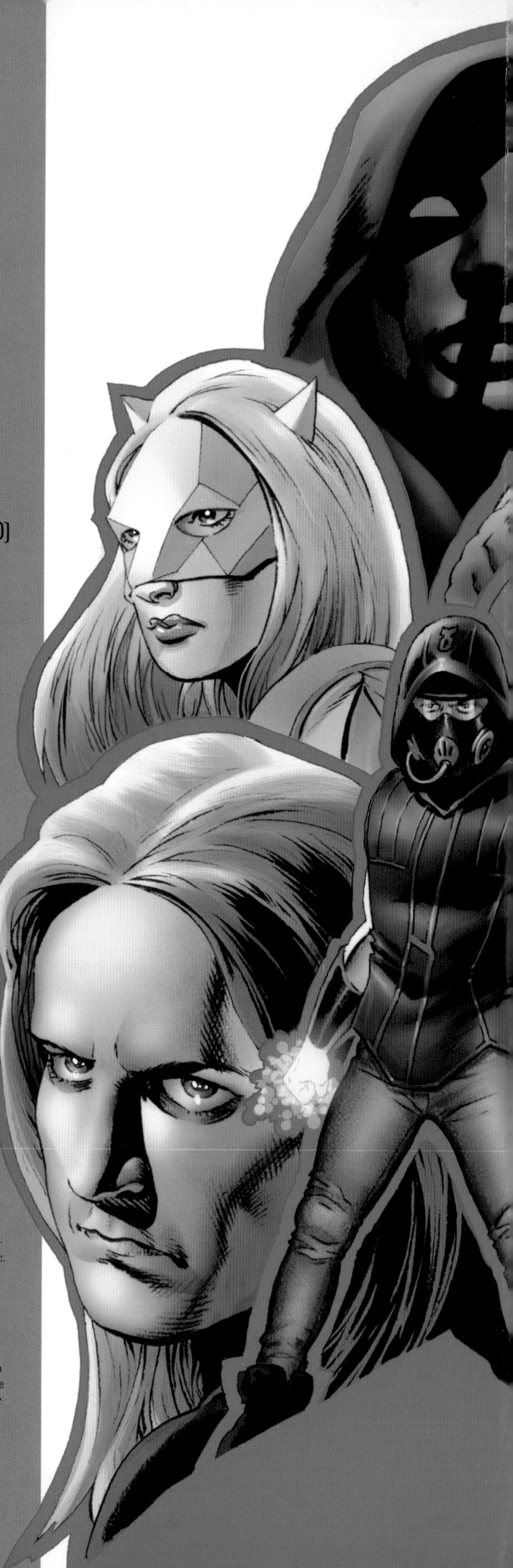

HUMANOIDS

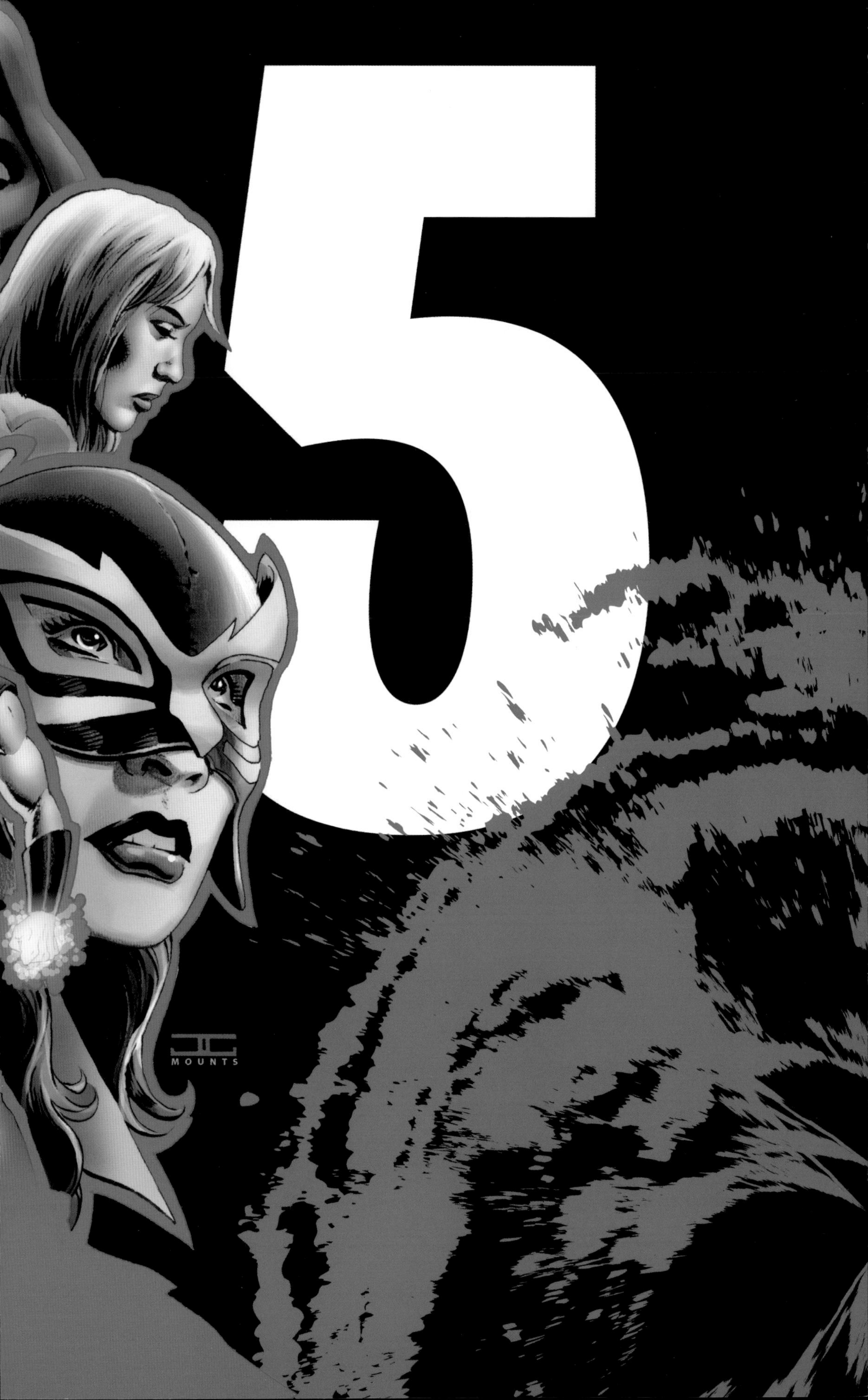
5
MOUNTS

OUR WORLD'S DNA IS CHANGING.

UNPRECEDENTED TECTONIC SHIFTS.
SPONTANEOUS, RADICAL CHANGES IN THE ECO SYSTEMS.

IN MOMENTS OF UNIMAGINABLE AGITATION,
THE HUMAN RACE ACTS OUT IN UNIMAGINABLE WAYS.

AND THOSE ARE JUST INDIVIDUAL SPECIES. NOW EARTH ITSELF IS PUSHING BACK.

CERTAIN PEOPLE WORLDWIDE ARE... CHANGING. **TRANSFORMING**.

IGNITING WITH **POWER**.

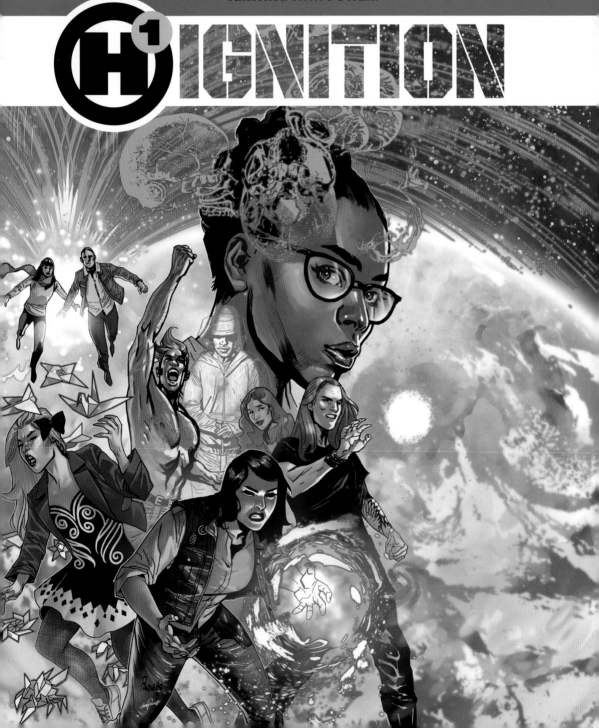

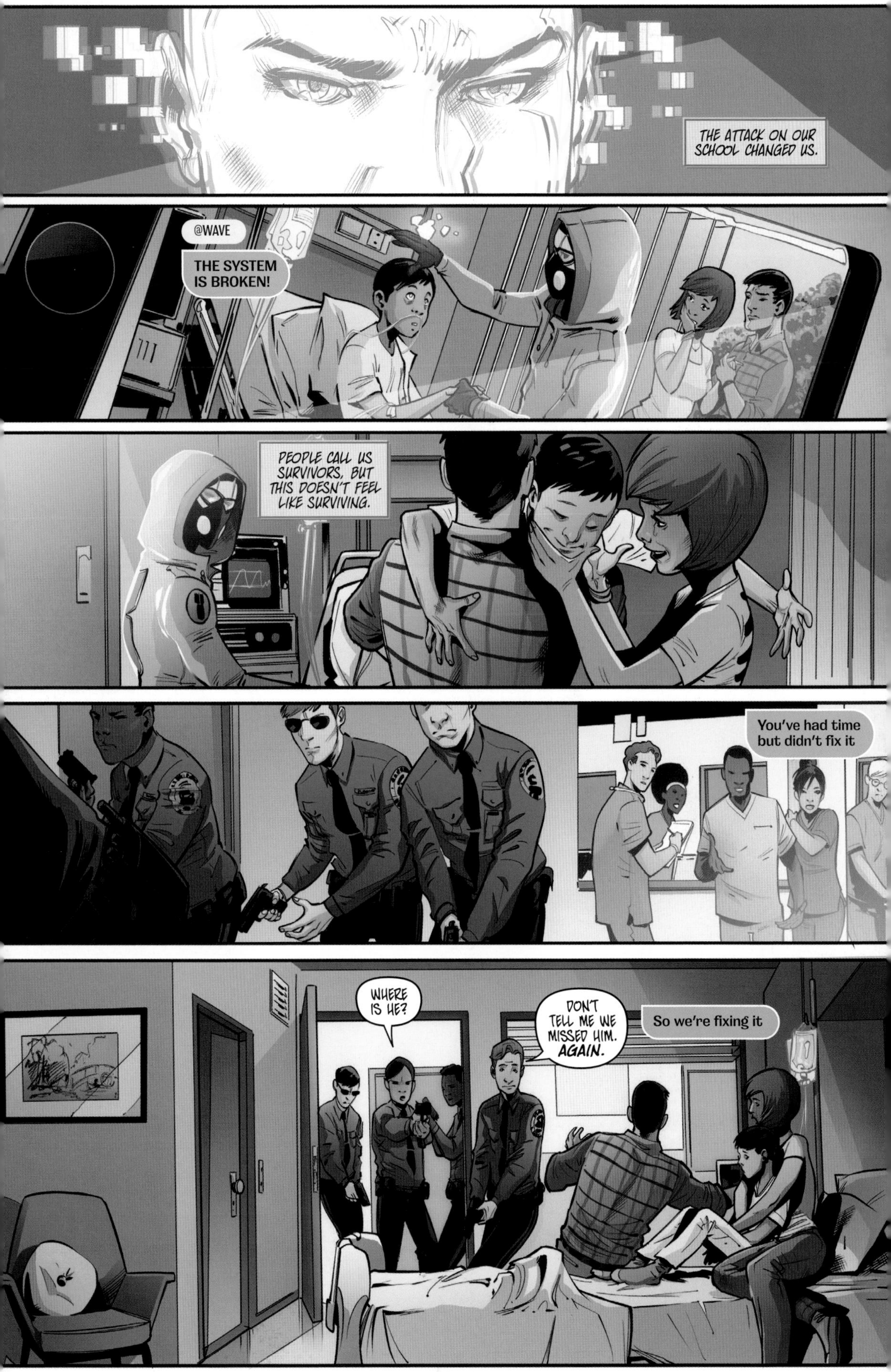
THE ATTACK ON OUR SCHOOL CHANGED US.
@WAVE
THE SYSTEM IS BROKEN!
PEOPLE CALL US SURVIVORS, BUT THIS DOESN'T FEEL LIKE SURVIVING.
You've had time but didn't fix it
WHERE IS HE?
DON'T TELL ME WE MISSED HIM. AGAIN.
So we're fixing it

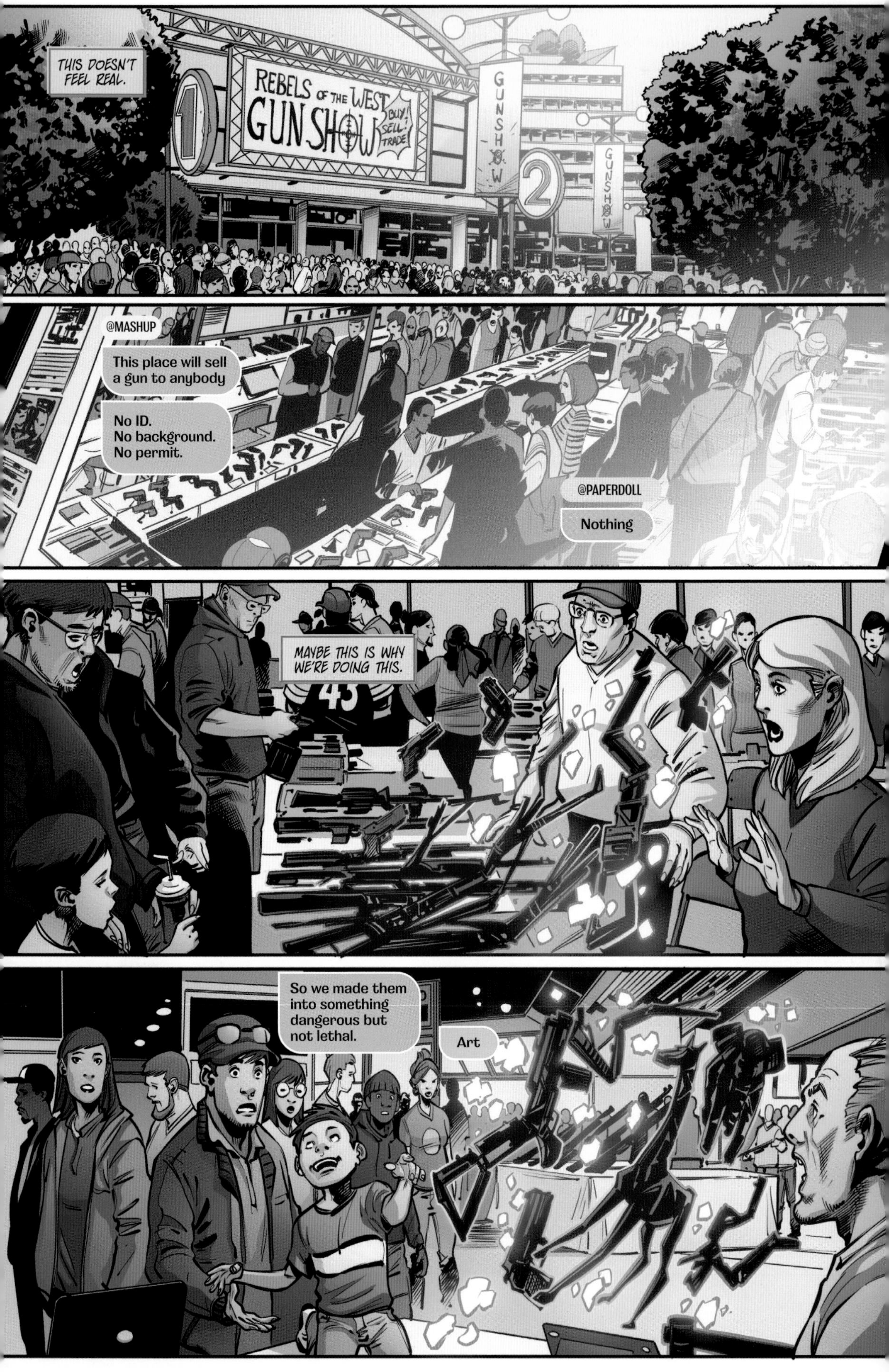
THIS DOESN'T FEEL REAL.
REBELS OF THE WEST GUN SHOW
BUY! SELL! TRADE!
1
GUNSHOW
2
GUNSHOW
@MASHUP
This place will sell a gun to anybody
No ID.
No background.
No permit.
@PAPERDOLL
Nothing
MAYBE THIS IS WHY WE'RE DOING THIS.
So we made them into something dangerous but not lethal.
Art

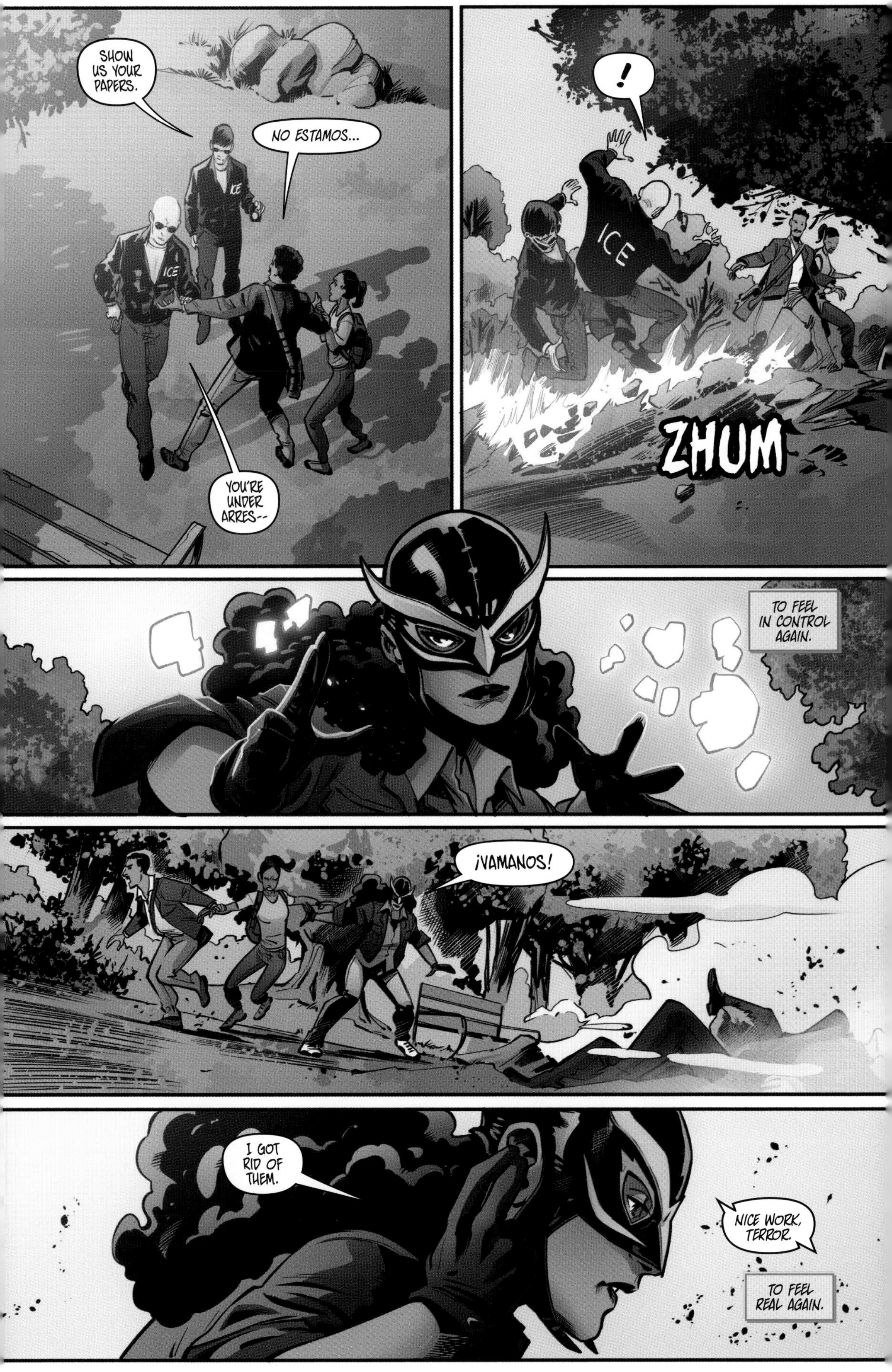
SHOW US YOUR PAPERS.
NO ESTAMOS...
YOU'RE UNDER ARRES--
!
ZHUM
TO FEEL IN CONTROL AGAIN.
¡VAMANOS!
I GOT RID OF THEM.
NICE WORK, TERROR.
TO FEEL REAL AGAIN.

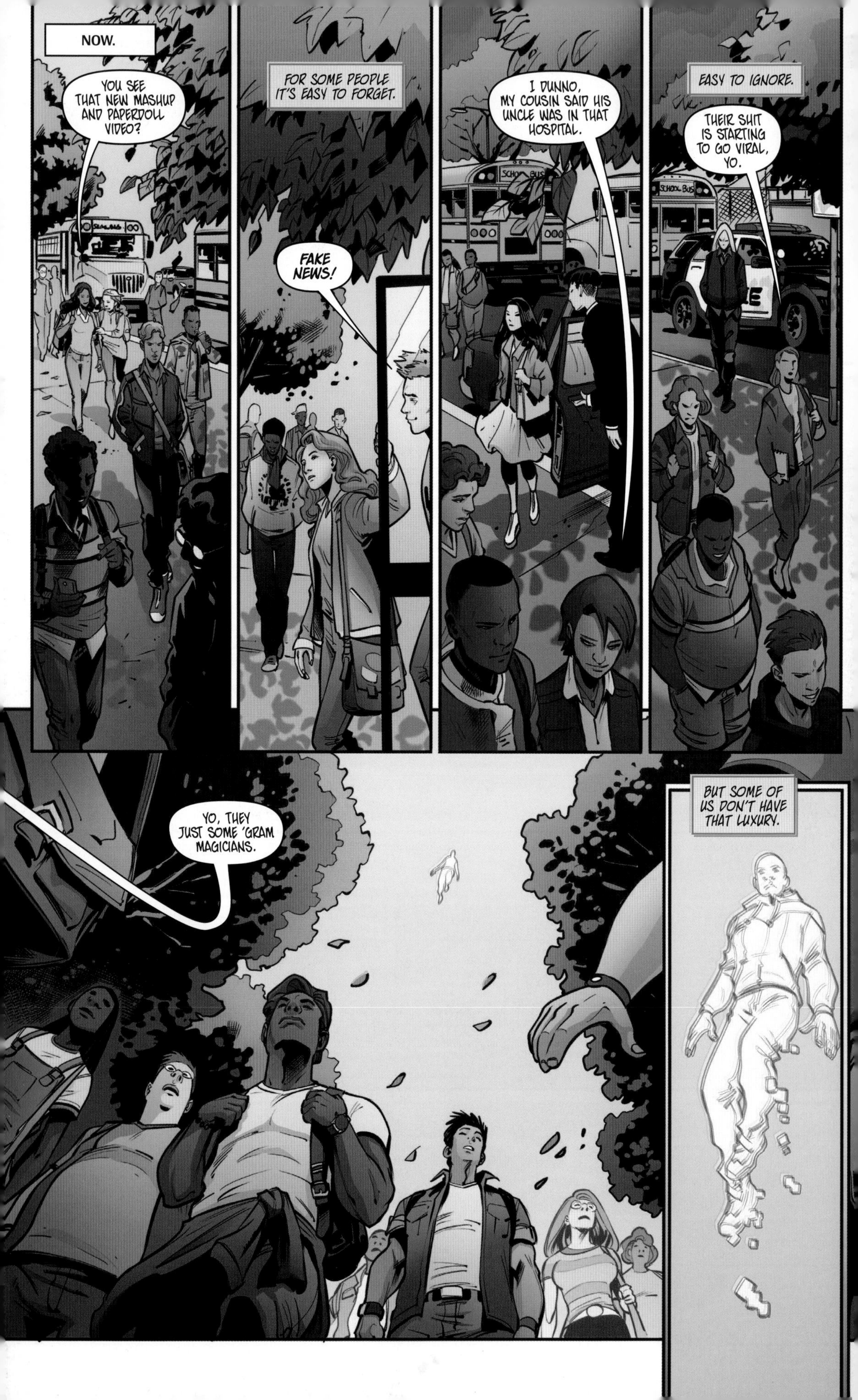
NOW.
YOU SEE THAT NEW MASHUP AND PAPERDOLL VIDEO?
FOR SOME PEOPLE IT'S EASY TO FORGET.
FAKE NEWS!
I DUNNO, MY COUSIN SAID HIS UNCLE WAS IN THAT HOSPITAL.
EASY TO IGNORE.
THEIR SHIT IS STARTING TO GO VIRAL, YO.
YO, THEY JUST SOME 'GRAM MAGICIANS.
BUT SOME OF US DON'T HAVE THAT LUXURY.

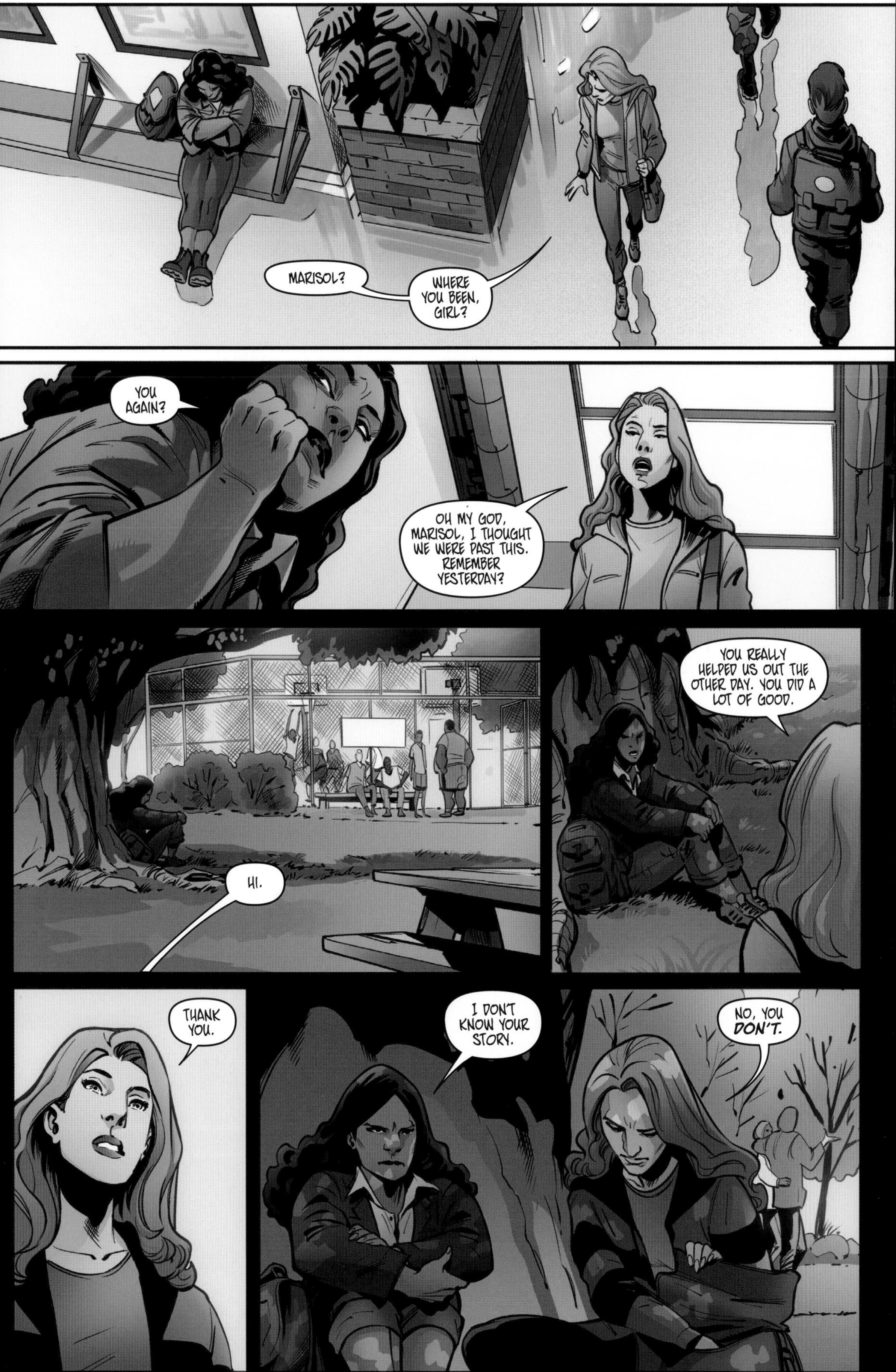
MARISOL?
WHERE YOU BEEN, GIRL?
YOU AGAIN?
OH MY GOD, MARISOL, I THOUGHT WE WERE PAST THIS. REMEMBER YESTERDAY?
HI.
YOU REALLY HELPED US OUT THE OTHER DAY. YOU DID A LOT OF GOOD.
THANK YOU.
I DON'T KNOW YOUR STORY.
NO, YOU **DON'T.**

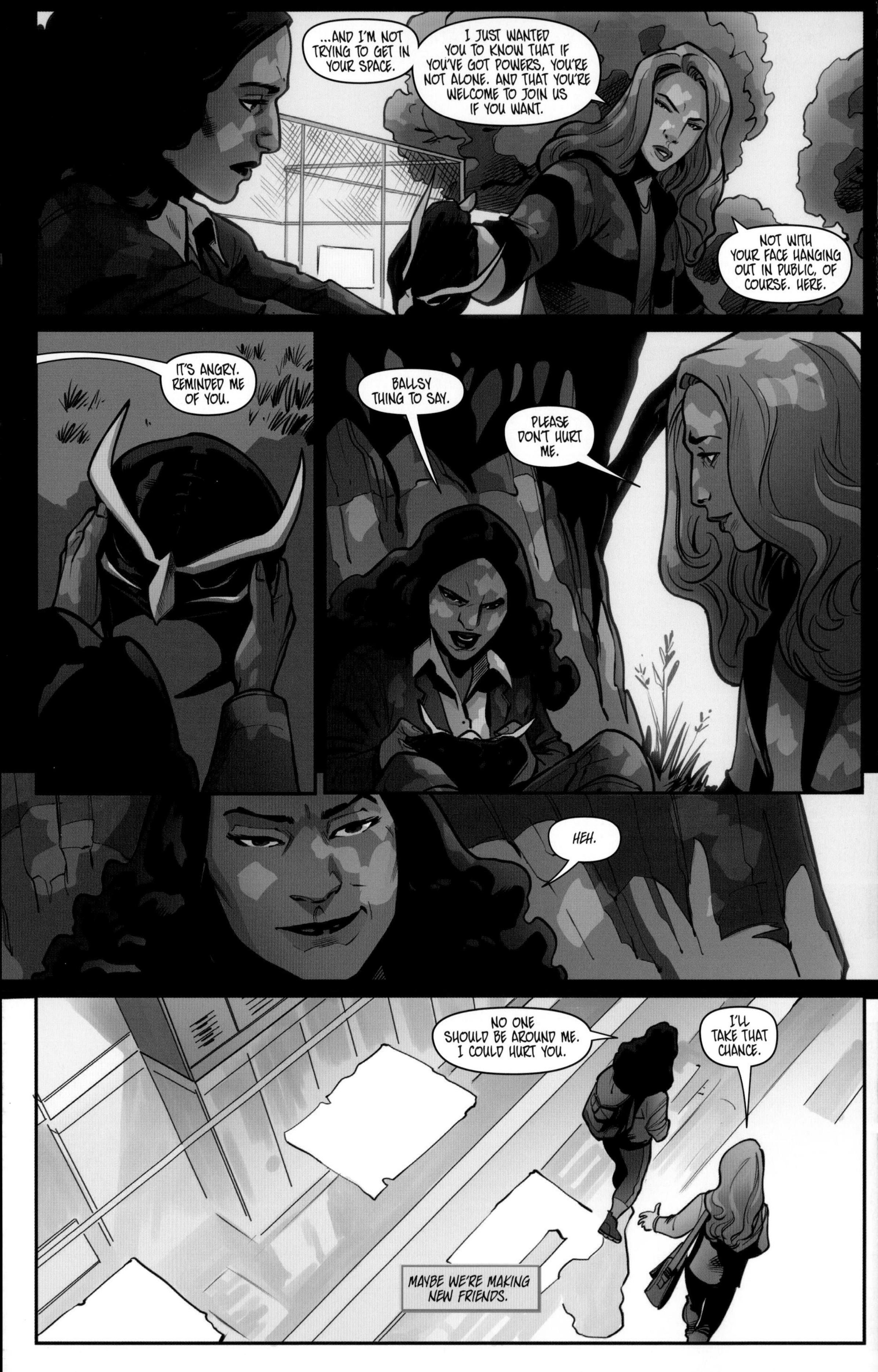
...AND I'M NOT TRYING TO GET IN YOUR SPACE.
I JUST WANTED YOU TO KNOW THAT IF YOU'VE GOT POWERS, YOU'RE NOT ALONE. AND THAT YOU'RE WELCOME TO JOIN US IF YOU WANT.
NOT WITH YOUR FACE HANGING OUT IN PUBLIC, OF COURSE. HERE.
IT'S ANGRY. REMINDED ME OF YOU.
BALLSY THING TO SAY.
PLEASE DON'T HURT ME.
HEH.
NO ONE SHOULD BE AROUND ME. I COULD HURT YOU.
I'LL TAKE THAT CHANCE.
MAYBE WE'RE MAKING NEW FRIENDS.

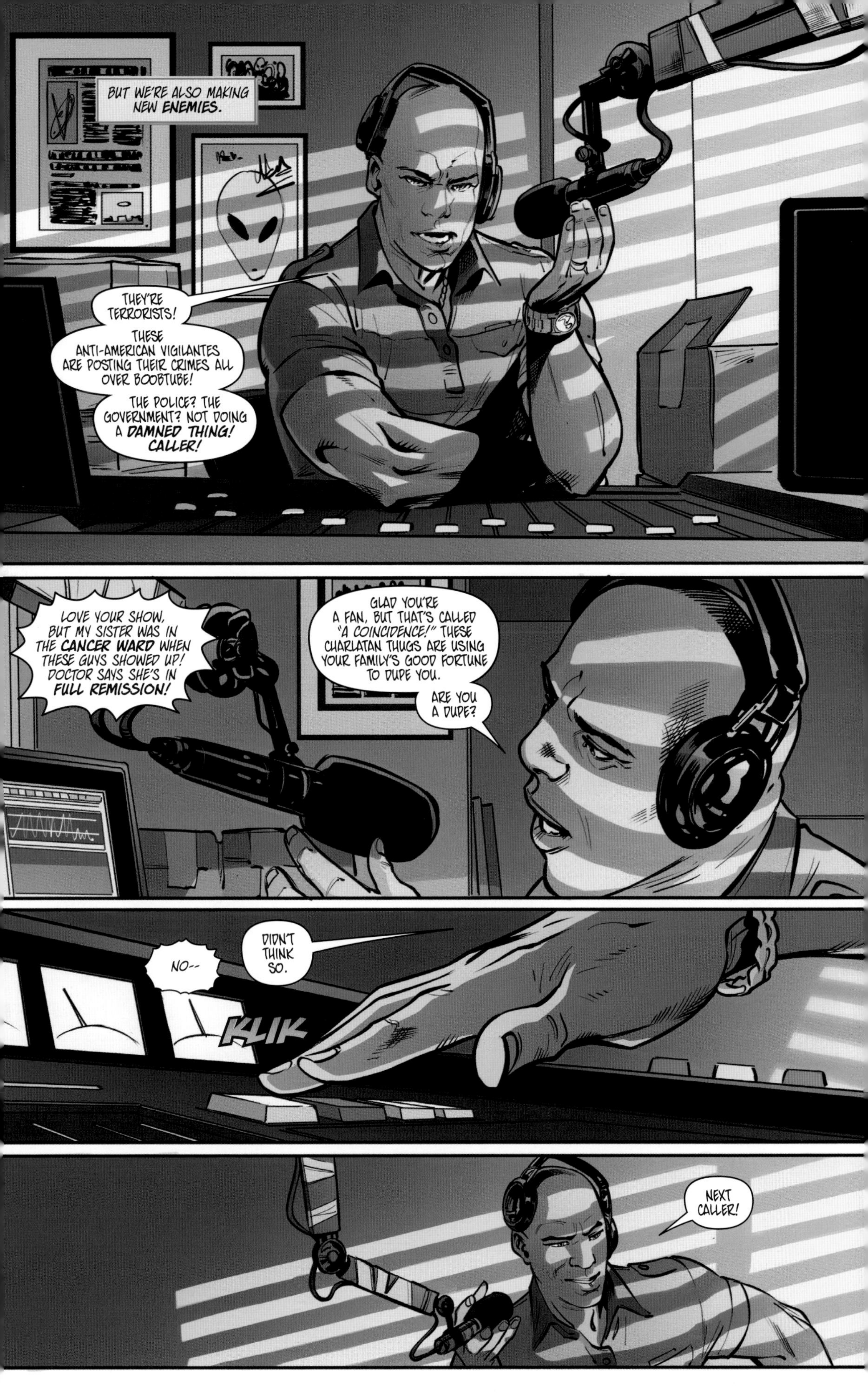
BUT WE'RE ALSO MAKING NEW ENEMIES.
THEY'RE TERRORISTS!
THESE ANTI-AMERICAN VIGILANTES ARE POSTING THEIR CRIMES ALL OVER BOOBTUBE!
THE POLICE? THE GOVERNMENT? NOT DOING A DAMNED THING! CALLER!
LOVE YOUR SHOW, BUT MY SISTER WAS IN THE CANCER WARD WHEN THESE GUYS SHOWED UP! DOCTOR SAYS SHE'S IN FULL REMISSION!
GLAD YOU'RE A FAN, BUT THAT'S CALLED "A COINCIDENCE!" THESE CHARLATAN THUGS ARE USING YOUR FAMILY'S GOOD FORTUNE TO DUPE YOU.
ARE YOU A DUPE?
NO--
DIDN'T THINK SO.
KLIK
NEXT CALLER!

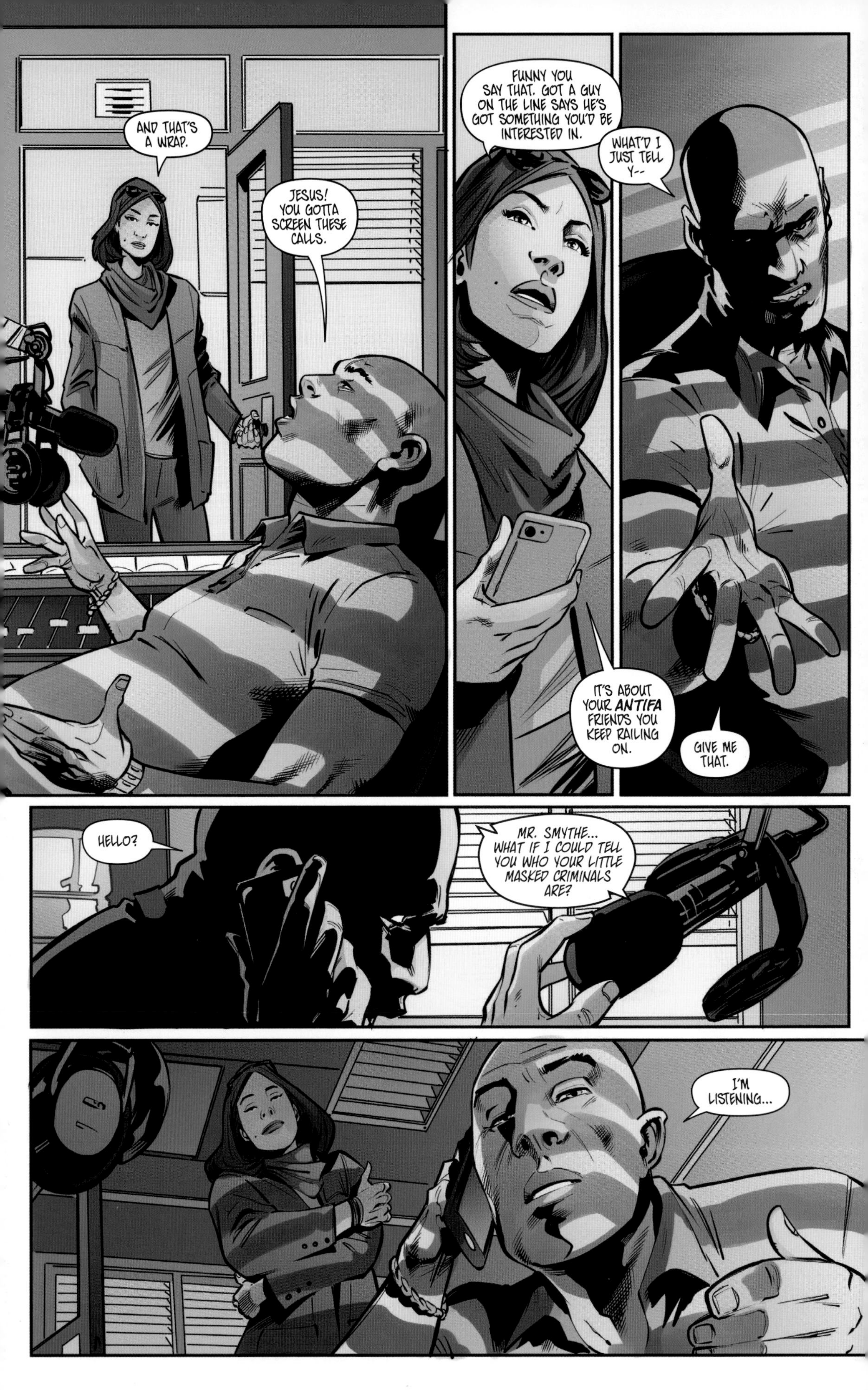
AND THAT'S A WRAP.
JESUS! YOU GOTTA SCREEN THESE CALLS.
FUNNY YOU SAY THAT. GOT A GUY ON THE LINE SAYS HE'S GOT SOMETHING YOU'D BE INTERESTED IN.
WHAT'D I JUST TELL Y--
IT'S ABOUT YOUR ANTIFA FRIENDS YOU KEEP RAILING ON.
GIVE ME THAT.
HELLO?
MR. SMYTHE... WHAT IF I COULD TELL YOU WHO YOUR LITTLE MASKED CRIMINALS ARE?
I'M LISTENING...

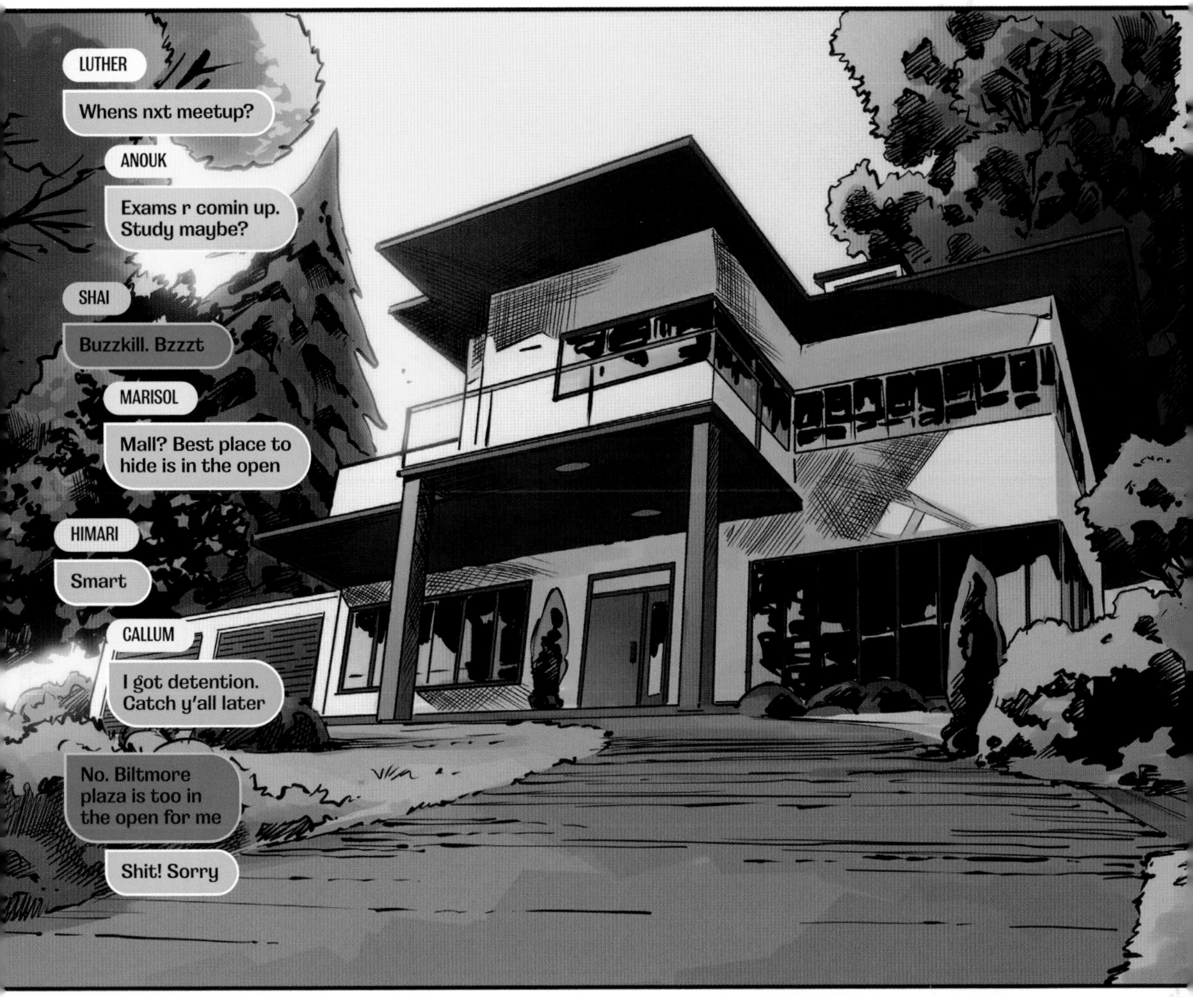
LUTHER
Whens nxt meetup?
ANOUK
Exams r comin up. Study maybe?
SHAI
Buzzkill. Bzzzt
MARISOL
Mall? Best place to hide is in the open
HIMARI
Smart
CALLUM
I got detention. Catch y'all later
No. Biltmore plaza is too in the open for me
Shit! Sorry

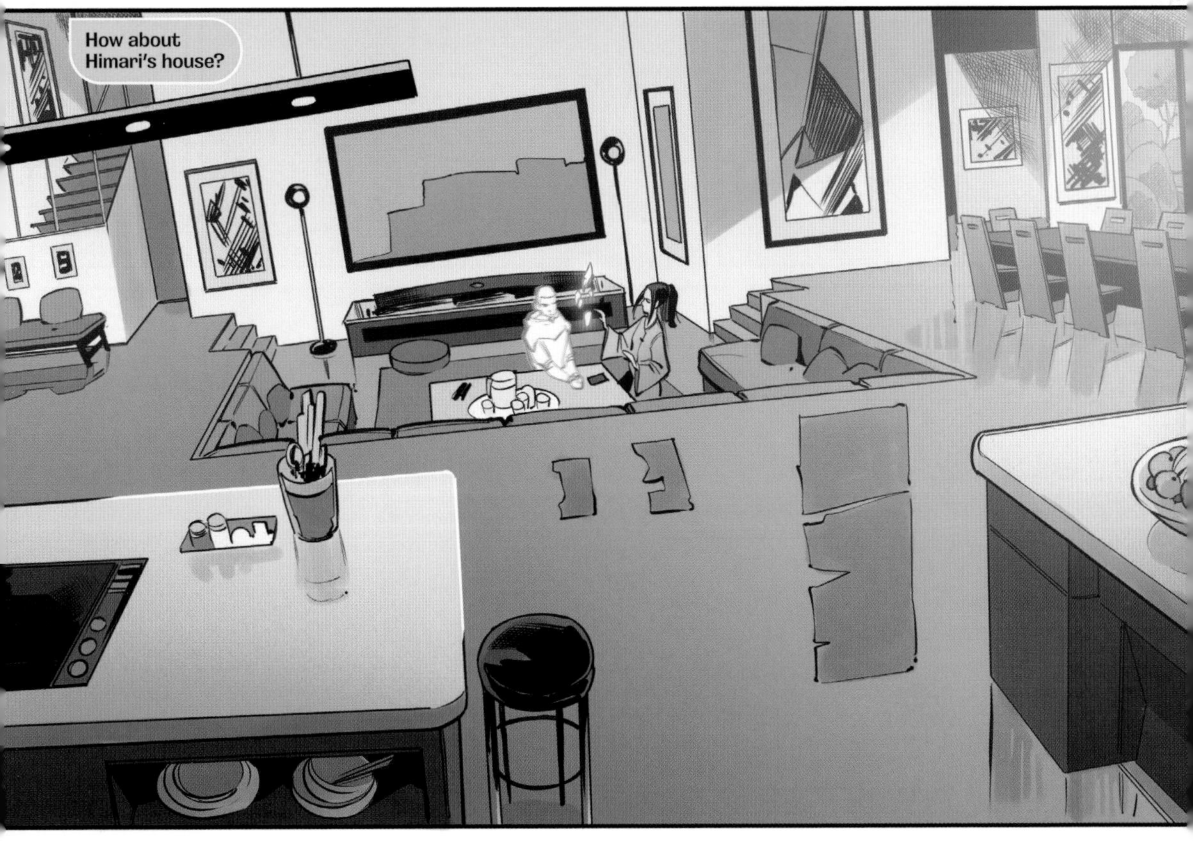
How about Himari's house?

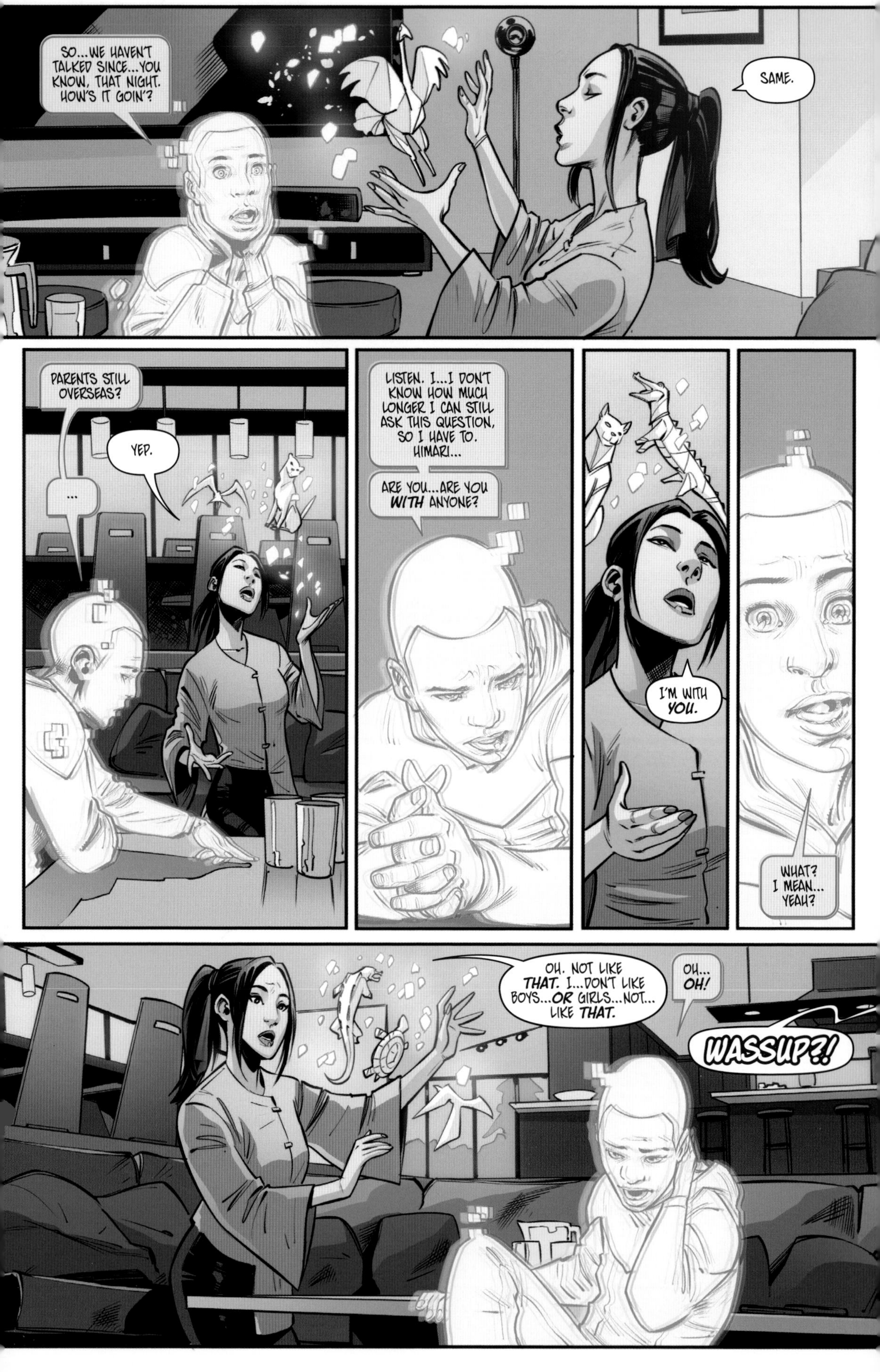
SO...WE HAVEN'T TALKED SINCE...YOU KNOW, THAT NIGHT. HOW'S IT GOIN'?
SAME.
PARENTS STILL OVERSEAS?
YEP.
...
LISTEN. I...I DON'T KNOW HOW MUCH LONGER I CAN STILL ASK THIS QUESTION, SO I HAVE TO. HIMARI...
ARE YOU...ARE YOU WITH ANYONE?
I'M WITH YOU.
WHAT? I MEAN... YEAH?
OH. NOT LIKE THAT. I...DON'T LIKE BOYS...OR GIRLS...NOT... LIKE THAT.
OH... OH!
WASSUP?!

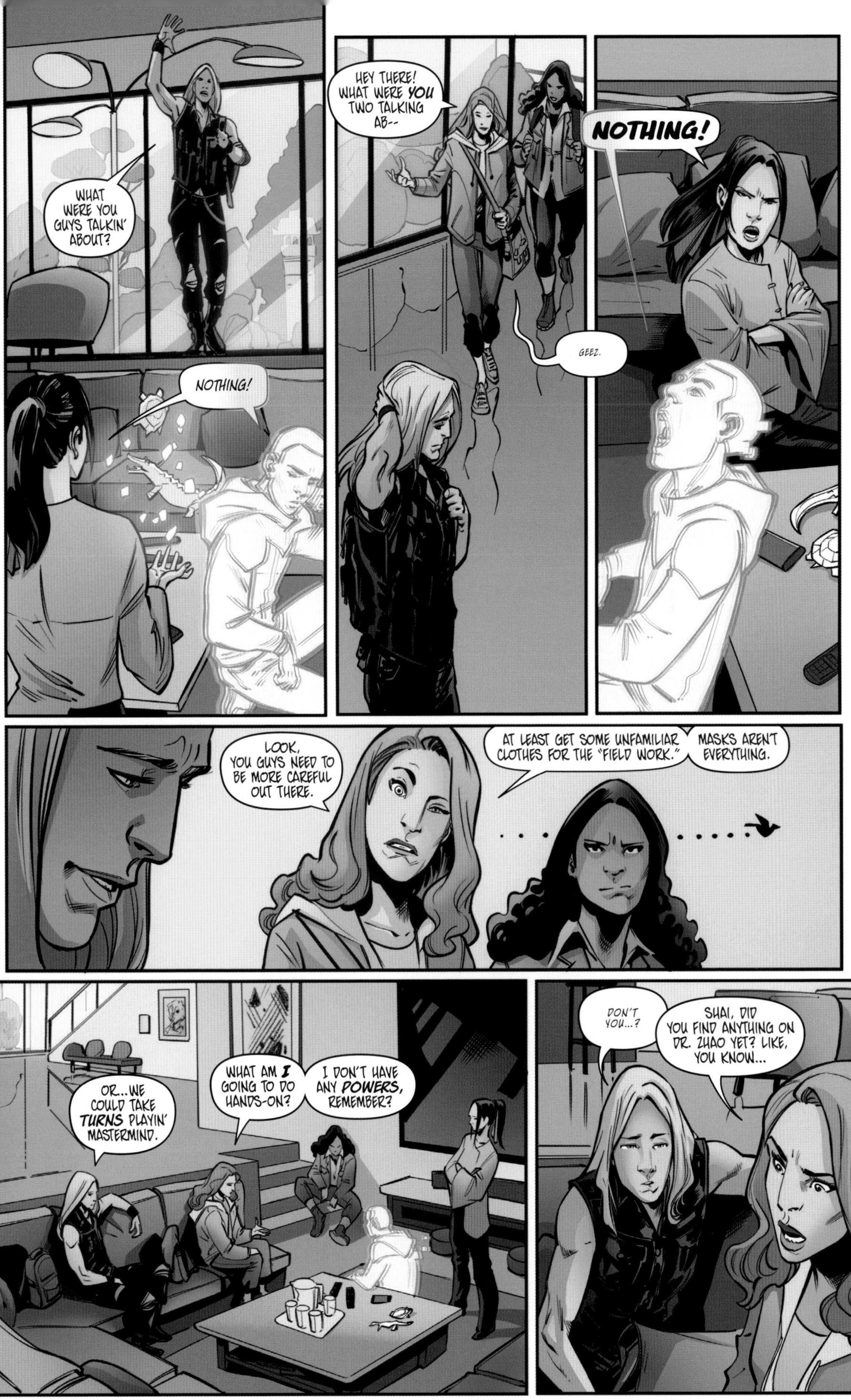
WHAT WERE YOU GUYS TALKIN' ABOUT?
HEY THERE! WHAT WERE YOU TWO TALKING AB--
NOTHING!
NOTHING!
GEEZ.
LOOK, YOU GUYS NEED TO BE MORE CAREFUL OUT THERE.
AT LEAST GET SOME UNFAMILIAR CLOTHES FOR THE "FIELD WORK."
MASKS AREN'T EVERYTHING.
OR...WE COULD TAKE TURNS PLAYIN' MASTERMIND.
WHAT AM I GOING TO DO HANDS-ON?
I DON'T HAVE ANY POWERS, REMEMBER?
DON'T YOU...?
SHAI, DID YOU FIND ANYTHING ON DR. ZHAO YET? LIKE, YOU KNOW...

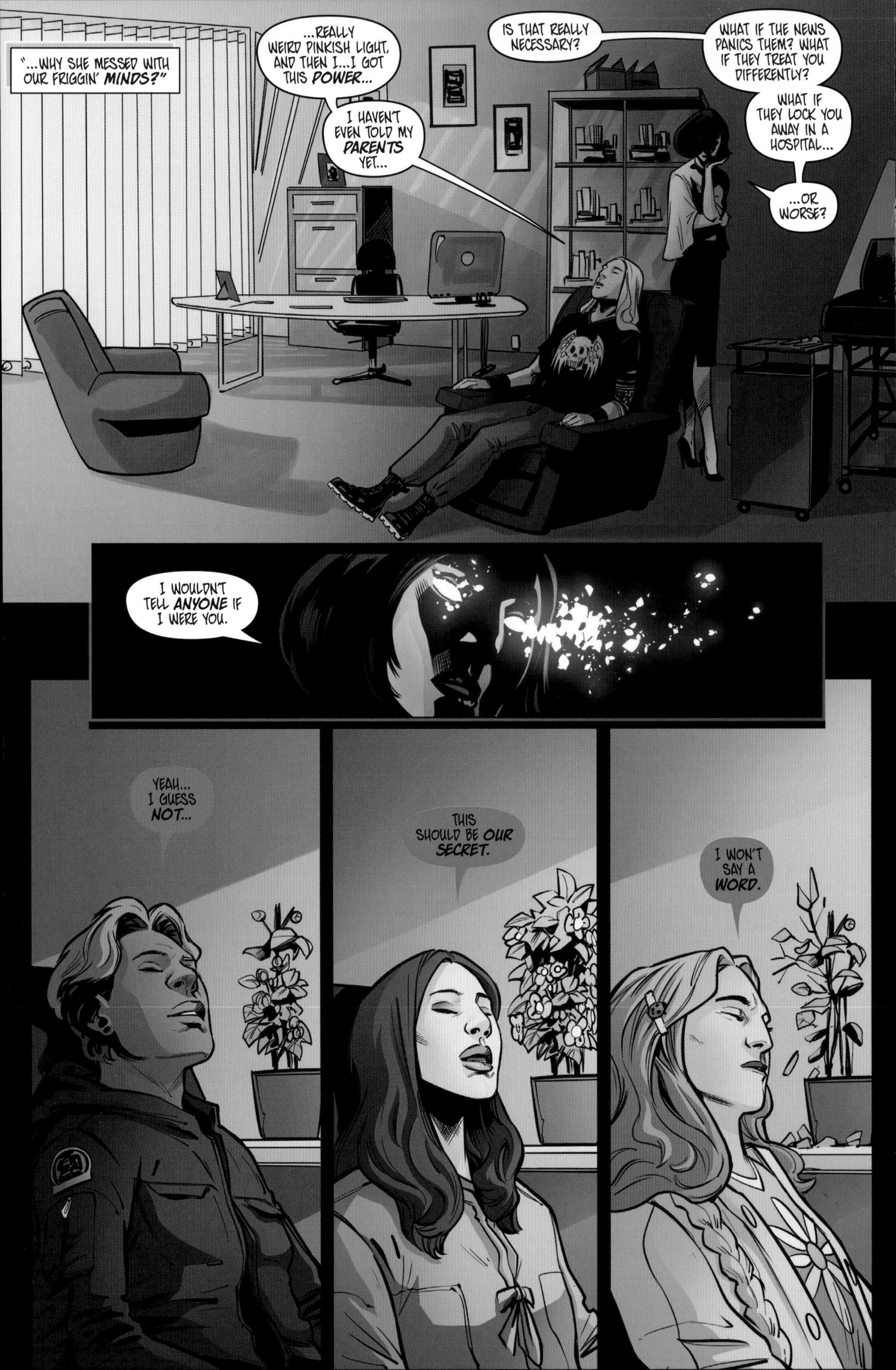
"...WHY SHE MESSED WITH OUR FRIGGIN' MINDS?"
...REALLY WEIRD PINKISH LIGHT, AND THEN I...I GOT THIS POWER...
I HAVEN'T EVEN TOLD MY PARENTS YET...
IS THAT REALLY NECESSARY?
WHAT IF THE NEWS PANICS THEM? WHAT IF THEY TREAT YOU DIFFERENTLY?
WHAT IF THEY LOCK YOU AWAY IN A HOSPITAL...
...OR WORSE?
I WOULDN'T TELL ANYONE IF I WERE YOU.
YEAH... I GUESS NOT...
THIS SHOULD BE OUR SECRET.
I WON'T SAY A WORD.

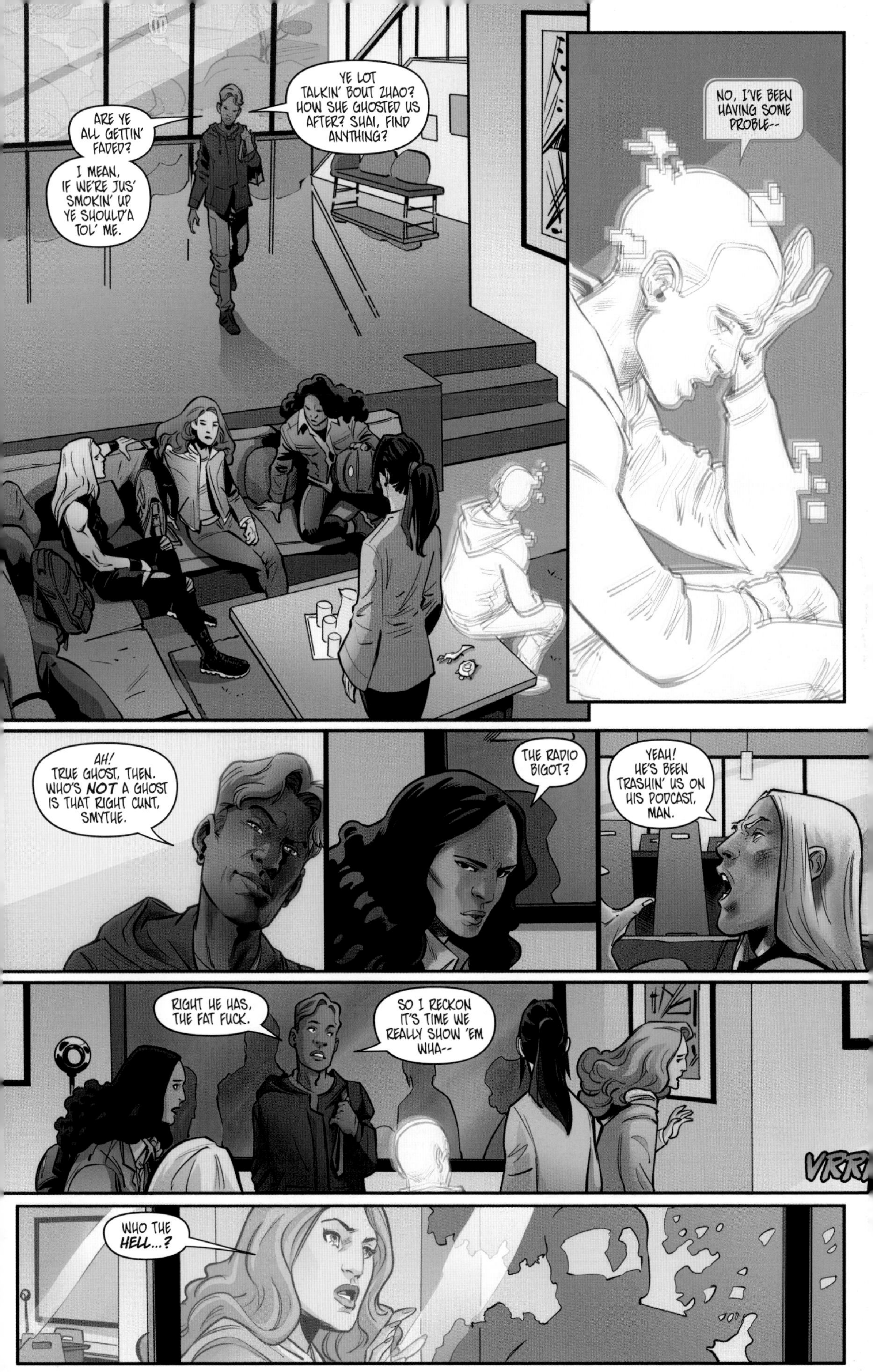
ARE YE ALL GETTIN' FADED?
I MEAN, IF WE'RE JUS' SMOKIN' UP YE SHOULD'A TOL' ME.
YE LOT TALKIN' BOUT ZHAO? HOW SHE GHOSTED US AFTER? SHAI, FIND ANYTHING?
NO, I'VE BEEN HAVING SOME PROBLE--
AH! TRUE GHOST, THEN. WHO'S **NOT** A GHOST IS THAT RIGHT CUNT, SMYTHE.
THE RADIO BIGOT?
YEAH! HE'S BEEN TRASHIN' US ON HIS PODCAST, MAN.
RIGHT HE HAS, THE FAT FUCK.
SO I RECKON IT'S TIME WE REALLY SHOW 'EM WHA--
VRR
WHO THE **HELL...?**

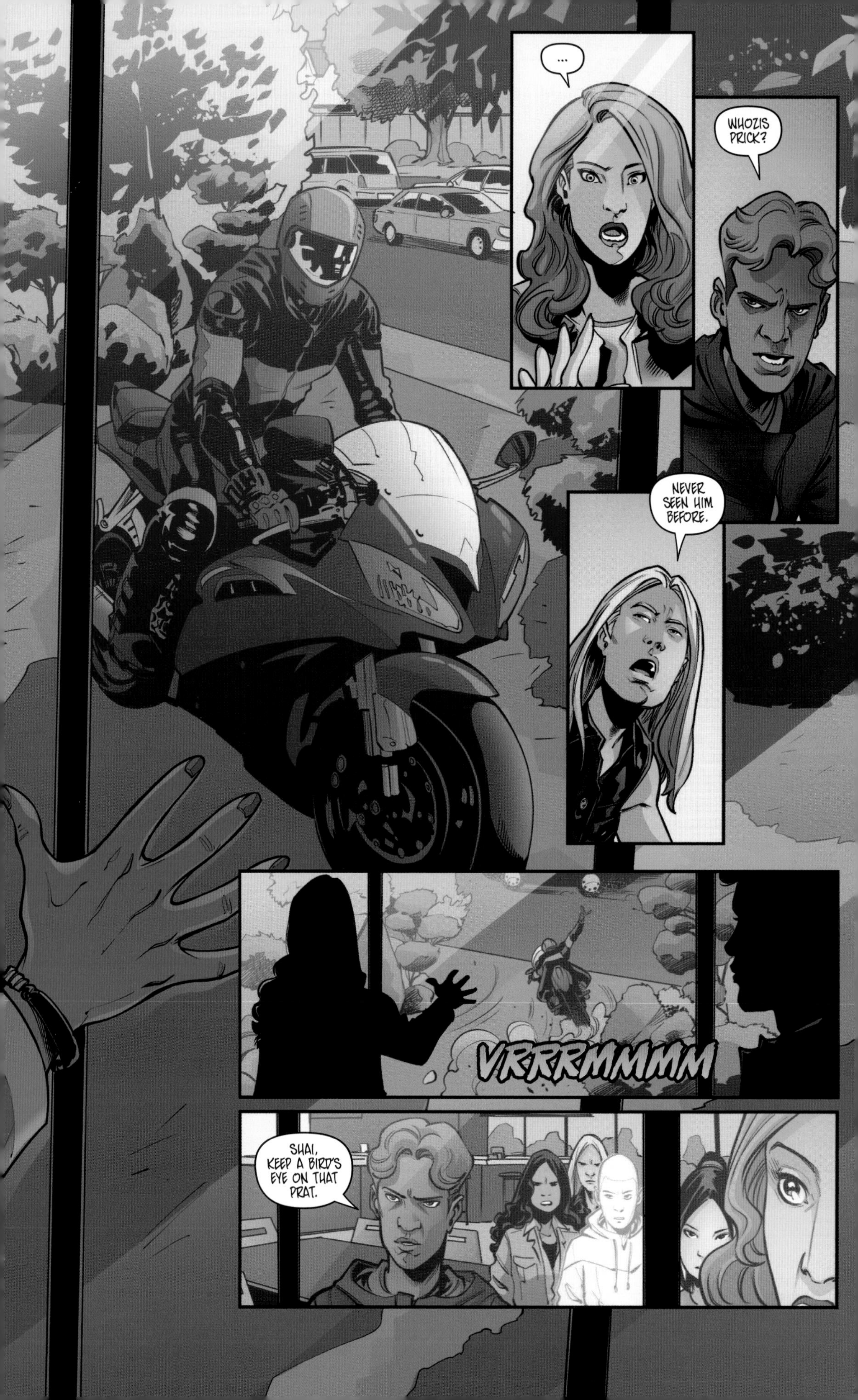
...
WHOZIS PRICK?
NEVER SEEN HIM BEFORE.
VRRRMMMMM
SHAI, KEEP A BIRD'S EYE ON THAT PRAT.

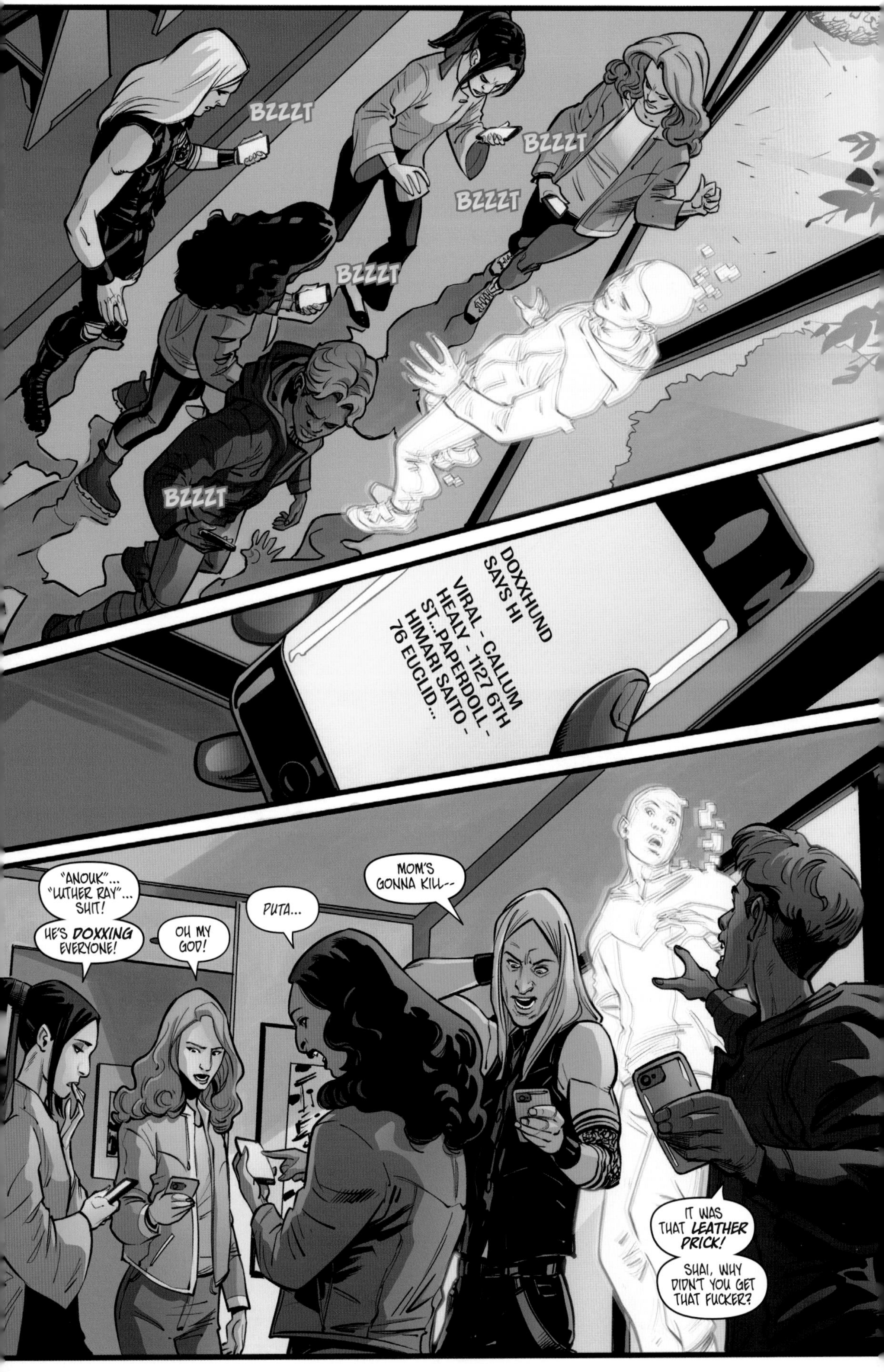
BZZZT
BZZZT
BZZZT
BZZZT
BZZZT
DOXXHUND SAYS HI
VIRAL - CALLUM HEALY - 1127 6TH ST...PAPERDOLL - HIMARI SAITO - 76 EUCLID...
"ANOUK"... "LUTHER RAY"... SHIT!
HE'S DOXXING EVERYONE!
OH MY GOD!
PUTA...
MOM'S GONNA KILL--
IT WAS THAT LEATHER PRICK!
SHAI, WHY DIDN'T YOU GET THAT FUCKER?

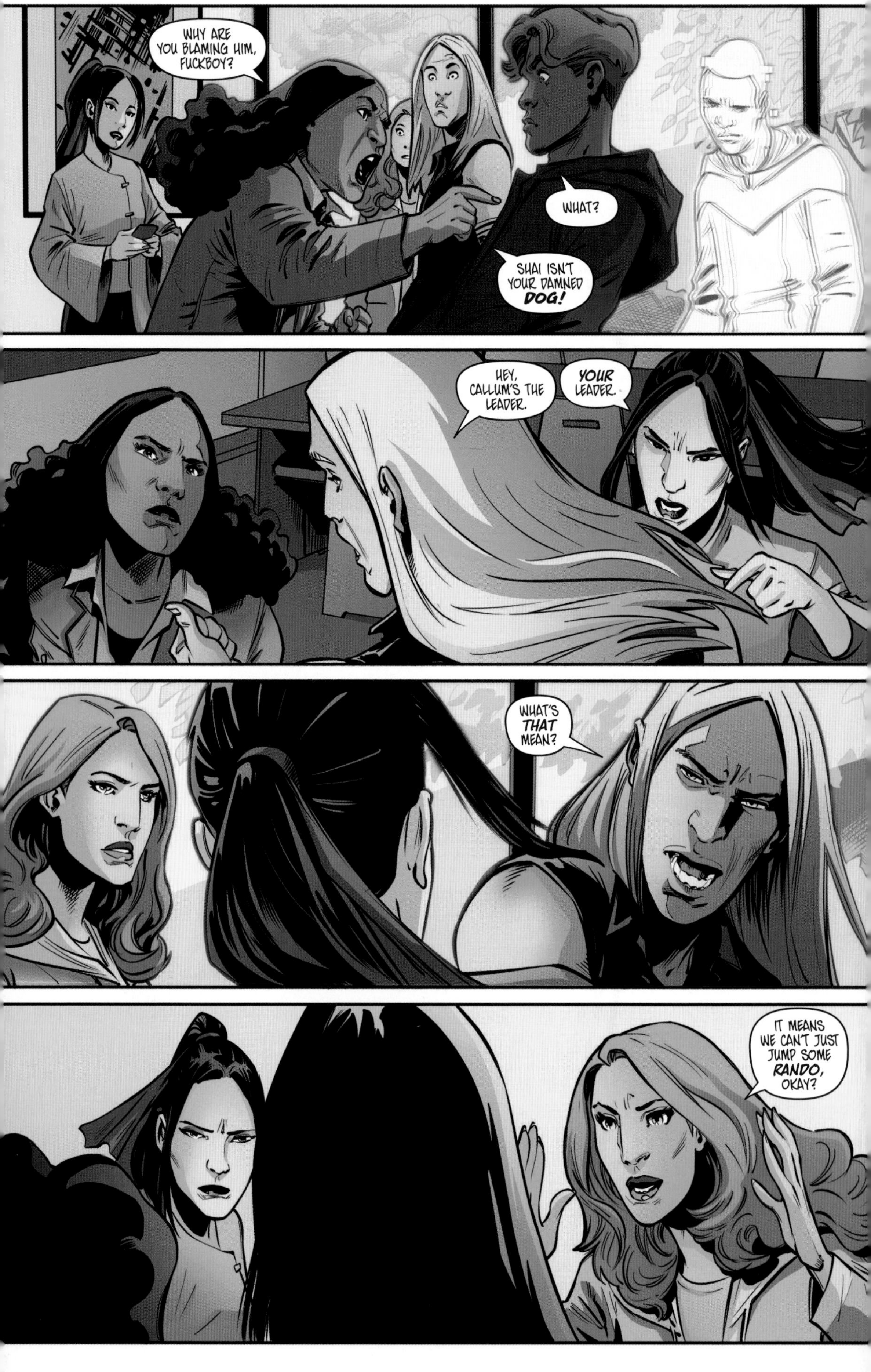
WHY ARE YOU BLAMING HIM, FUCKBOY?
WHAT?
SHAI ISN'T YOUR DAMNED DOG!
HEY, CALLUM'S THE LEADER.
YOUR LEADER.
WHAT'S THAT MEAN?
IT MEANS WE CAN'T JUST JUMP SOME RANDO, OKAY?

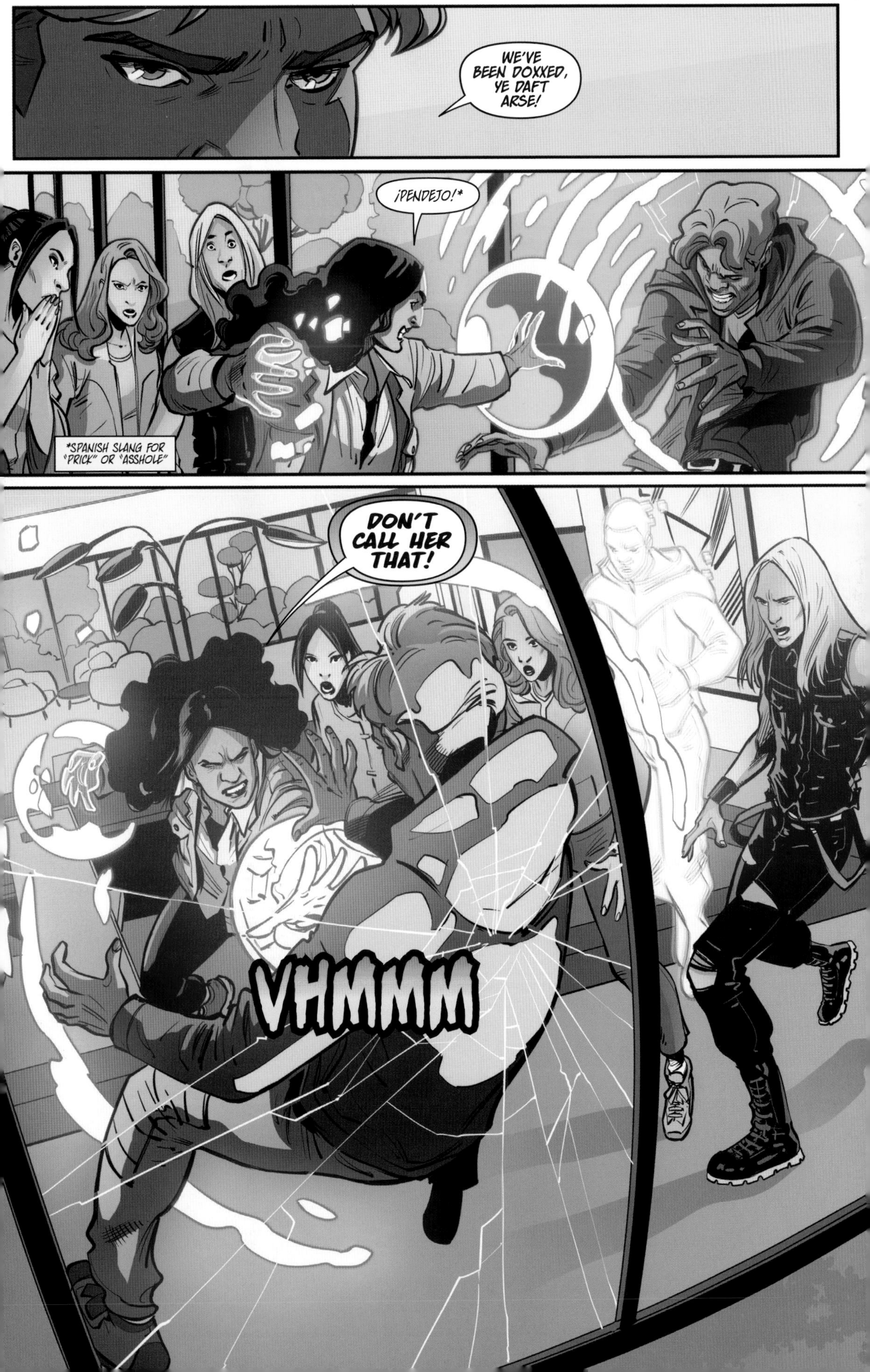
WE'VE BEEN DOXXED, YE DAFT ARSE!
¡PENDEJO!*
*SPANISH SLANG FOR "PRICK" OR "ASSHOLE"
DON'T CALL HER THAT!
VHMMM

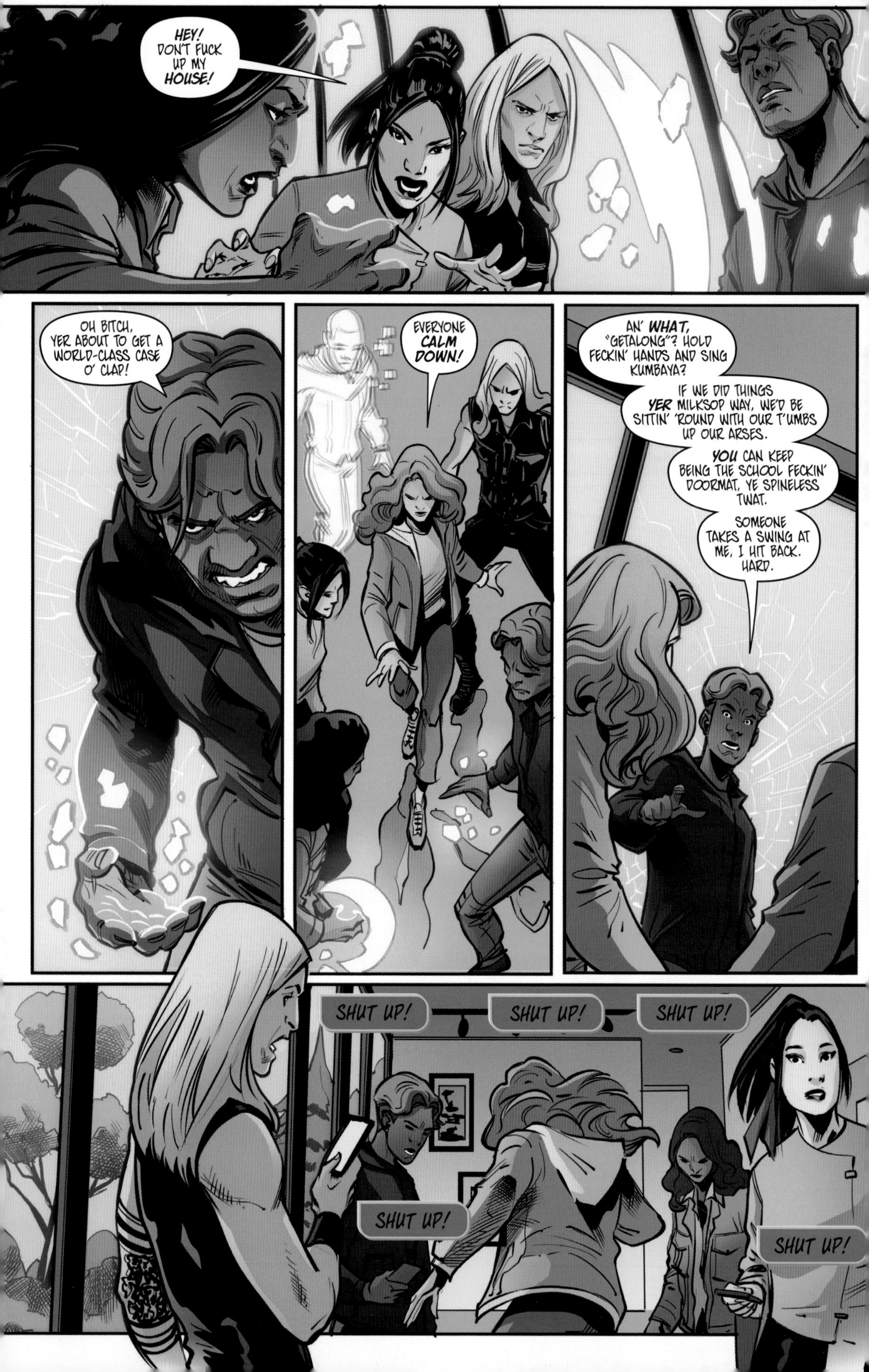
HEY! DON'T FUCK UP MY HOUSE!
OH BITCH, YER ABOUT TO GET A WORLD-CLASS CASE O' CLAP!
EVERYONE CALM DOWN!
AN' WHAT, "GETALONG"? HOLD FECKIN' HANDS AND SING KUMBAYA?
IF WE DID THINGS YER MILKSOP WAY, WE'D BE SITTIN' 'ROUND WITH OUR T'UMBS UP OUR ARSES.
YOU CAN KEEP BEING THE SCHOOL FECKIN' DOORMAT, YE SPINELESS TWAT.
SOMEONE TAKES A SWING AT ME, I HIT BACK. HARD.
SHUT UP!
SHUT UP!
SHUT UP!
SHUT UP!
SHUT UP!

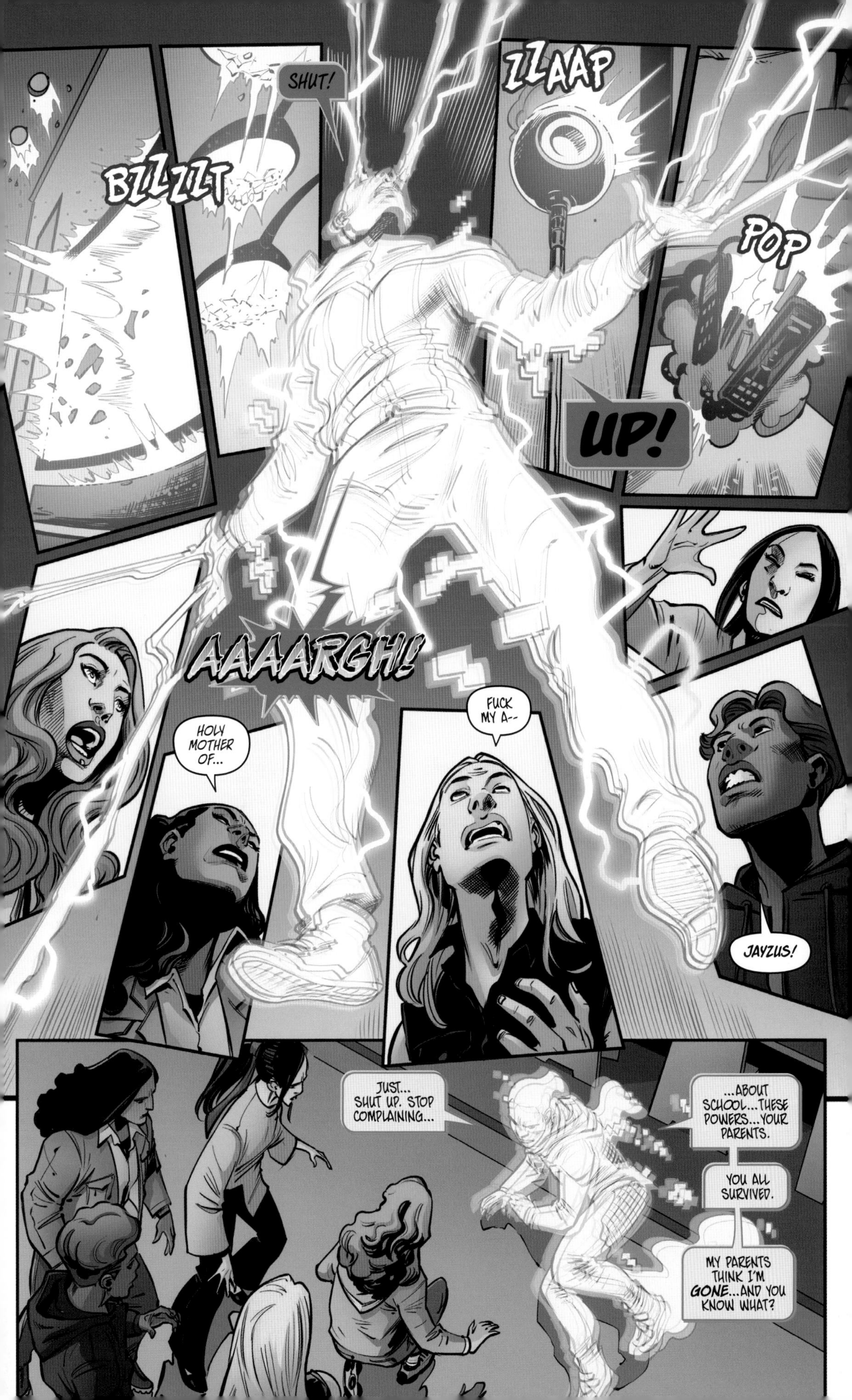
BZZZZT
SHUT!
ZZAAP
POP
UP!
AAAARGH!
HOLY MOTHER OF...
FUCK MY A--
JAYZUS!
JUST... SHUT UP. STOP COMPLAINING...
...ABOUT SCHOOL...THESE POWERS...YOUR PARENTS.
YOU ALL SURVIVED.
MY PARENTS THINK I'M **GONE**...AND YOU KNOW WHAT?

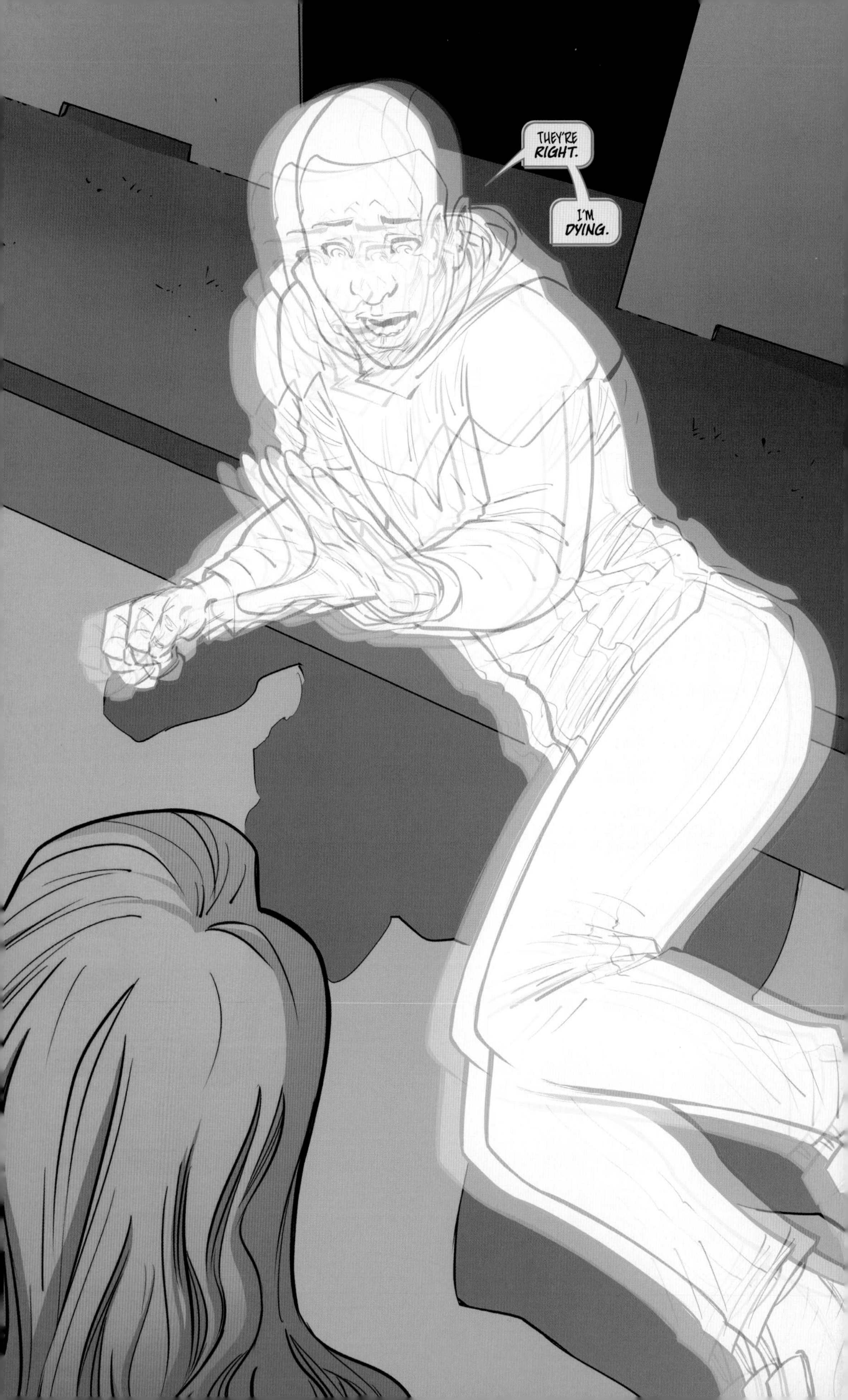
THEY'RE RIGHT.
I'M DYING.

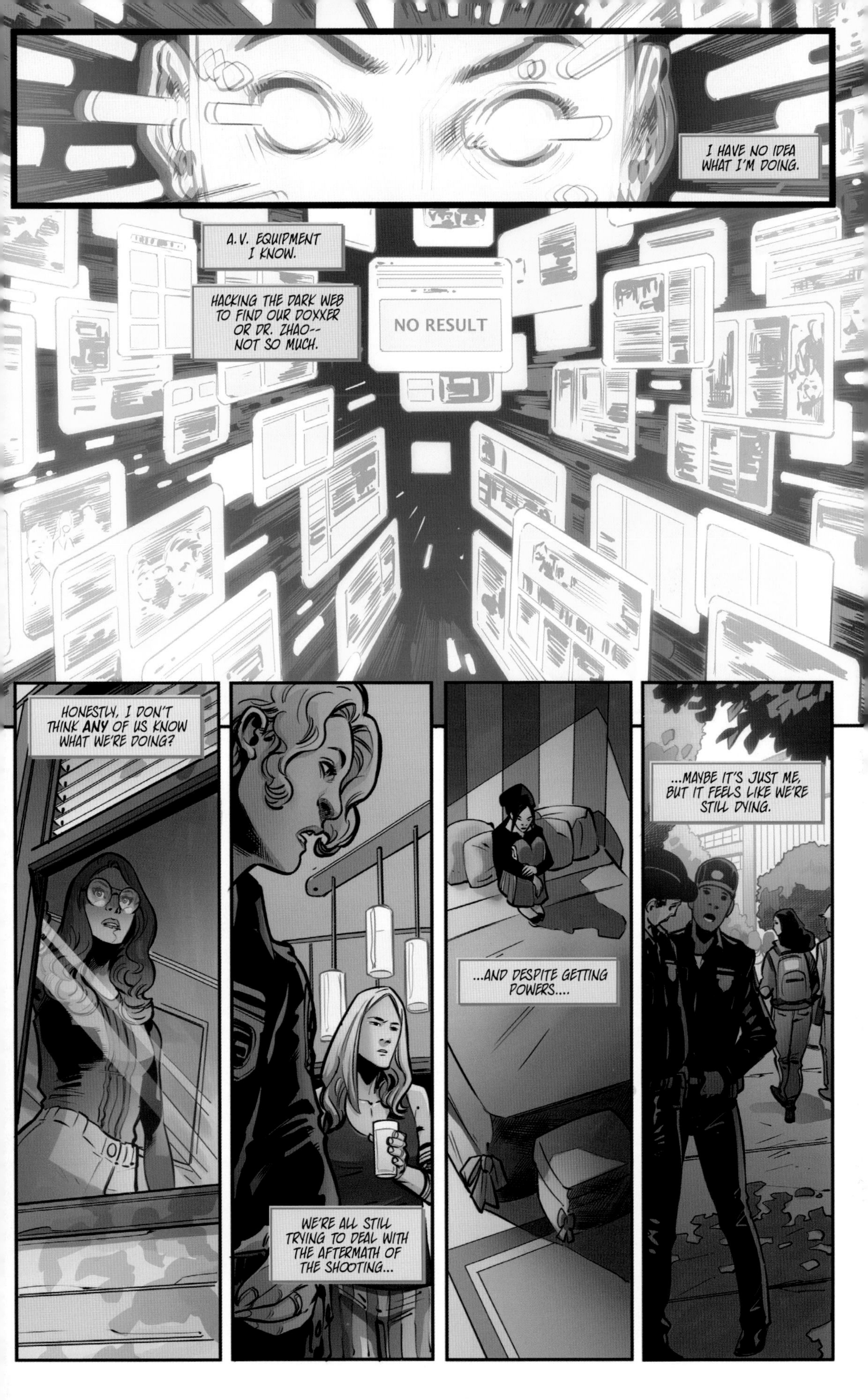
I HAVE NO IDEA WHAT I'M DOING.
A.V. EQUIPMENT I KNOW.
HACKING THE DARK WEB TO FIND OUR DOXXER OR DR. ZHAO-- NOT SO MUCH.
NO RESULT
HONESTLY, I DON'T THINK ANY OF US KNOW WHAT WE'RE DOING?
WE'RE ALL STILL TRYING TO DEAL WITH THE AFTERMATH OF THE SHOOTING...
...AND DESPITE GETTING POWERS....
...MAYBE IT'S JUST ME, BUT IT FEELS LIKE WE'RE STILL DYING.

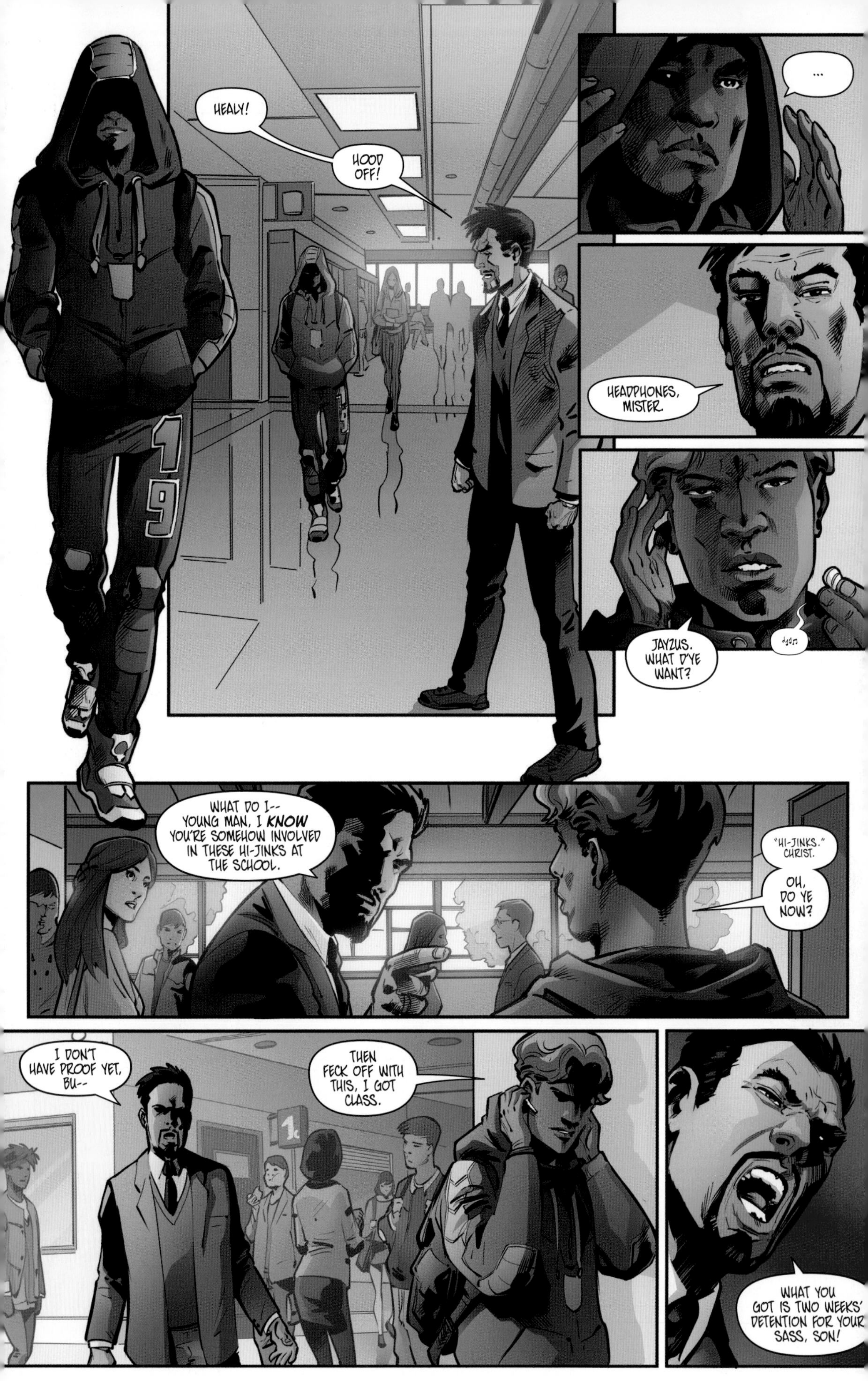
HEALY!
HOOD OFF!
...
HEADPHONES, MISTER.
JAYZUS. WHAT D'YE WANT?
WHAT DO I-- YOUNG MAN, I **KNOW** YOU'RE SOMEHOW INVOLVED IN THESE HI-JINKS AT THE SCHOOL.
"HI-JINKS." CHRIST.
OH, DO YE NOW?
I DON'T HAVE PROOF YET, BU--
THEN FECK OFF WITH THIS, I GOT CLASS.
WHAT YOU GOT IS TWO WEEKS' DETENTION FOR YOUR SASS, SON!

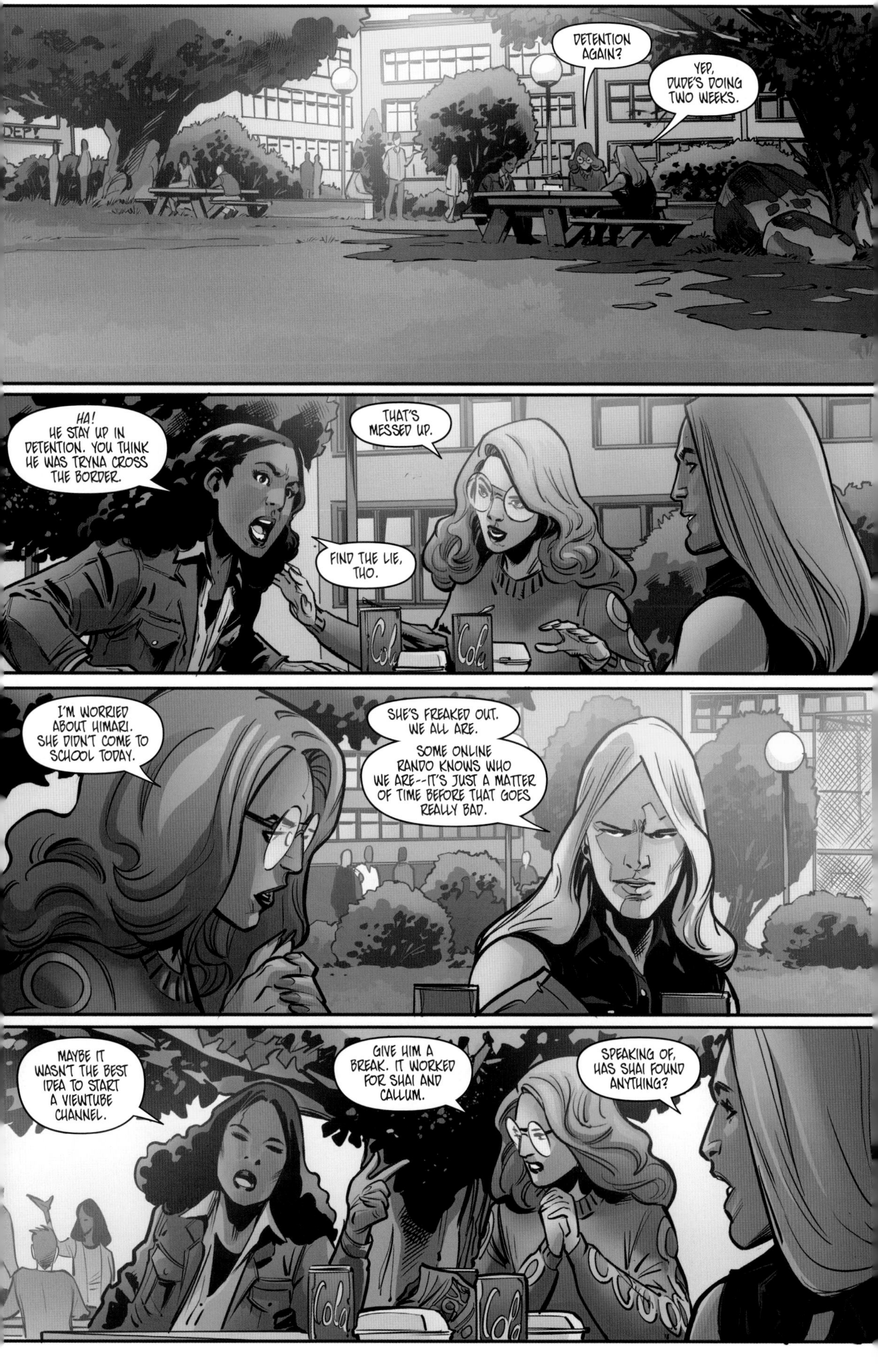
DETENTION AGAIN?
YEP, DUDE'S DOING TWO WEEKS.
HA! HE STAY UP IN DETENTION. YOU THINK HE WAS TRYNA CROSS THE BORDER.
THAT'S MESSED UP.
FIND THE LIE, THO.
I'M WORRIED ABOUT HIMARI. SHE DIDN'T COME TO SCHOOL TODAY.
SHE'S FREAKED OUT. WE ALL ARE.
SOME ONLINE RANDO KNOWS WHO WE ARE--IT'S JUST A MATTER OF TIME BEFORE THAT GOES REALLY BAD.
MAYBE IT WASN'T THE BEST IDEA TO START A VIEWTUBE CHANNEL.
GIVE HIM A BREAK. IT WORKED FOR SHAI AND CALLUM.
SPEAKING OF, HAS SHAI FOUND ANYTHING?

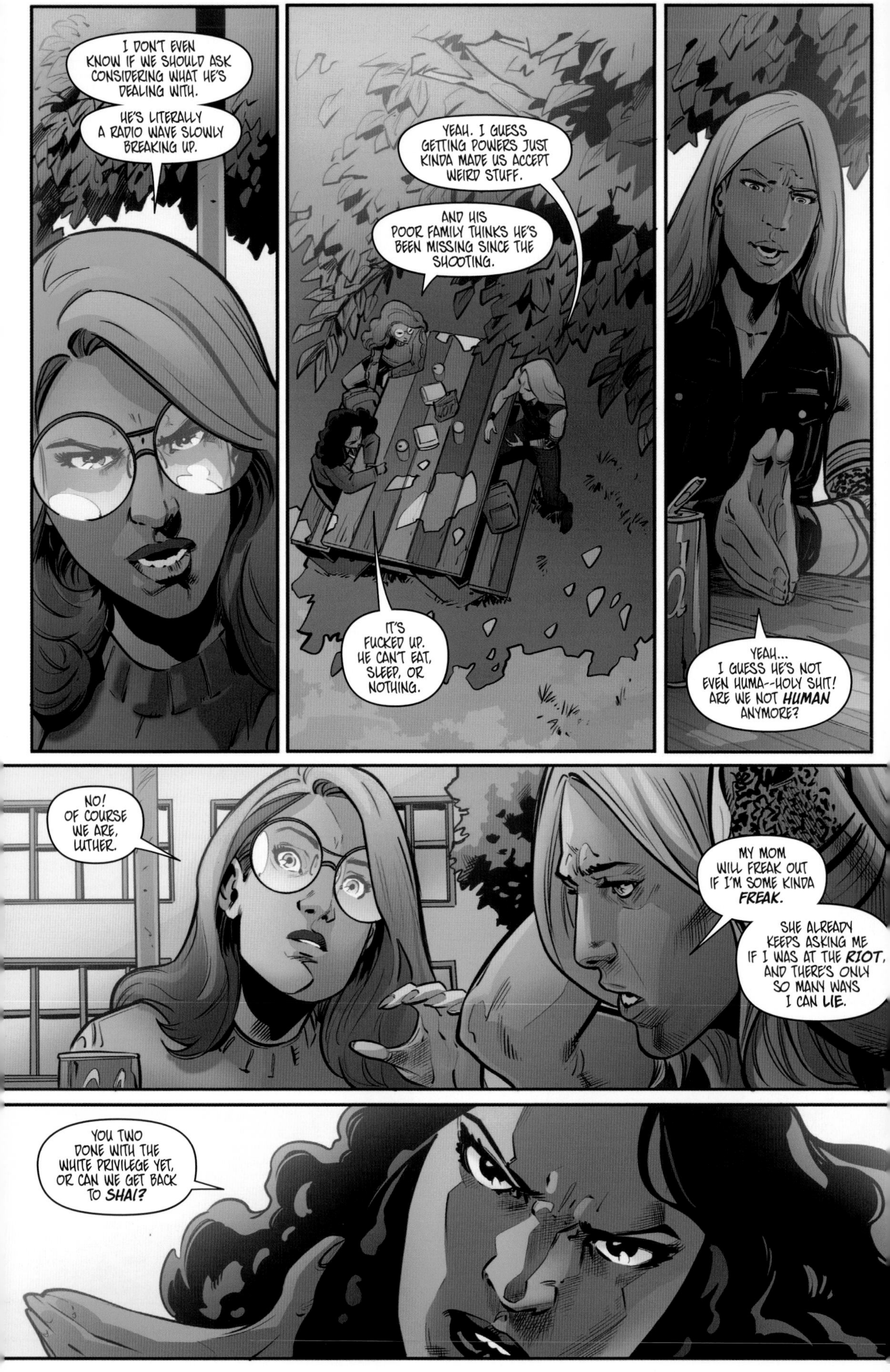
I DON'T EVEN KNOW IF WE SHOULD ASK CONSIDERING WHAT HE'S DEALING WITH.
HE'S LITERALLY A RADIO WAVE SLOWLY BREAKING UP.
YEAH. I GUESS GETTING POWERS JUST KINDA MADE US ACCEPT WEIRD STUFF.
AND HIS POOR FAMILY THINKS HE'S BEEN MISSING SINCE THE SHOOTING.
IT'S FUCKED UP. HE CAN'T EAT, SLEEP, OR NOTHING.
YEAH... I GUESS HE'S NOT EVEN HUMA--HOLY SHIT! ARE WE NOT HUMAN ANYMORE?
NO! OF COURSE WE ARE, LUTHER.
MY MOM WILL FREAK OUT IF I'M SOME KINDA FREAK.
SHE ALREADY KEEPS ASKING ME IF I WAS AT THE RIOT, AND THERE'S ONLY SO MANY WAYS I CAN LIE.
YOU TWO DONE WITH THE WHITE PRIVILEGE YET, OR CAN WE GET BACK TO SHAI?

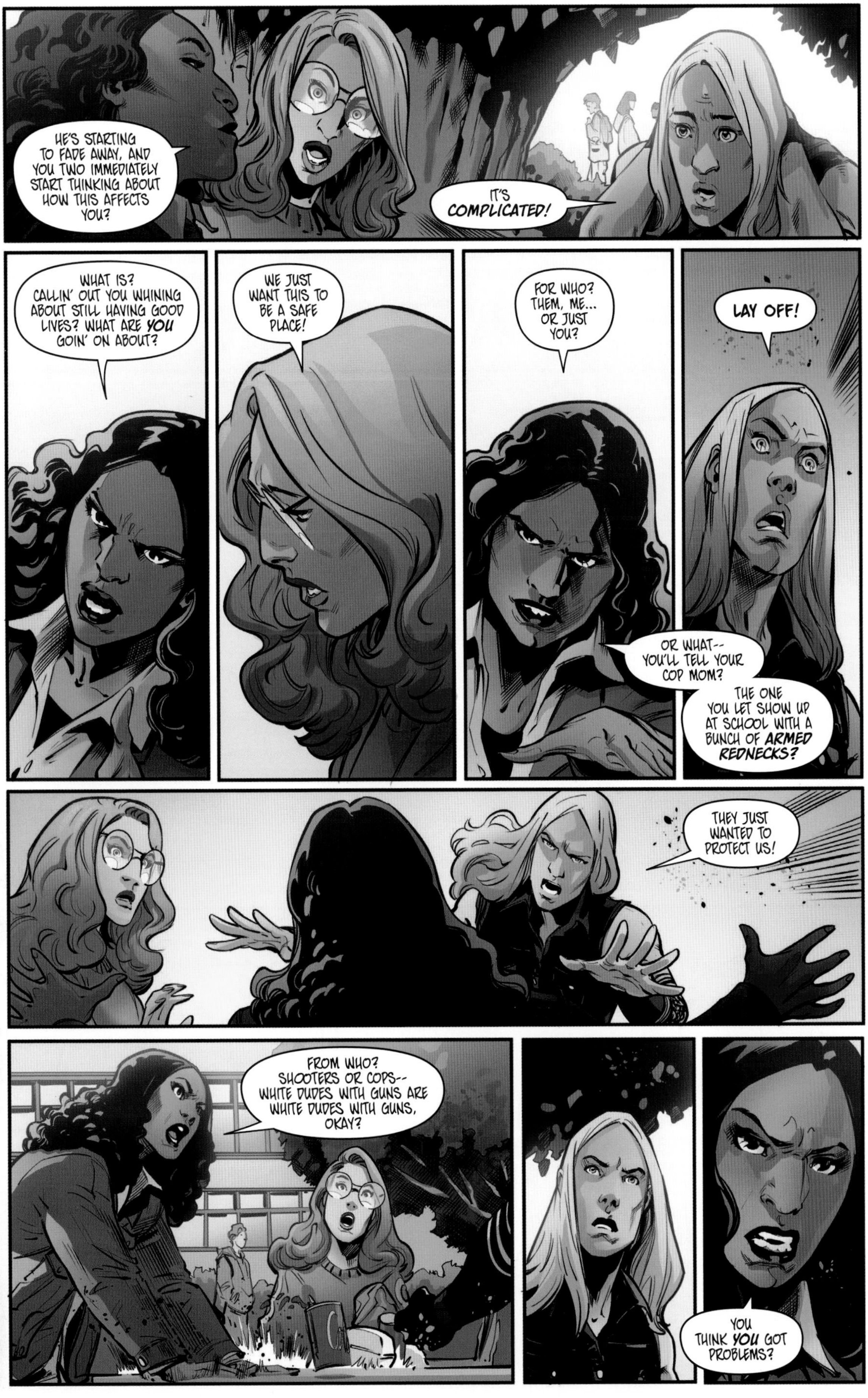
HE'S STARTING TO FADE AWAY, AND YOU TWO IMMEDIATELY START THINKING ABOUT HOW THIS AFFECTS YOU?
IT'S COMPLICATED!
WHAT IS? CALLIN' OUT YOU WHINING ABOUT STILL HAVING GOOD LIVES? WHAT ARE YOU GOIN' ON ABOUT?
WE JUST WANT THIS TO BE A SAFE PLACE!
FOR WHO? THEM, ME... OR JUST YOU?
LAY OFF!
OR WHAT-- YOU'LL TELL YOUR COP MOM?
THE ONE YOU LET SHOW UP AT SCHOOL WITH A BUNCH OF ARMED REDNECKS?
THEY JUST WANTED TO PROTECT US!
FROM WHO? SHOOTERS OR COPS-- WHITE DUDES WITH GUNS ARE WHITE DUDES WITH GUNS, OKAY?
YOU THINK YOU GOT PROBLEMS?

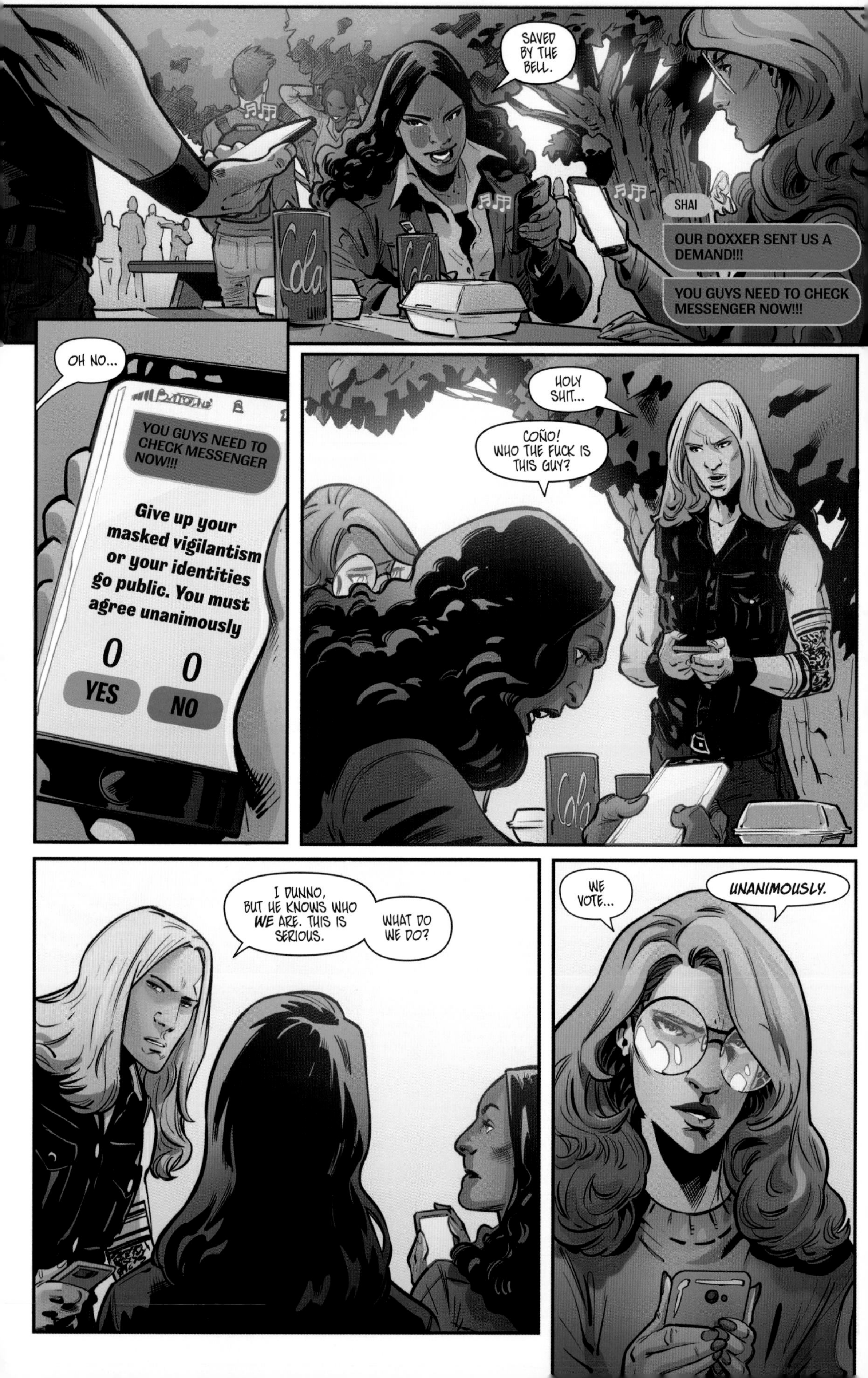
SAVED BY THE BELL.
SHAI
OUR DOXXER SENT US A DEMAND!!!
YOU GUYS NEED TO CHECK MESSENGER NOW!!!
OH NO...
YOU GUYS NEED TO CHECK MESSENGER NOW!!!
Give up your masked vigilantism or your identities go public. You must agree unanimously
0 0
YES NO
HOLY SHIT...
COÑO! WHO THE FUCK IS THIS GUY?
I DUNNO, BUT HE KNOWS WHO WE ARE. THIS IS SERIOUS.
WHAT DO WE DO?
WE VOTE...
UNANIMOUSLY.

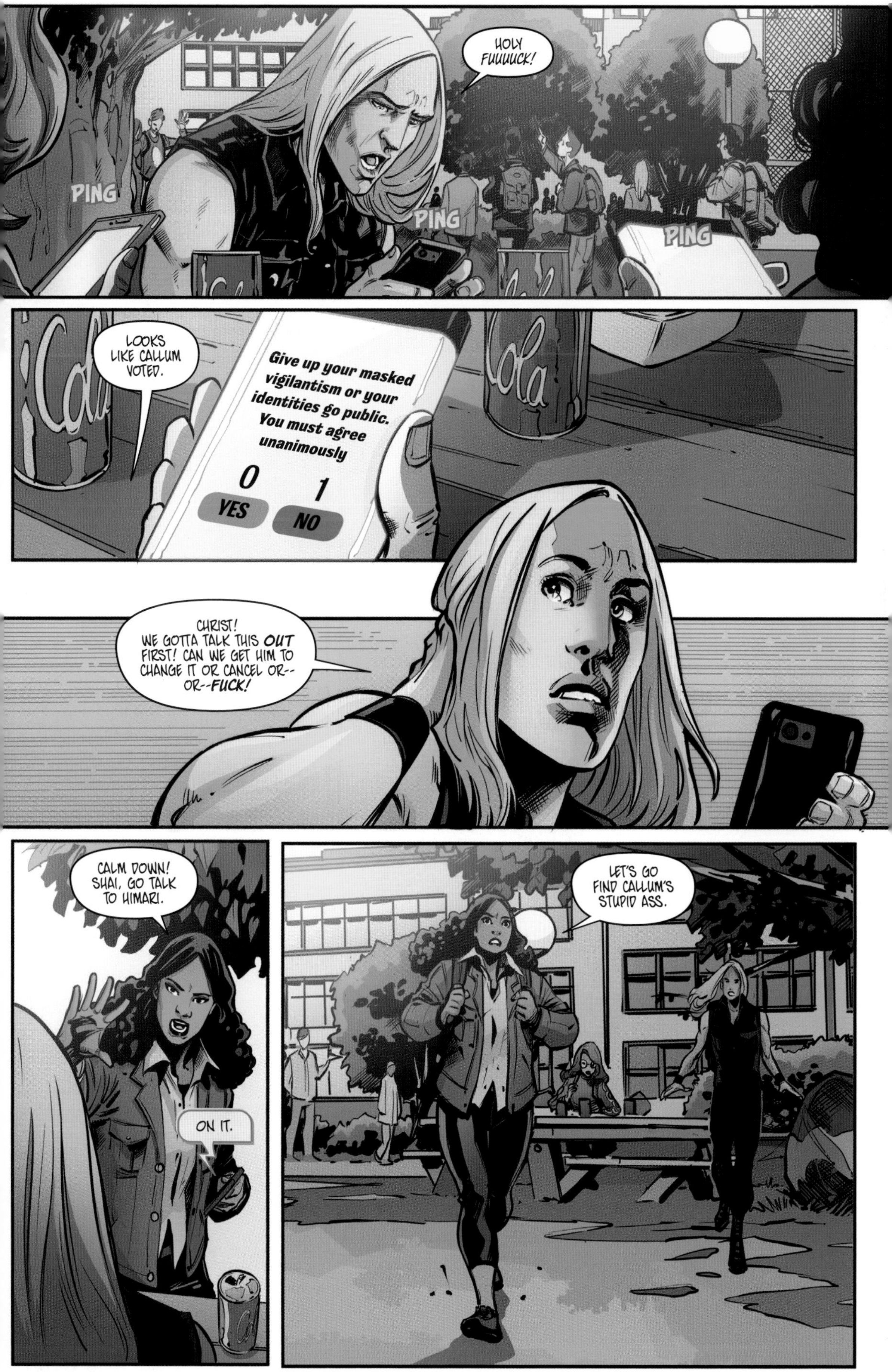
HOLY FUUUUCK!
PING
PING
PING
LOOKS LIKE CALLUM VOTED.
Give up your masked vigilantism or your identities go public. You must agree unanimously
0
1
YES
NO
CHRIST! WE GOTTA TALK THIS OUT FIRST! CAN WE GET HIM TO CHANGE IT OR CANCEL OR-- OR--FUCK!
CALM DOWN! SHAI, GO TALK TO HIMARI.
ON IT.
LET'S GO FIND CALLUM'S STUPID ASS.

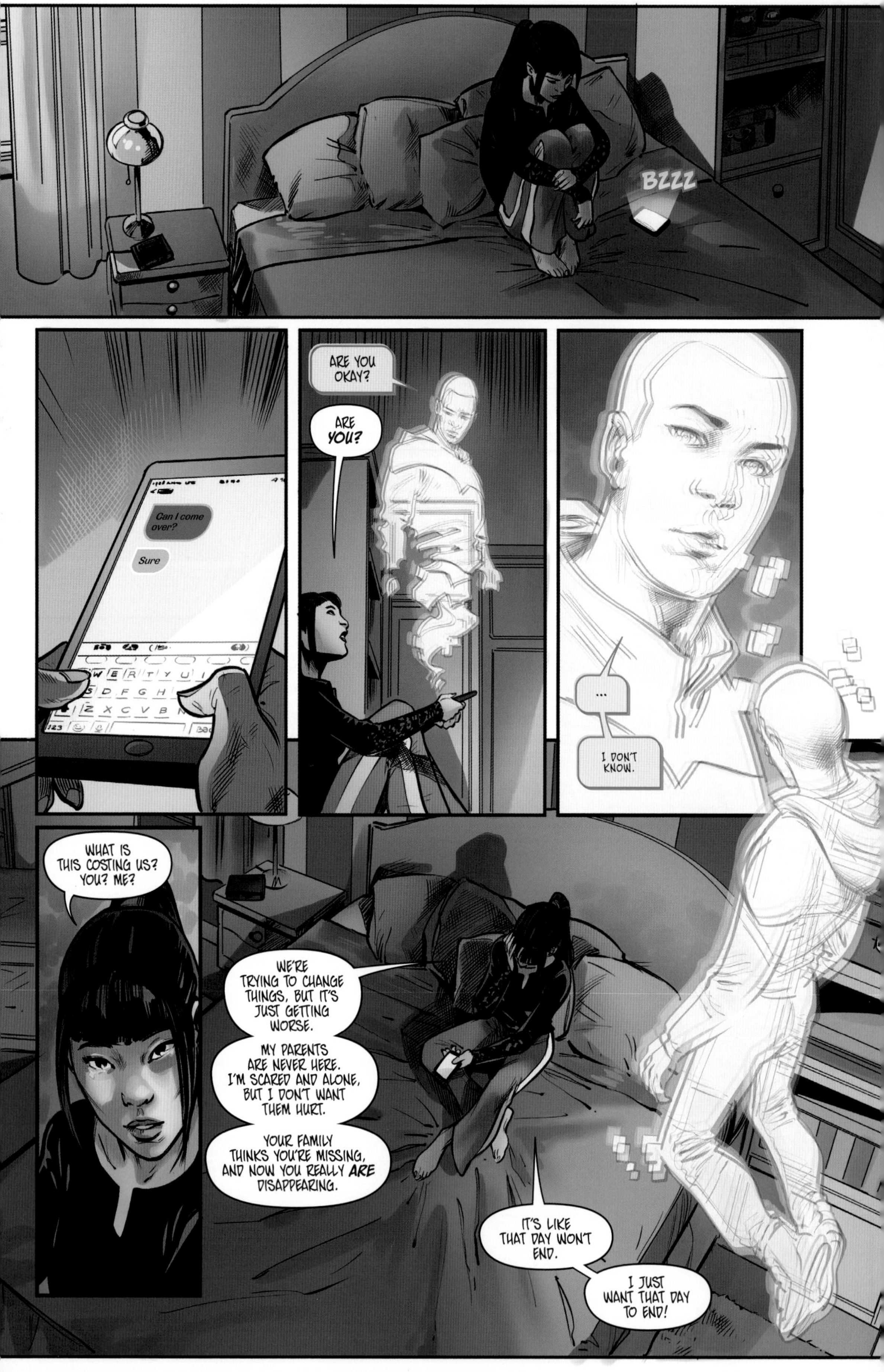

BZZZ
Can I come over?
Sure
ARE YOU OKAY?
ARE YOU?
...
I DON'T KNOW.
WHAT IS THIS COSTING US? YOU? ME?
WE'RE TRYING TO CHANGE THINGS, BUT IT'S JUST GETTING WORSE.
MY PARENTS ARE NEVER HERE. I'M SCARED AND ALONE, BUT I DON'T WANT THEM HURT.
YOUR FAMILY THINKS YOU'RE MISSING, AND NOW YOU REALLY ARE DISAPPEARING.
IT'S LIKE THAT DAY WON'T END.
I JUST WANT THAT DAY TO END!

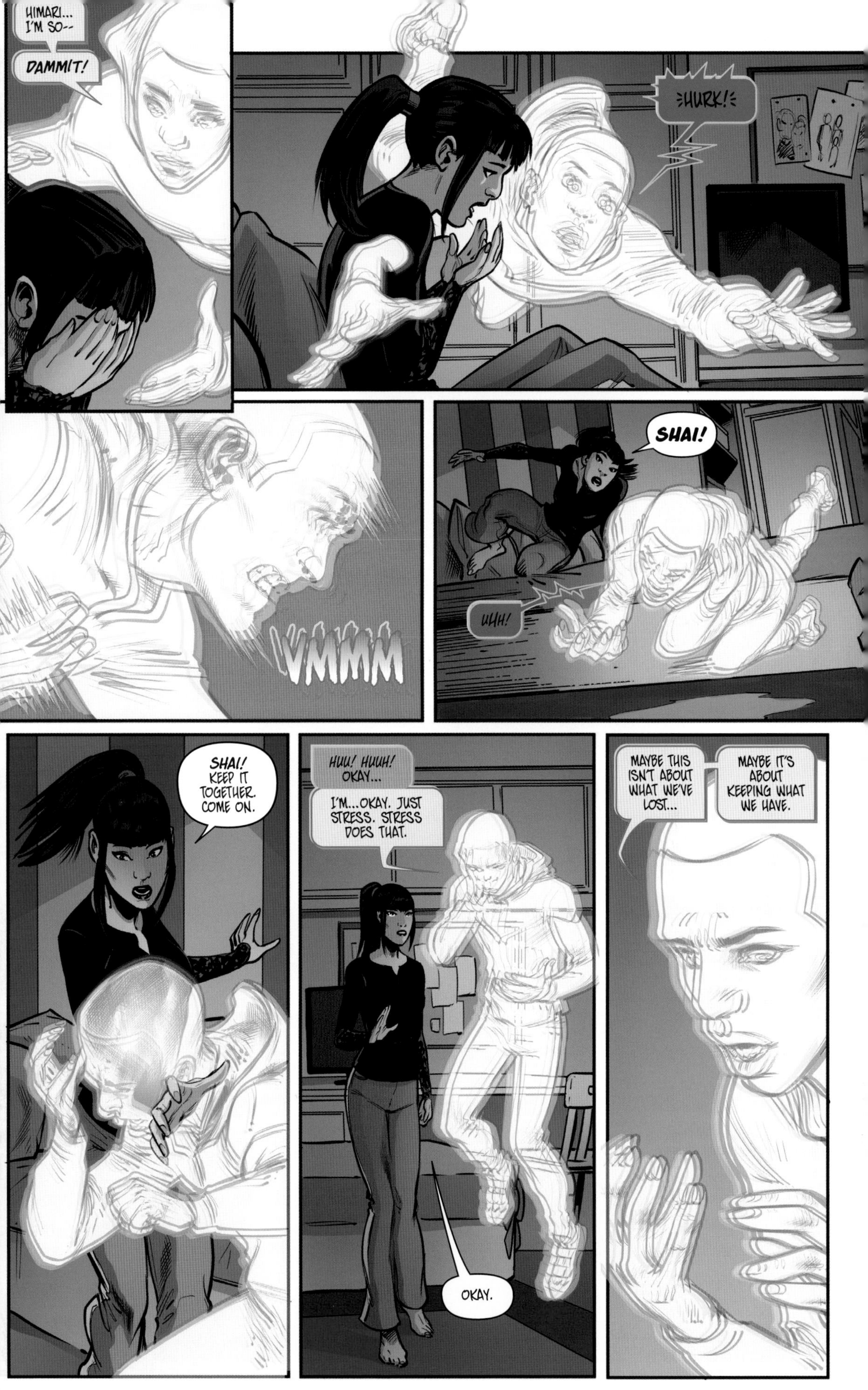
HIMARI... I'M SO--
DAMMIT!
HURK!
VMMM
SHAI!
UHH!
SHAI! KEEP IT TOGETHER. COME ON.
HUU! HUUH! OKAY...
I'M...OKAY. JUST STRESS. STRESS DOES THAT.
OKAY.
MAYBE THIS ISN'T ABOUT WHAT WE'VE LOST...
MAYBE IT'S ABOUT KEEPING WHAT WE HAVE.

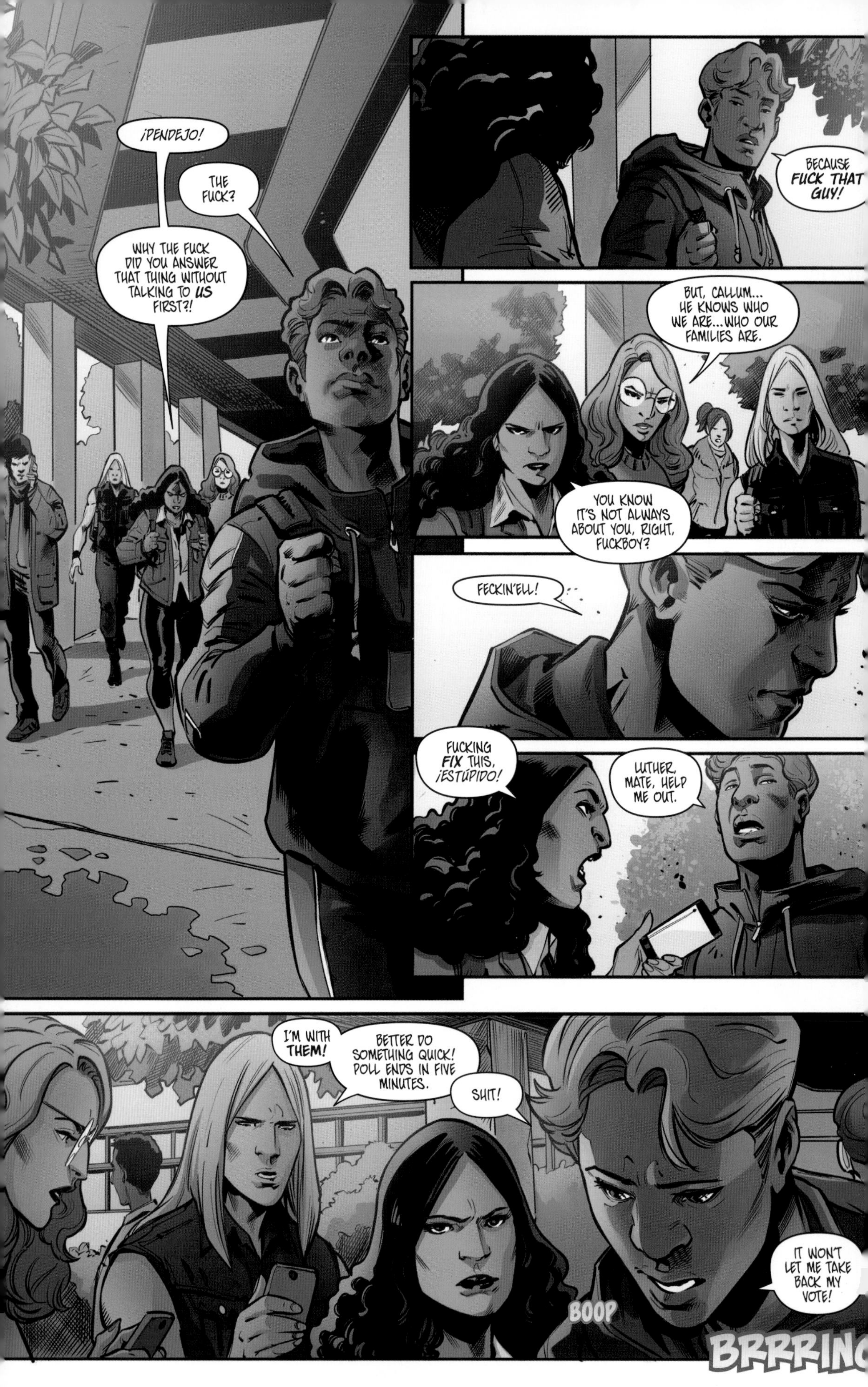
¡PENDEJO!
THE FUCK?
WHY THE FUCK DID YOU ANSWER THAT THING WITHOUT TALKING TO US FIRST?!
BECAUSE FUCK THAT GUY!
BUT, CALLUM... HE KNOWS WHO WE ARE...WHO OUR FAMILIES ARE.
YOU KNOW IT'S NOT ALWAYS ABOUT YOU, RIGHT, FUCKBOY?
FECKIN'ELL!
FUCKING FIX THIS, ¡ESTÚPIDO!
LUTHER, MATE, HELP ME OUT.
I'M WITH THEM!
BETTER DO SOMETHING QUICK! POLL ENDS IN FIVE MINUTES.
SHIT!
IT WON'T LET ME TAKE BACK MY VOTE!
BOOP
BRRRING

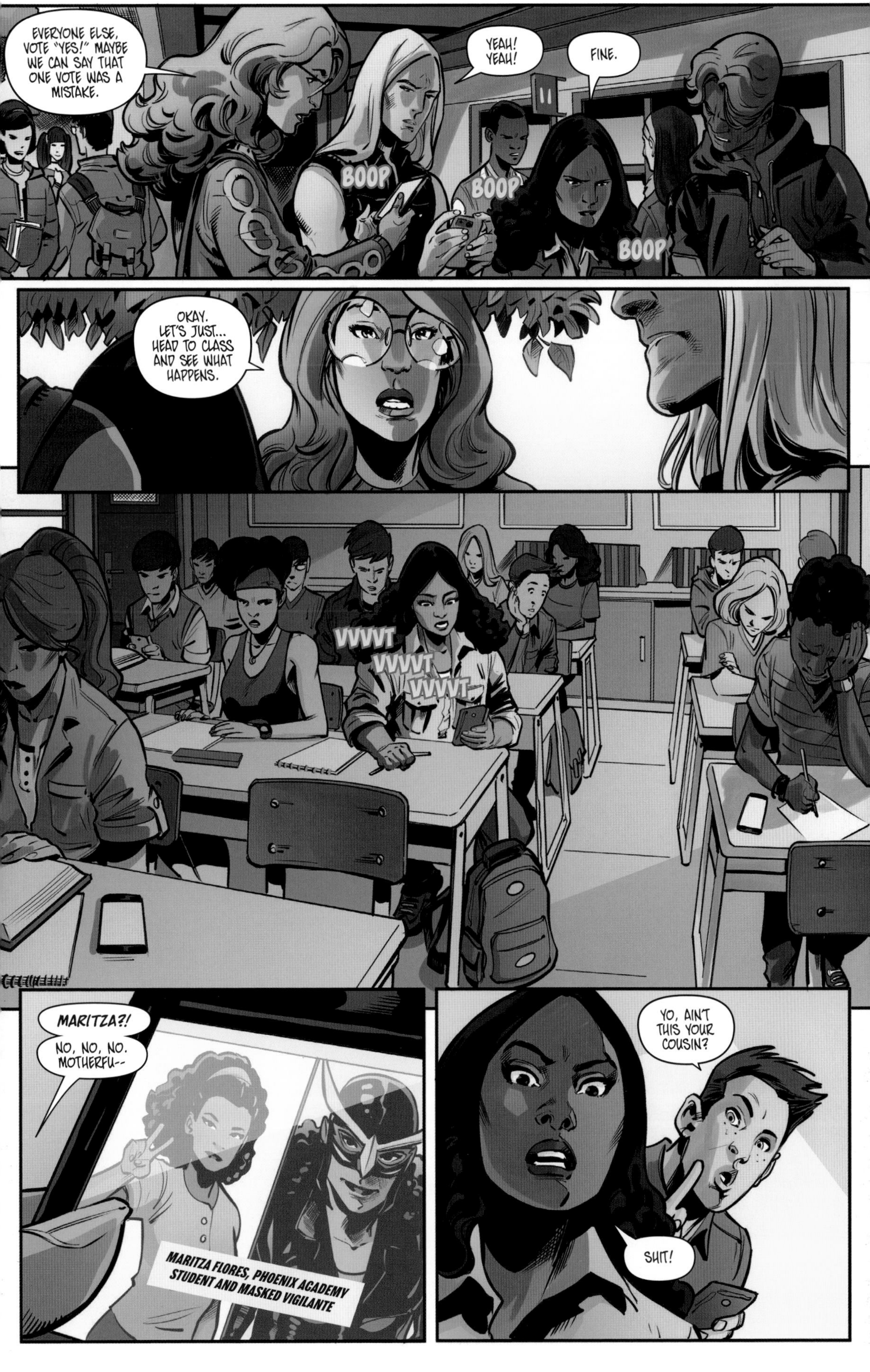
EVERYONE ELSE, VOTE "YES!" MAYBE WE CAN SAY THAT ONE VOTE WAS A MISTAKE.
YEAH! YEAH!
FINE.
BOOP
BOOP
BOOP
OKAY. LET'S JUST... HEAD TO CLASS AND SEE WHAT HAPPENS.
VVVVT
VVVVT
VVVVT
MARITZA?!
NO, NO, NO. MOTHERFU--
MARITZA FLORES, PHOENIX ACADEMY STUDENT AND MASKED VIGILANTE
YO, AIN'T THIS YOUR COUSIN?
SHIT!

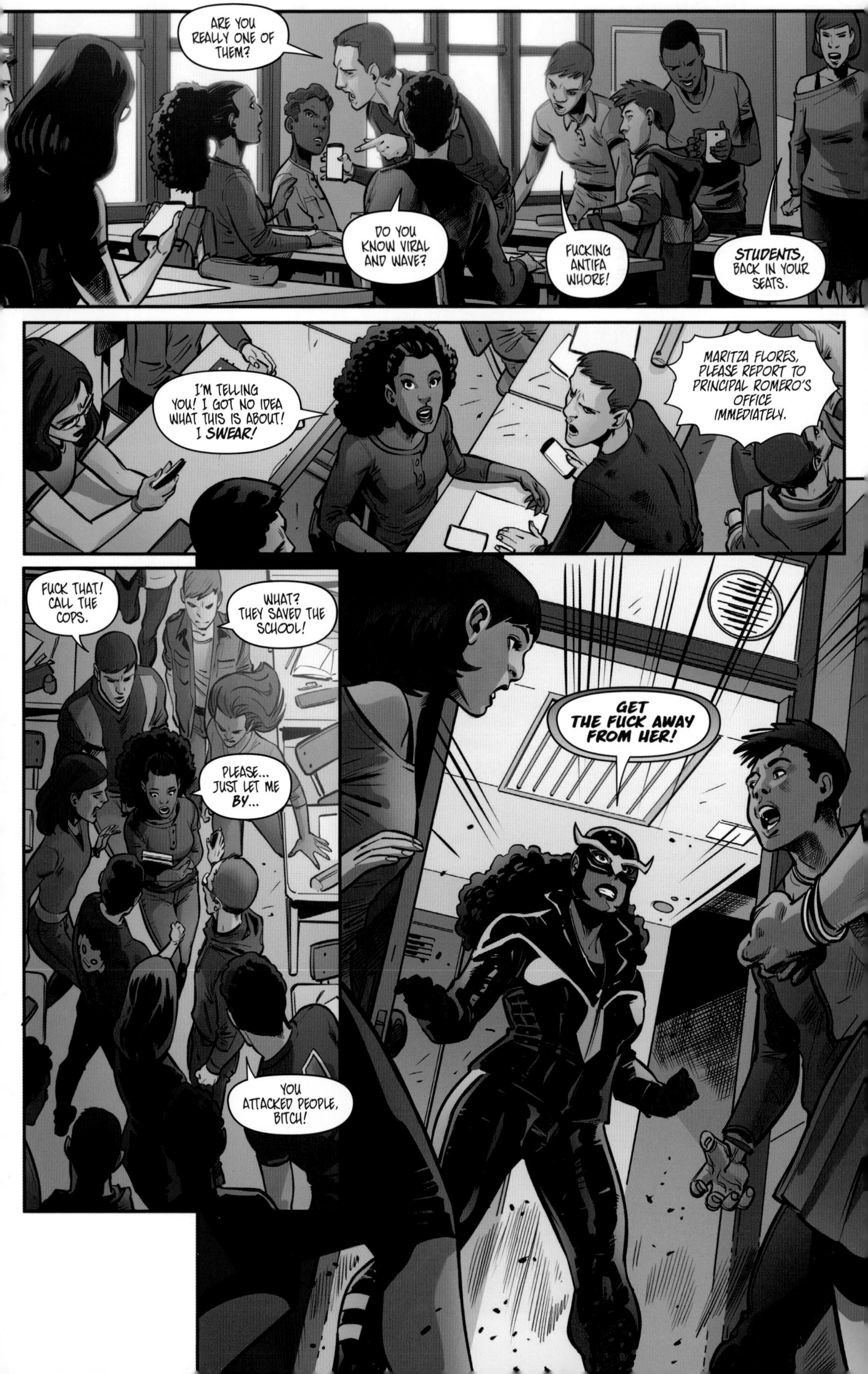
ARE YOU REALLY ONE OF THEM?
DO YOU KNOW VIRAL AND WAVE?
FUCKING ANTIFA WHORE!
STUDENTS, BACK IN YOUR SEATS.
I'M TELLING YOU! I GOT NO IDEA WHAT THIS IS ABOUT! I SWEAR!
MARITZA FLORES, PLEASE REPORT TO PRINCIPAL ROMERO'S OFFICE IMMEDIATELY.
FUCK THAT! CALL THE COPS.
WHAT? THEY SAVED THE SCHOOL!
PLEASE... JUST LET ME BY...
YOU ATTACKED PEOPLE, BITCH!
GET THE FUCK AWAY FROM HER!

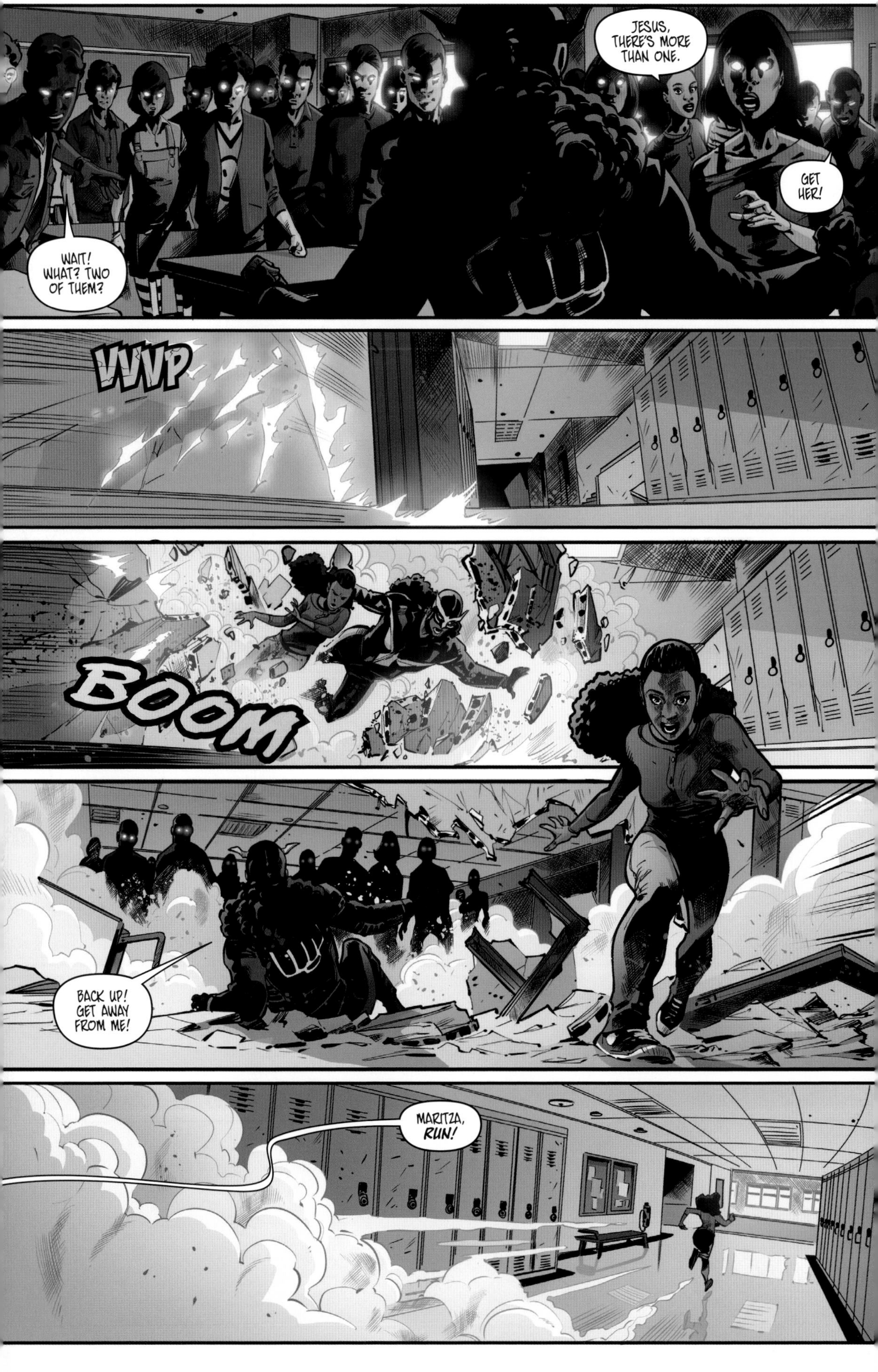
JESUS, THERE'S MORE THAN ONE.
GET HER!
WAIT! WHAT? TWO OF THEM?
VVVP
BOOM
BACK UP! GET AWAY FROM ME!
MARITZA, RUN!

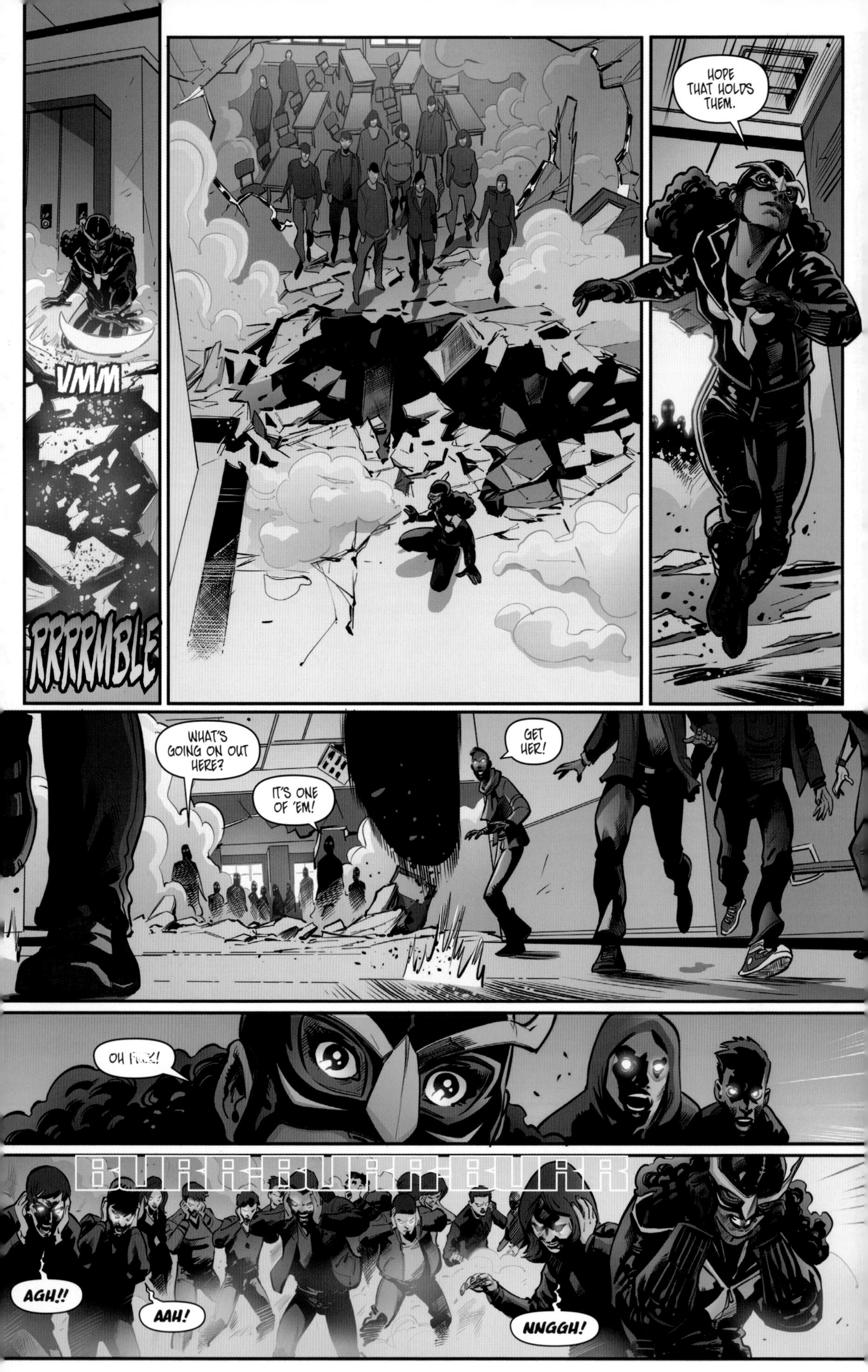
VMM
RRRRMBLE
HOPE THAT HOLDS THEM.
WHAT'S GOING ON OUT HERE?
IT'S ONE OF 'EM!
GET HER!
OH FUCK!
BURR-BURR-BURR
AGH!!
AAH!
NNGGH!

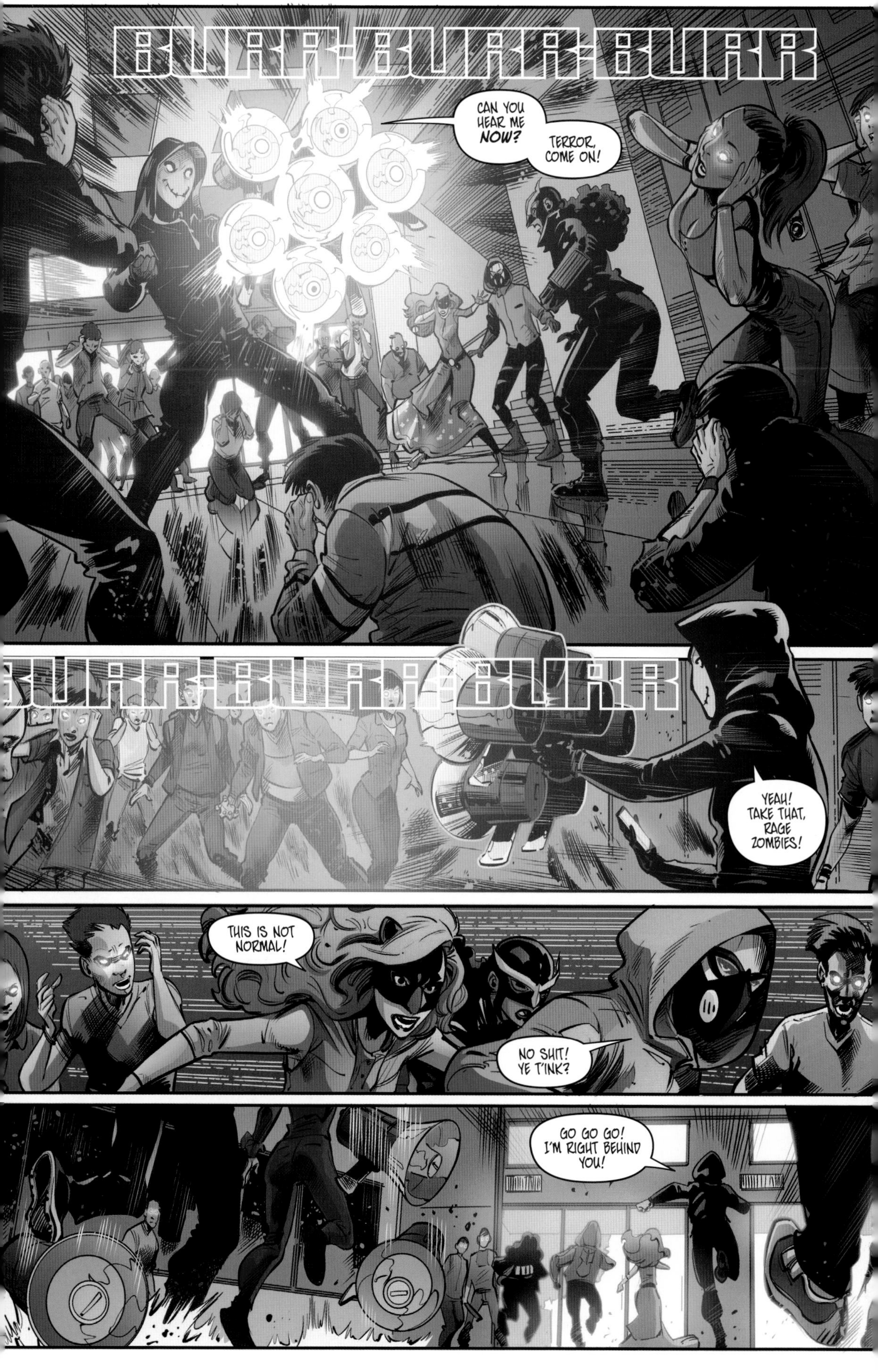
BURR-BURR-BURR
CAN YOU HEAR ME NOW?
TERROR, COME ON!
BURR-BURR-BURR
YEAH! TAKE THAT, RAGE ZOMBIES!
THIS IS NOT NORMAL!
NO SHIT! YE T'INK?
GO GO GO! I'M RIGHT BEHIND YOU!

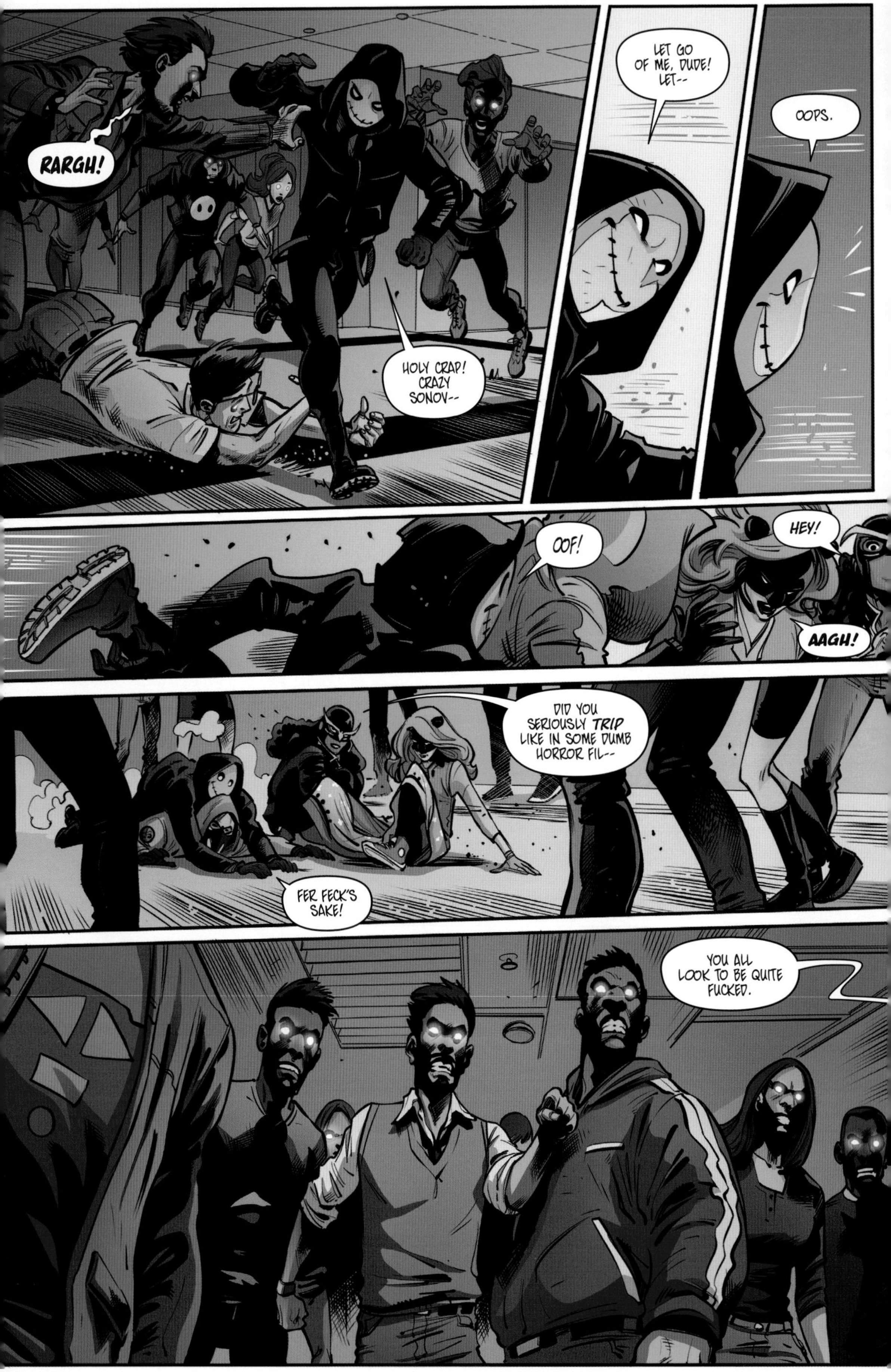
RARGH!
HOLY CRAP! CRAZY SONOV--
LET GO OF ME, DUDE! LET--
OOPS.
OOF!
HEY!
AAGH!
DID YOU SERIOUSLY TRIP LIKE IN SOME DUMB HORROR FIL--
FER FECK'S SAKE!
YOU ALL LOOK TO BE QUITE FUCKED.

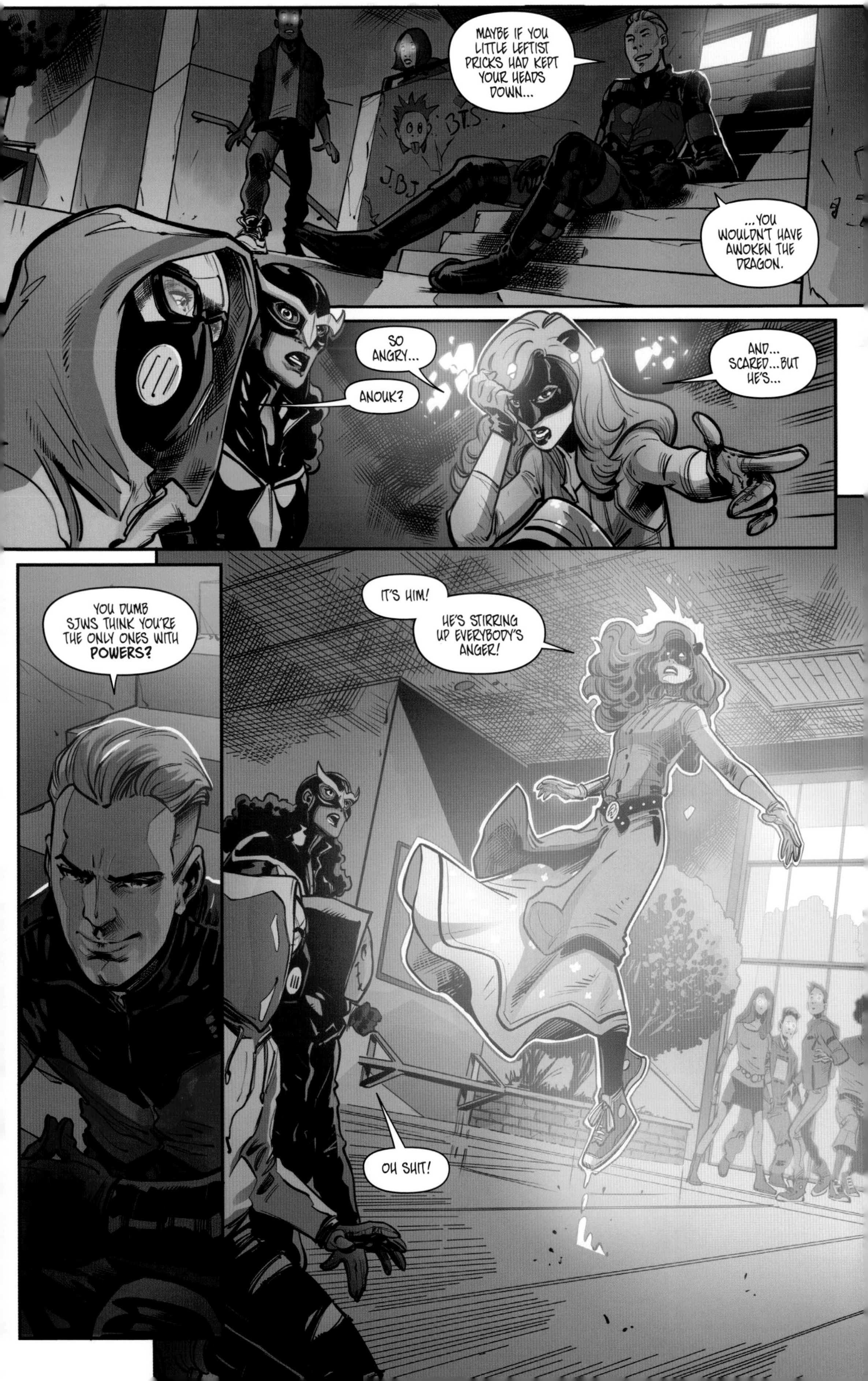
MAYBE IF YOU LITTLE LEFTIST PRICKS HAD KEPT YOUR HEADS DOWN...
...YOU WOULDN'T HAVE AWOKEN THE DRAGON.
SO ANGRY...
ANOUK?
AND... SCARED...BUT HE'S...
YOU DUMB SJWS THINK YOU'RE THE ONLY ONES WITH **POWERS?**
IT'S HIM!
HE'S STIRRING UP EVERYBODY'S ANGER!
OH SHIT!

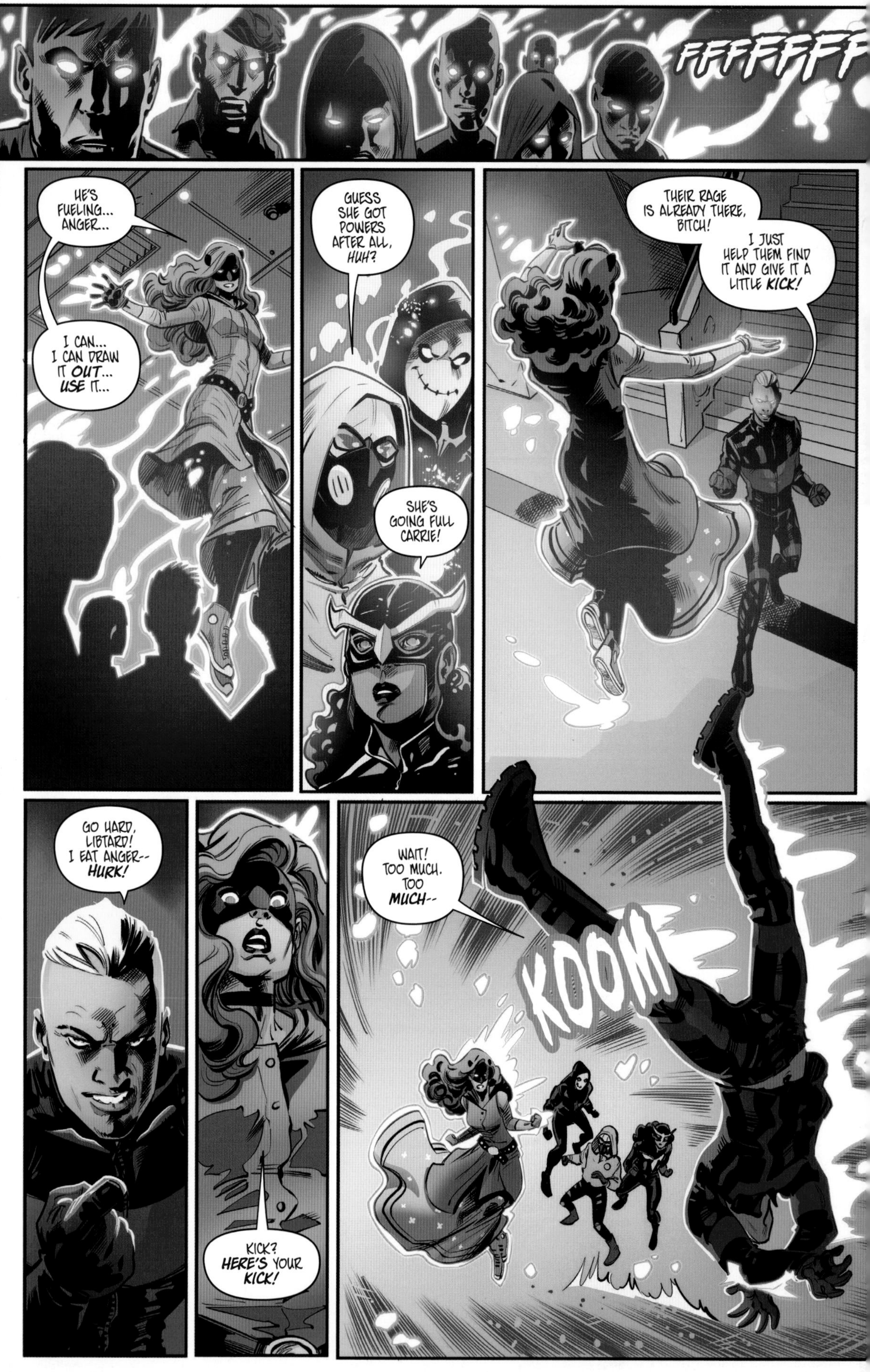
FFFFFFF
HE'S FUELING... ANGER...
I CAN... I CAN DRAW IT OUT... USE IT...
GUESS SHE GOT POWERS AFTER ALL, HUH?
SHE'S GOING FULL CARRIE!
THEIR RAGE IS ALREADY THERE, BITCH!
I JUST HELP THEM FIND IT AND GIVE IT A LITTLE KICK!
GO HARD, LIBTARD! I EAT ANGER-- HURK!
KICK? HERE'S YOUR KICK!
WAIT! TOO MUCH. TOO MUCH--
KOOM

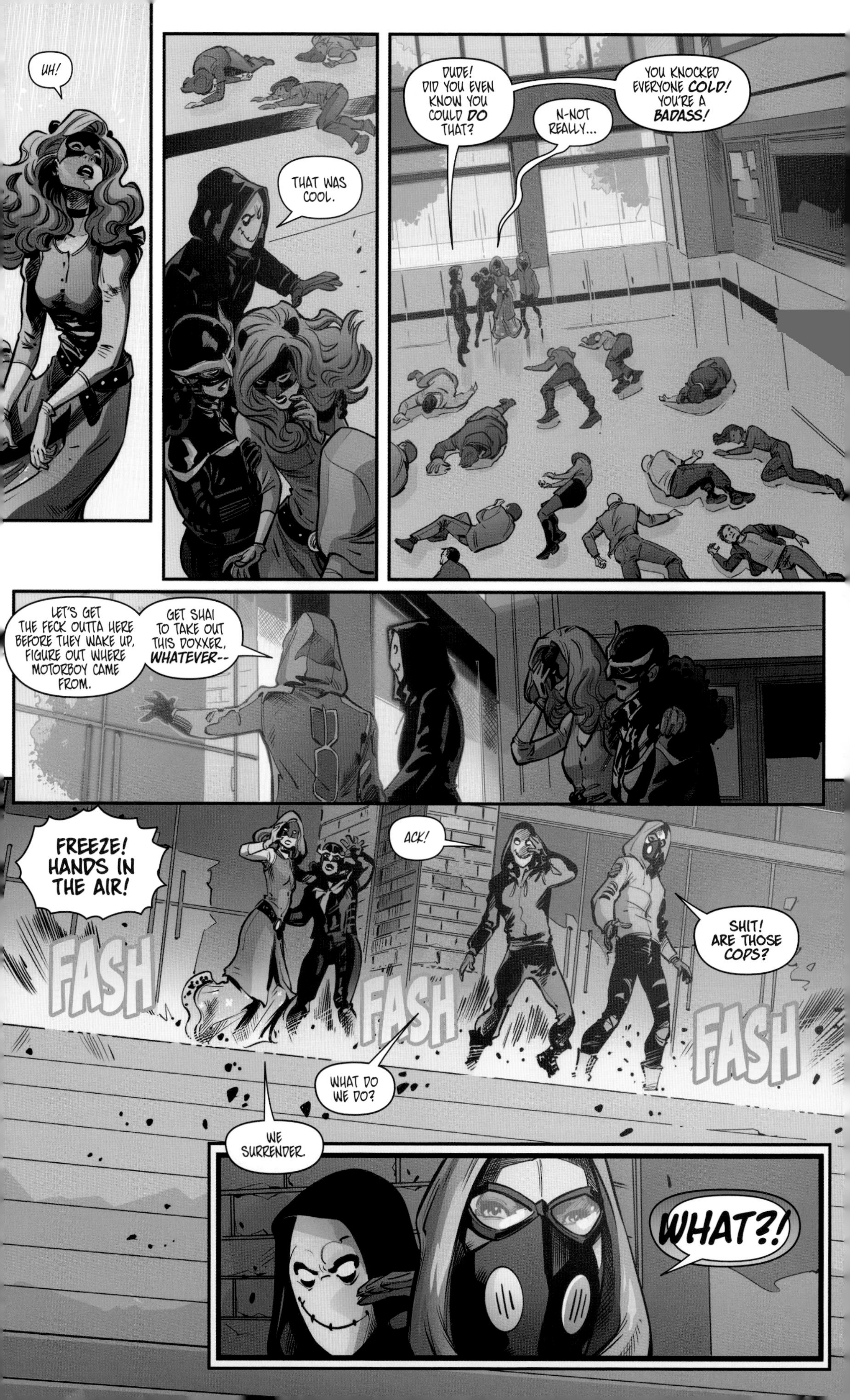
UH!
THAT WAS COOL.
DUDE! DID YOU EVEN KNOW YOU COULD DO THAT?
N-NOT REALLY...
YOU KNOCKED EVERYONE COLD! YOU'RE A BADASS!
LET'S GET THE FECK OUTTA HERE BEFORE THEY WAKE UP, FIGURE OUT WHERE MOTORBOY CAME FROM.
GET SHAI TO TAKE OUT THIS DOXXER, WHATEVER--
FREEZE! HANDS IN THE AIR!
ACK!
SHIT! ARE THOSE COPS?
FASH
FASH
FASH
WHAT DO WE DO?
WE SURRENDER.
WHAT?!

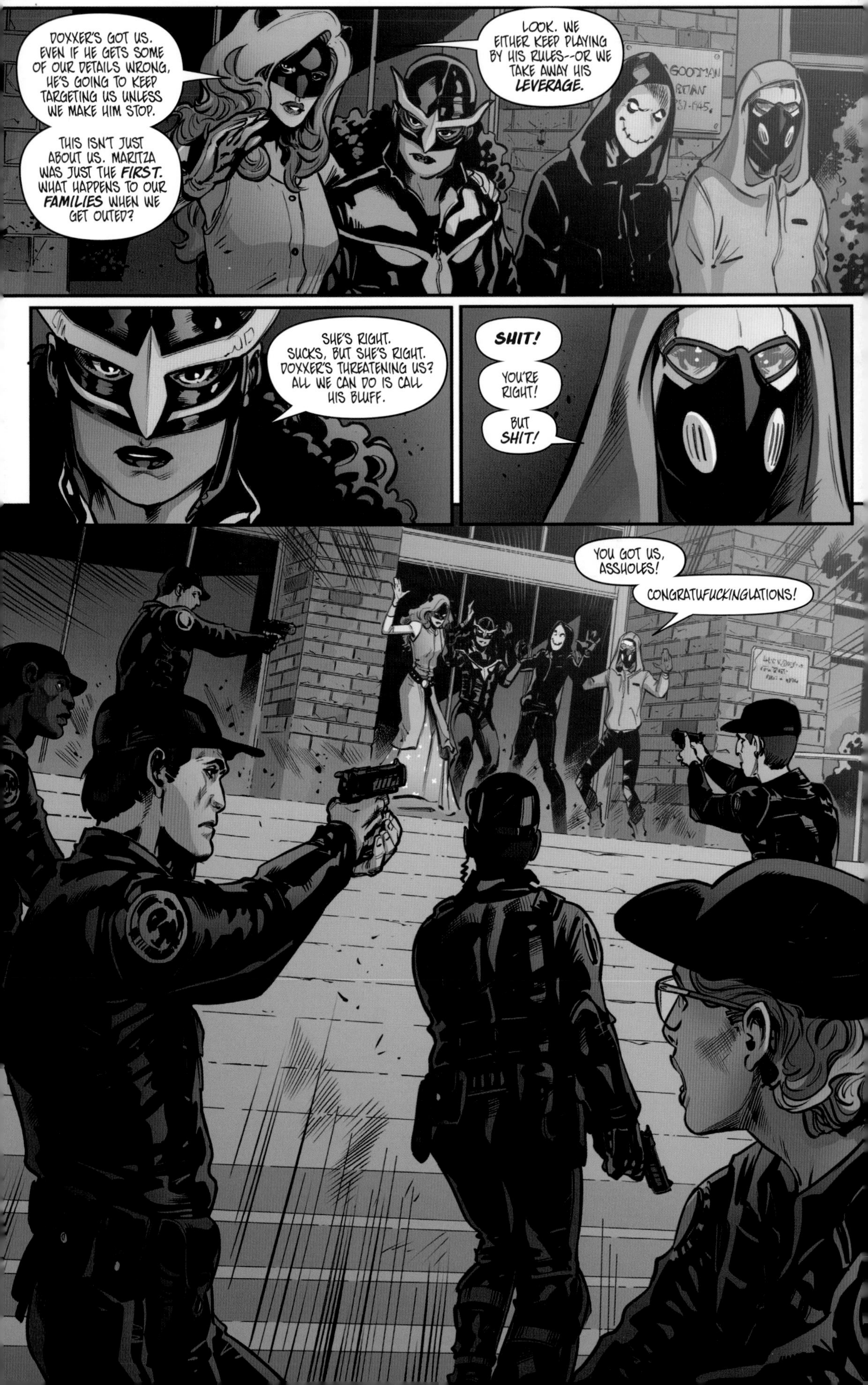
DOXXER'S GOT US. EVEN IF HE GETS SOME OF OUR DETAILS WRONG, HE'S GOING TO KEEP TARGETING US UNLESS WE MAKE HIM STOP.
THIS ISN'T JUST ABOUT US. MARITZA WAS JUST THE FIRST. WHAT HAPPENS TO OUR FAMILIES WHEN WE GET OUTED?
LOOK. WE EITHER KEEP PLAYING BY HIS RULES--OR WE TAKE AWAY HIS LEVERAGE.
SHE'S RIGHT. SUCKS, BUT SHE'S RIGHT. DOXXER'S THREATENING US? ALL WE CAN DO IS CALL HIS BLUFF.
SHIT!
YOU'RE RIGHT!
BUT SHIT!
YOU GOT US, ASSHOLES!
CONGRATUFUCKINGLATIONS!

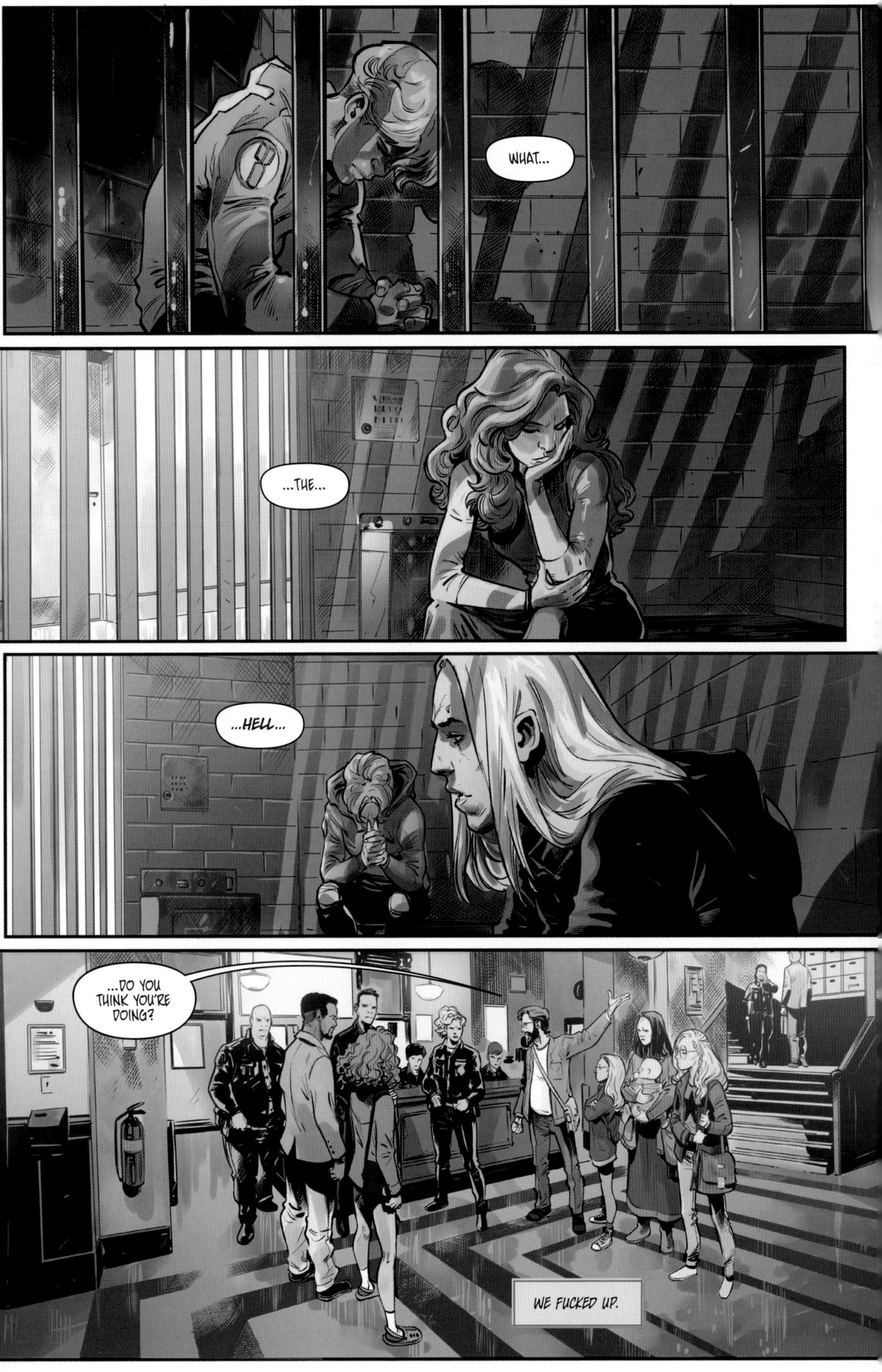
WHAT...
...THE...
...HELL...
...DO YOU THINK YOU'RE DOING?
WE FUCKED UP.

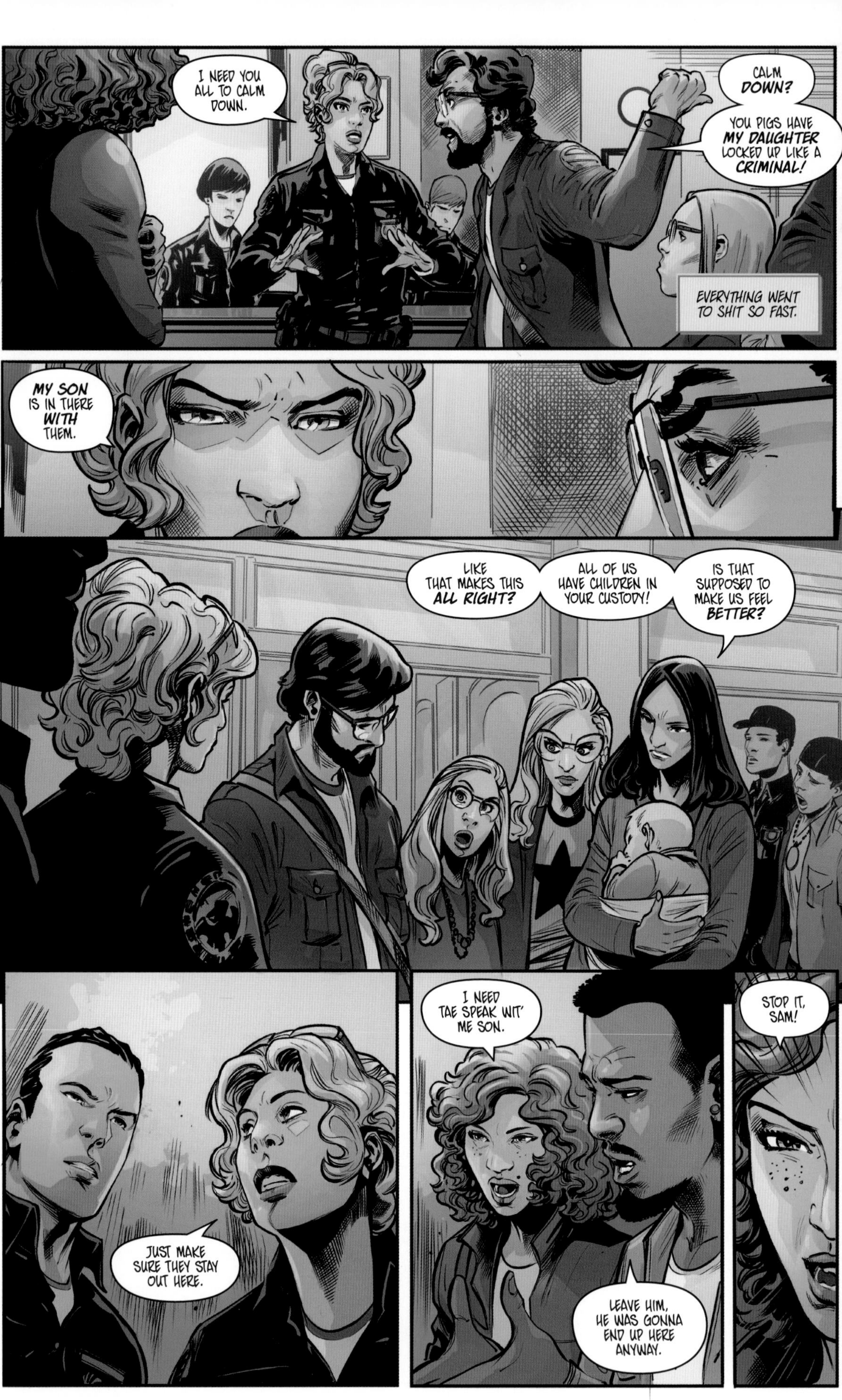
I NEED YOU ALL TO CALM DOWN.
CALM DOWN?
YOU PIGS HAVE MY DAUGHTER LOCKED UP LIKE A CRIMINAL!
EVERYTHING WENT TO SHIT SO FAST.
MY SON IS IN THERE WITH THEM.
LIKE THAT MAKES THIS ALL RIGHT?
ALL OF US HAVE CHILDREN IN YOUR CUSTODY!
IS THAT SUPPOSED TO MAKE US FEEL BETTER?
JUST MAKE SURE THEY STAY OUT HERE.
I NEED TAE SPEAK WIT' ME SON.
LEAVE HIM, HE WAS GONNA END UP HERE ANYWAY.
STOP IT, SAM!

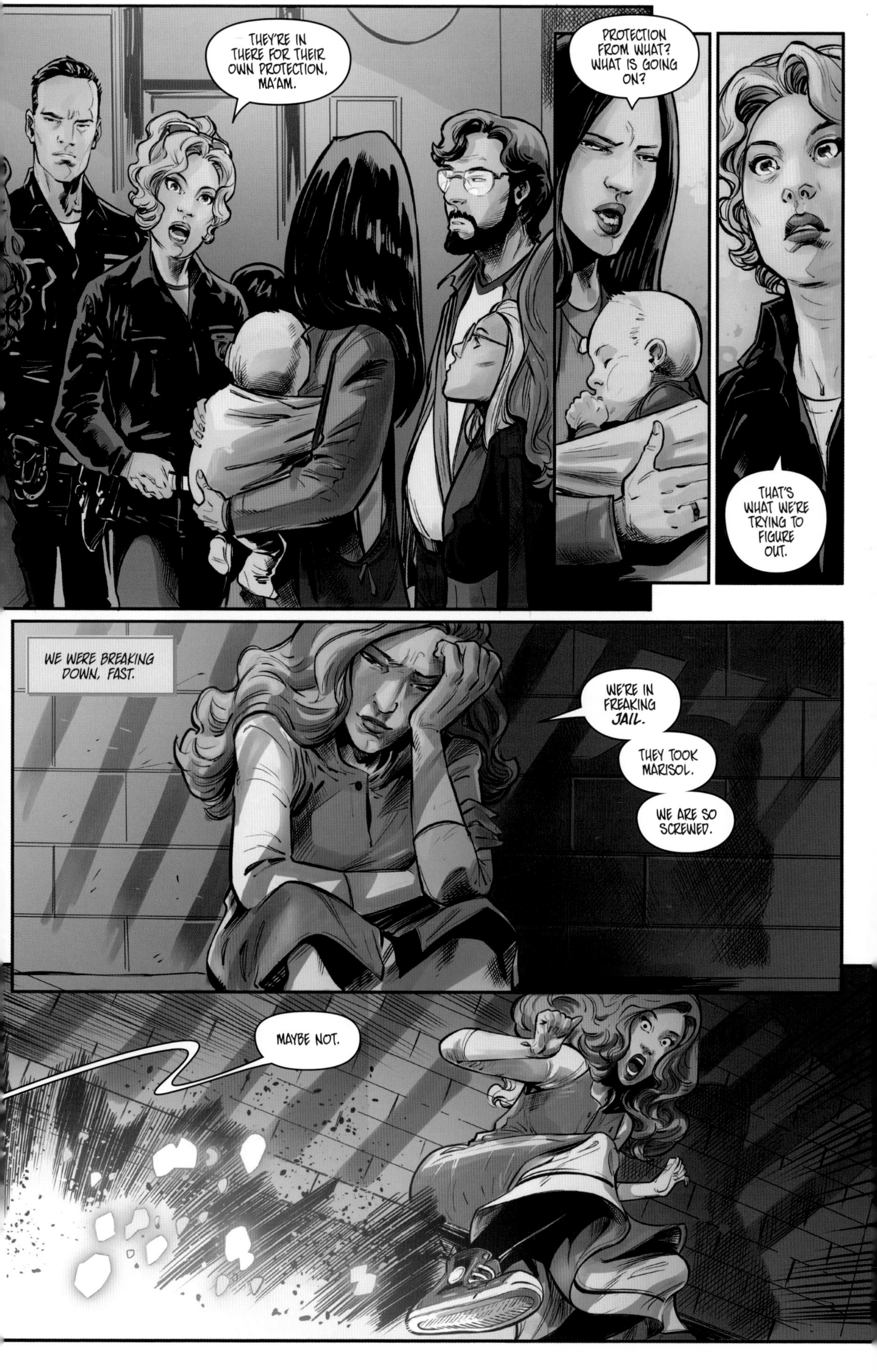
THEY'RE IN THERE FOR THEIR OWN PROTECTION, MA'AM.
PROTECTION FROM WHAT? WHAT IS GOING ON?
THAT'S WHAT WE'RE TRYING TO FIGURE OUT.
WE WERE BREAKING DOWN, FAST.
WE'RE IN FREAKING JAIL.
THEY TOOK MARISOL.
WE ARE SO SCREWED.
MAYBE NOT.

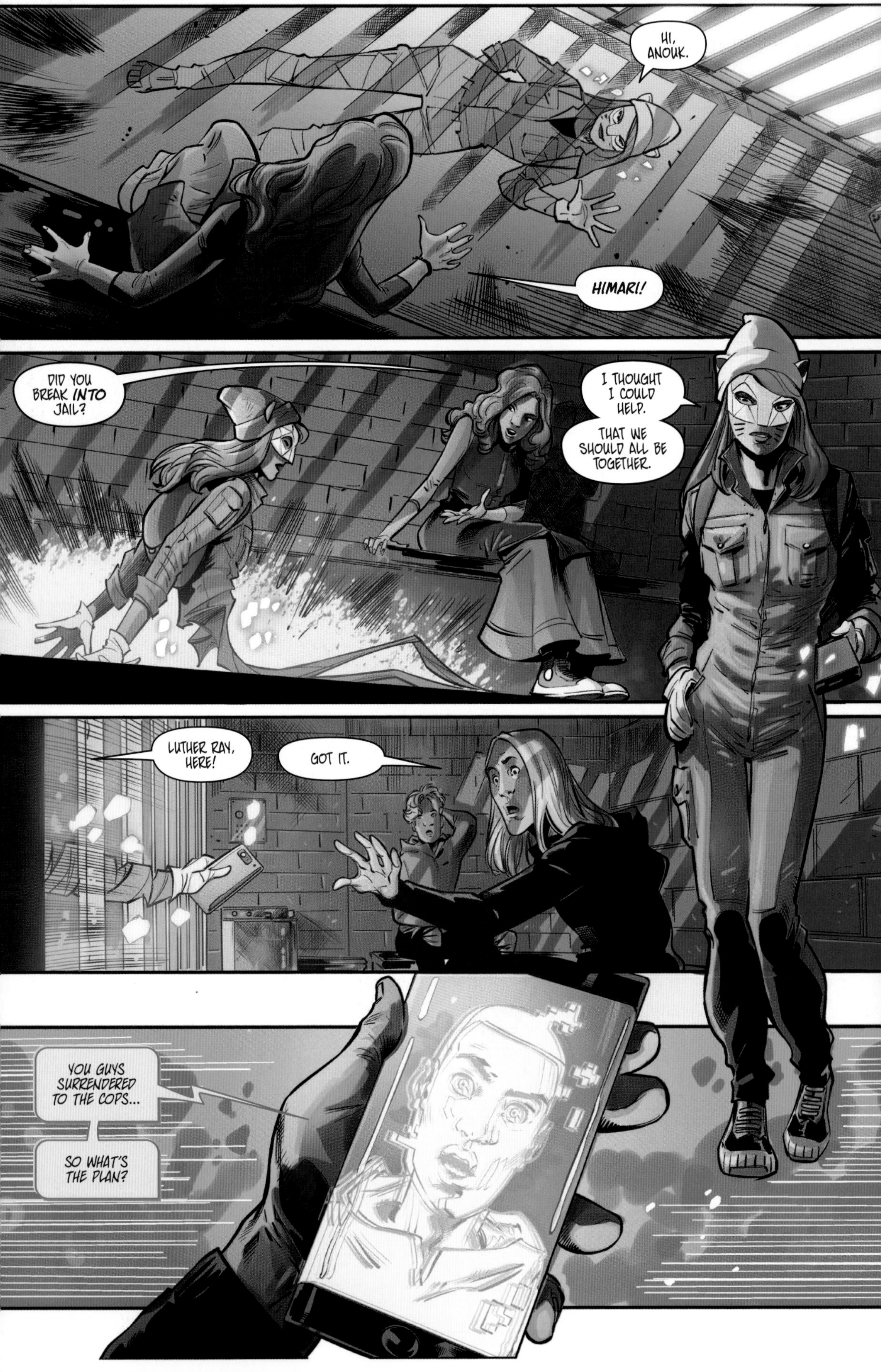
HI, ANOUK.
HIMARI!
DID YOU BREAK INTO JAIL?
I THOUGHT I COULD HELP.
THAT WE SHOULD ALL BE TOGETHER.
LUTHER RAY, HERE!
GOT IT.
YOU GUYS SURRENDERED TO THE COPS...
SO WHAT'S THE PLAN?

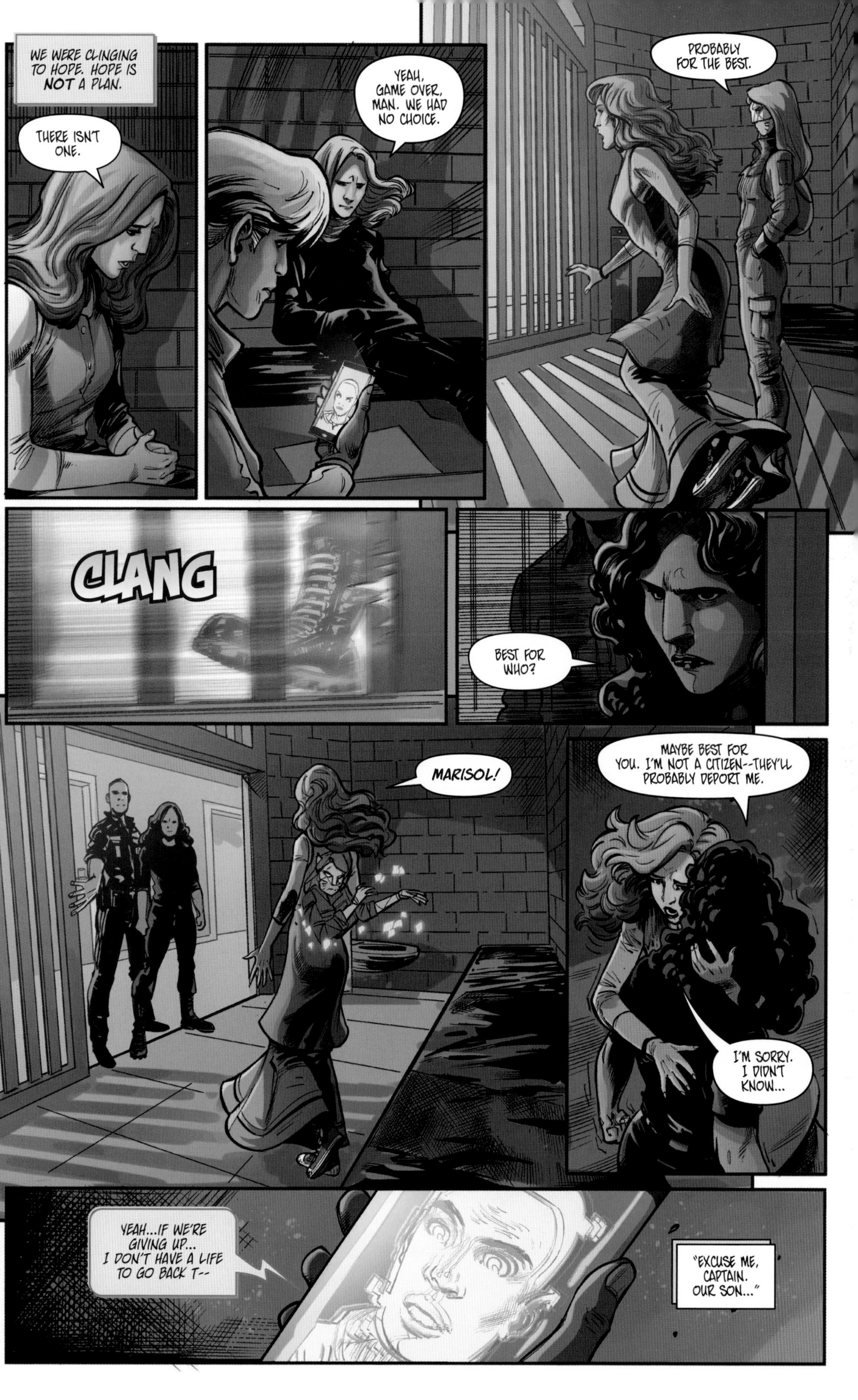

WE WERE CLINGING TO HOPE. HOPE IS NOT A PLAN.
THERE ISN'T ONE.
YEAH, GAME OVER, MAN. WE HAD NO CHOICE.
PROBABLY FOR THE BEST.
CLANG
BEST FOR WHO?
MARISOL!
MAYBE BEST FOR YOU. I'M NOT A CITIZEN--THEY'LL PROBABLY DEPORT ME.
I'M SORRY. I DIDN'T KNOW...
YEAH...IF WE'RE GIVING UP... I DON'T HAVE A LIFE TO GO BACK T--
"EXCUSE ME, CAPTAIN. OUR SON..."

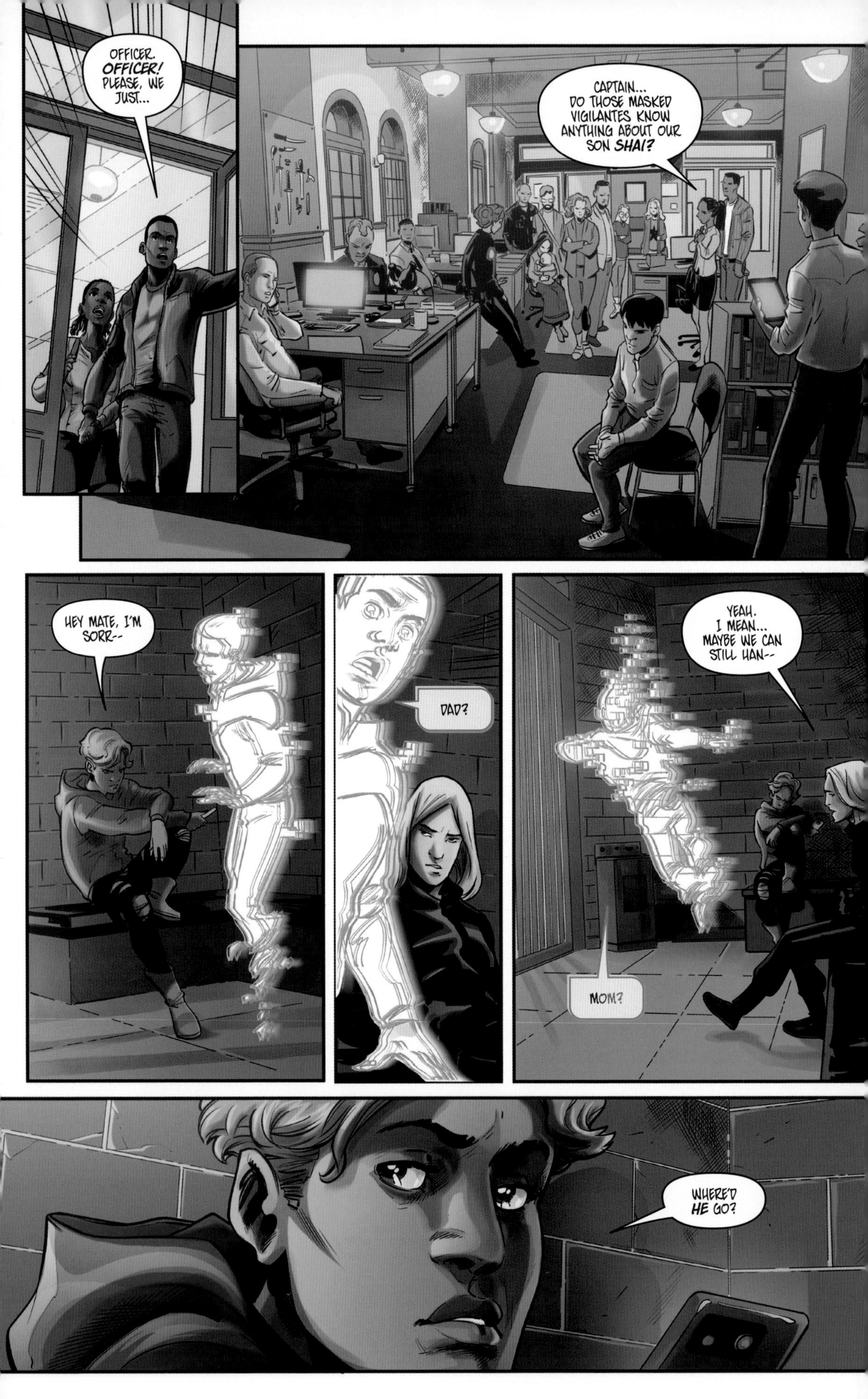
OFFICER. OFFICER! PLEASE, WE JUST...
CAPTAIN... DO THOSE MASKED VIGILANTES KNOW ANYTHING ABOUT OUR SON SHAI?
HEY MATE, I'M SORR--
DAD?
YEAH. I MEAN... MAYBE WE CAN STILL HAN--
MOM?
WHERE'D HE GO?

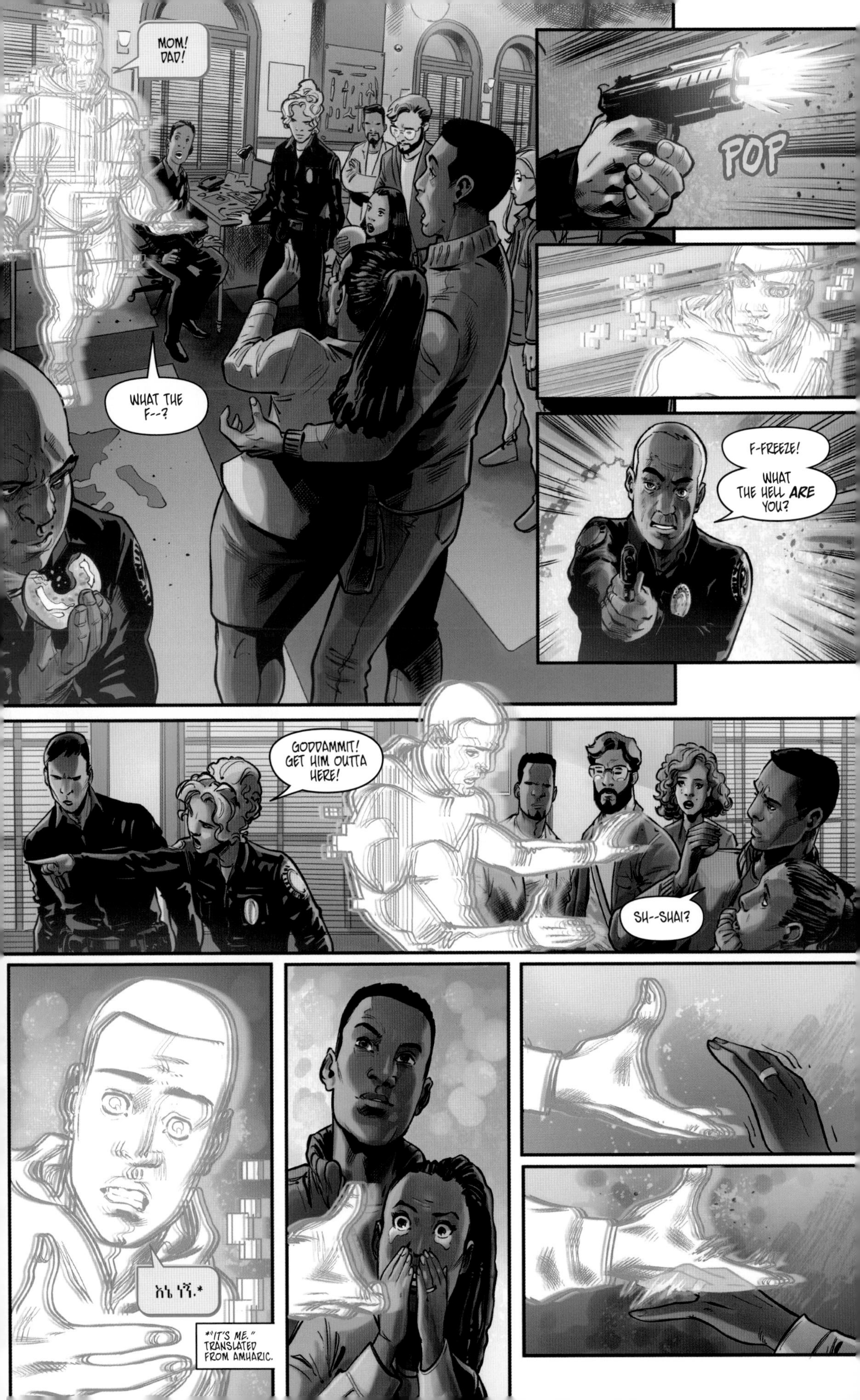
MOM! DAD!
WHAT THE F--?
POP
F-FREEZE!
WHAT THE HELL ARE YOU?
GODDAMMIT! GET HIM OUTTA HERE!
SH--SHAI?
እኔ ነኝ.*
*"IT'S ME." TRANSLATED FROM AMHARIC.

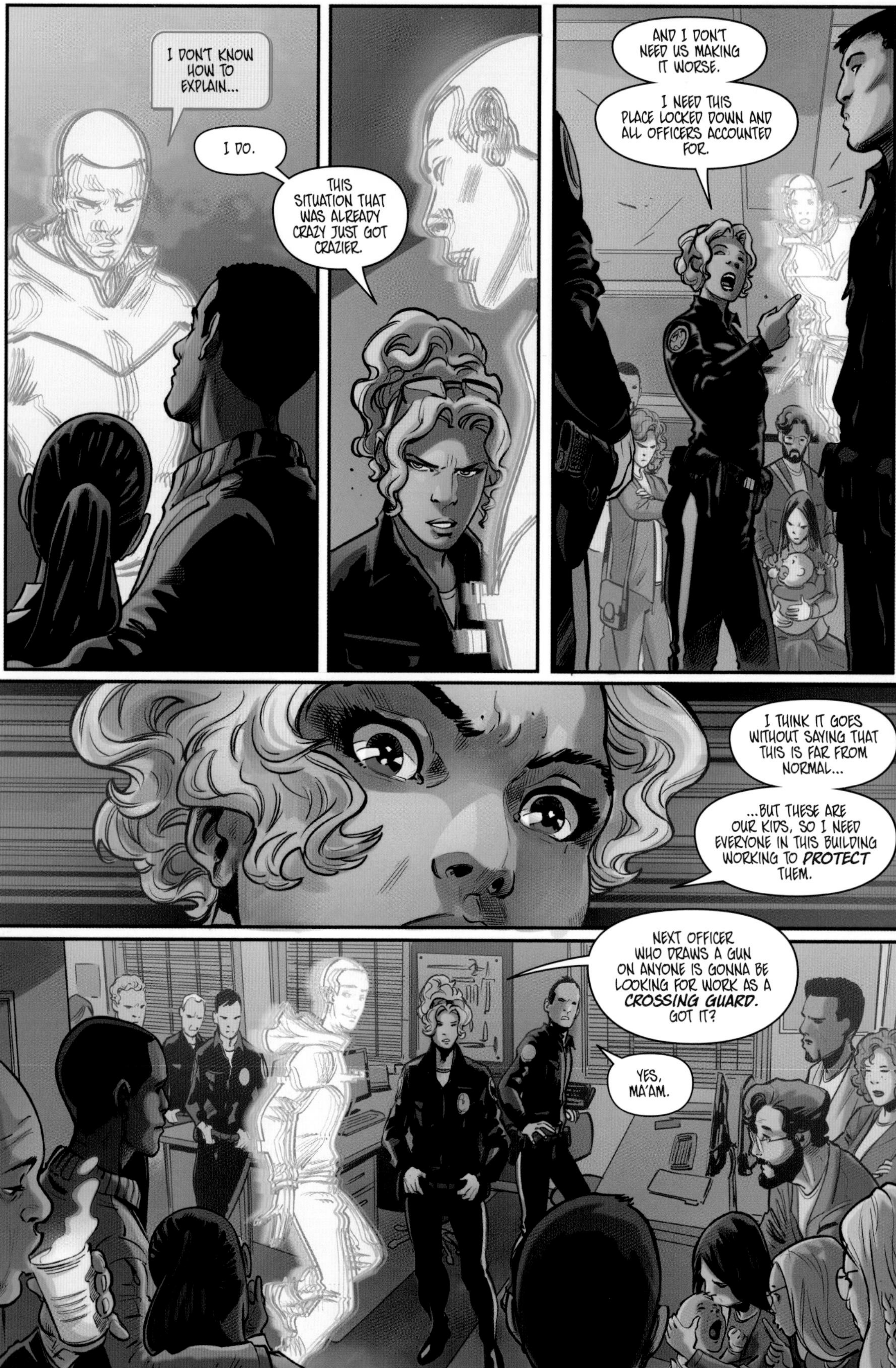
I DON'T KNOW HOW TO EXPLAIN...
I DO.
THIS SITUATION THAT WAS ALREADY CRAZY JUST GOT CRAZIER.
AND I DON'T NEED US MAKING IT WORSE.
I NEED THIS PLACE LOCKED DOWN AND ALL OFFICERS ACCOUNTED FOR.
I THINK IT GOES WITHOUT SAYING THAT THIS IS FAR FROM NORMAL...
...BUT THESE ARE OUR KIDS, SO I NEED EVERYONE IN THIS BUILDING WORKING TO PROTECT THEM.
NEXT OFFICER WHO DRAWS A GUN ON ANYONE IS GONNA BE LOOKING FOR WORK AS A CROSSING GUARD. GOT IT?
YES, MA'AM.

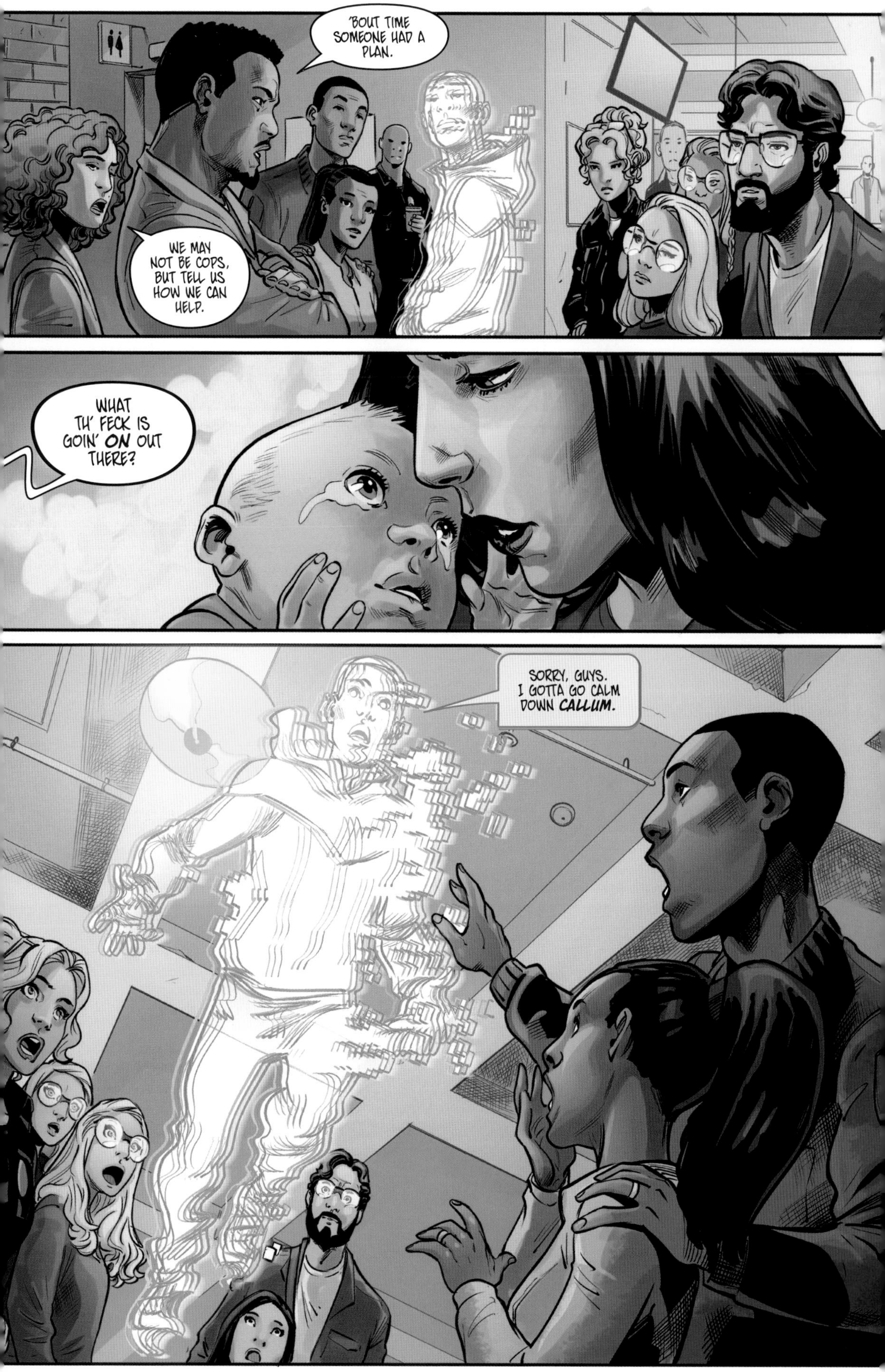
'BOUT TIME SOMEONE HAD A PLAN.
WE MAY NOT BE COPS, BUT TELL US HOW WE CAN HELP.
WHAT TH' FECK IS GOIN' **ON** OUT THERE?
SORRY, GUYS. I GOTTA GO CALM DOWN ***CALLUM.***

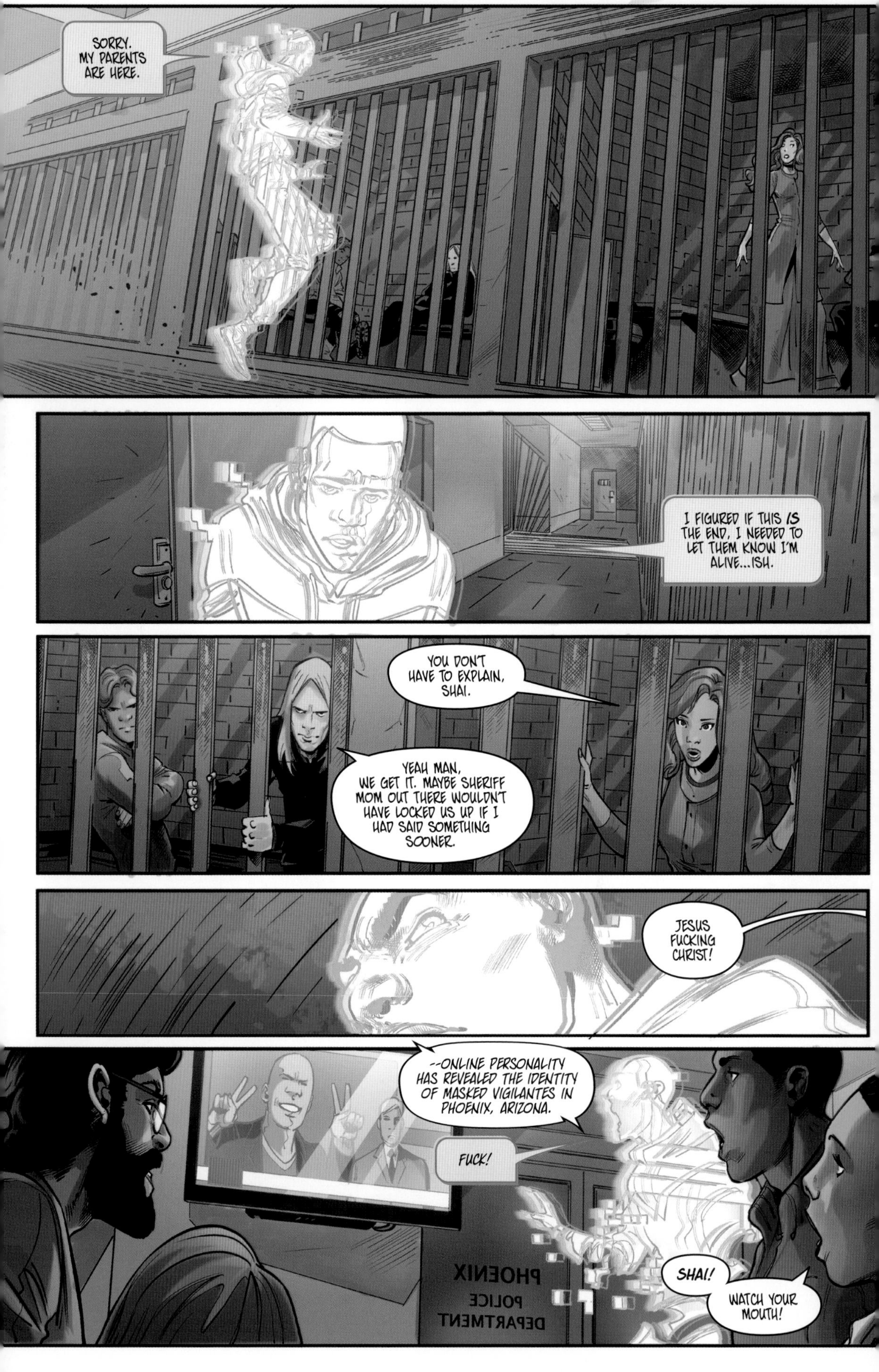
SORRY. MY PARENTS ARE HERE.
I FIGURED IF THIS IS THE END, I NEEDED TO LET THEM KNOW I'M ALIVE...ISH.
YOU DON'T HAVE TO EXPLAIN, SHAI.
YEAH MAN, WE GET IT. MAYBE SHERIFF MOM OUT THERE WOULDN'T HAVE LOCKED US UP IF I HAD SAID SOMETHING SOONER.
JESUS FUCKING CHRIST!
--ONLINE PERSONALITY HAS REVEALED THE IDENTITY OF MASKED VIGILANTES IN PHOENIX, ARIZONA.
FUCK!
PHOENIX POLICE DEPARTMENT
SHAI!
WATCH YOUR MOUTH!

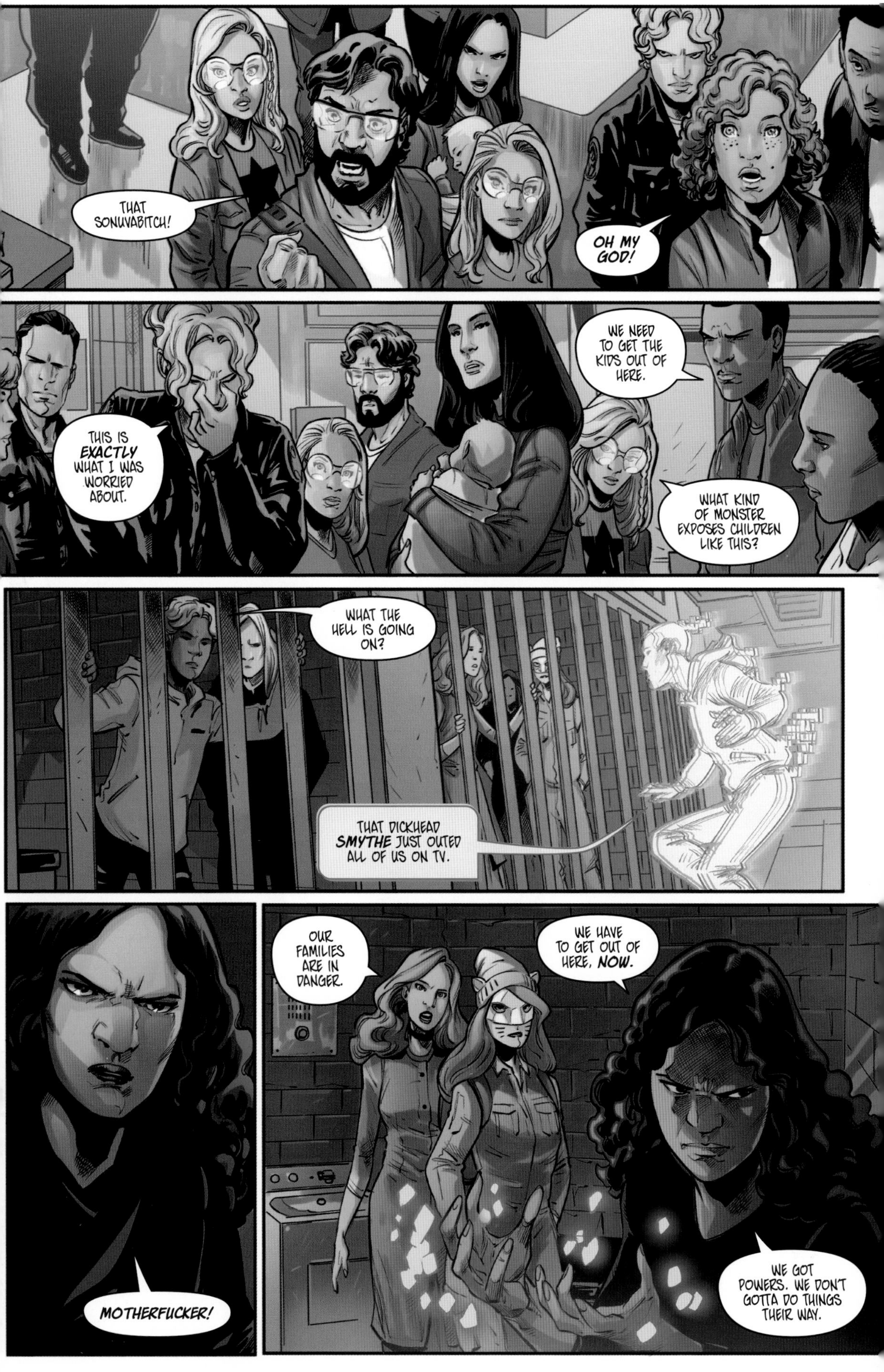
THAT SONUVABITCH!
OH MY GOD!
THIS IS EXACTLY WHAT I WAS WORRIED ABOUT.
WE NEED TO GET THE KIDS OUT OF HERE.
WHAT KIND OF MONSTER EXPOSES CHILDREN LIKE THIS?
WHAT THE HELL IS GOING ON?
THAT DICKHEAD SMYTHE JUST OUTED ALL OF US ON TV.
MOTHERFUCKER!
OUR FAMILIES ARE IN DANGER.
WE HAVE TO GET OUT OF HERE, NOW.
WE GOT POWERS. WE DON'T GOTTA DO THINGS THEIR WAY.

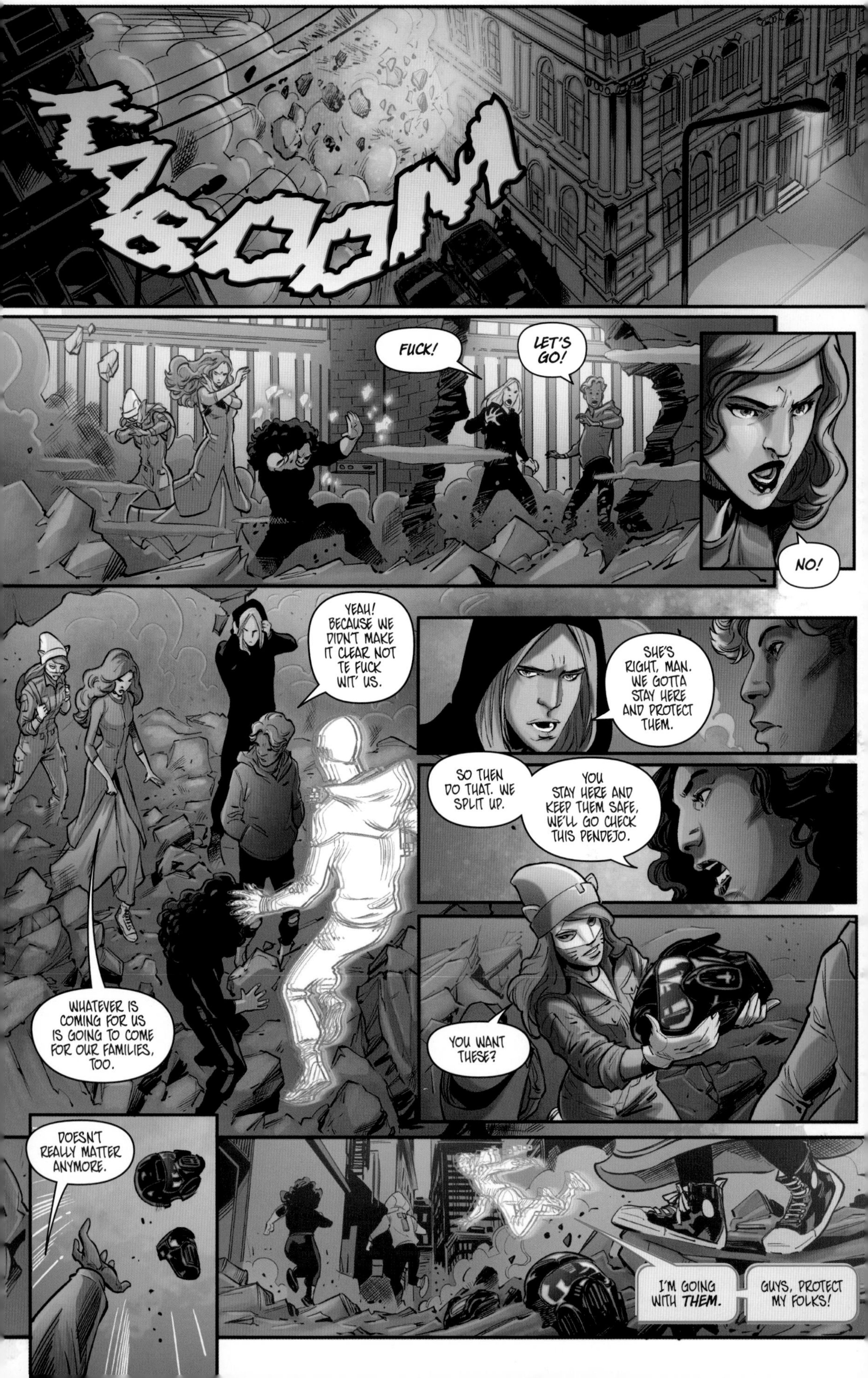
KA BOOM
FUCK!
LET'S GO!
NO!
YEAH! BECAUSE WE DIDN'T MAKE IT CLEAR NOT TE FUCK WIT' US.
WHATEVER IS COMING FOR US IS GOING TO COME FOR OUR FAMILIES, TOO.
SHE'S RIGHT, MAN. WE GOTTA STAY HERE AND PROTECT THEM.
SO THEN DO THAT. WE SPLIT UP.
YOU STAY HERE AND KEEP THEM SAFE, WE'LL GO CHECK THIS PENDEJO.
YOU WANT THESE?
DOESN'T REALLY MATTER ANYMORE.
I'M GOING WITH THEM.
GUYS, PROTECT MY FOLKS!

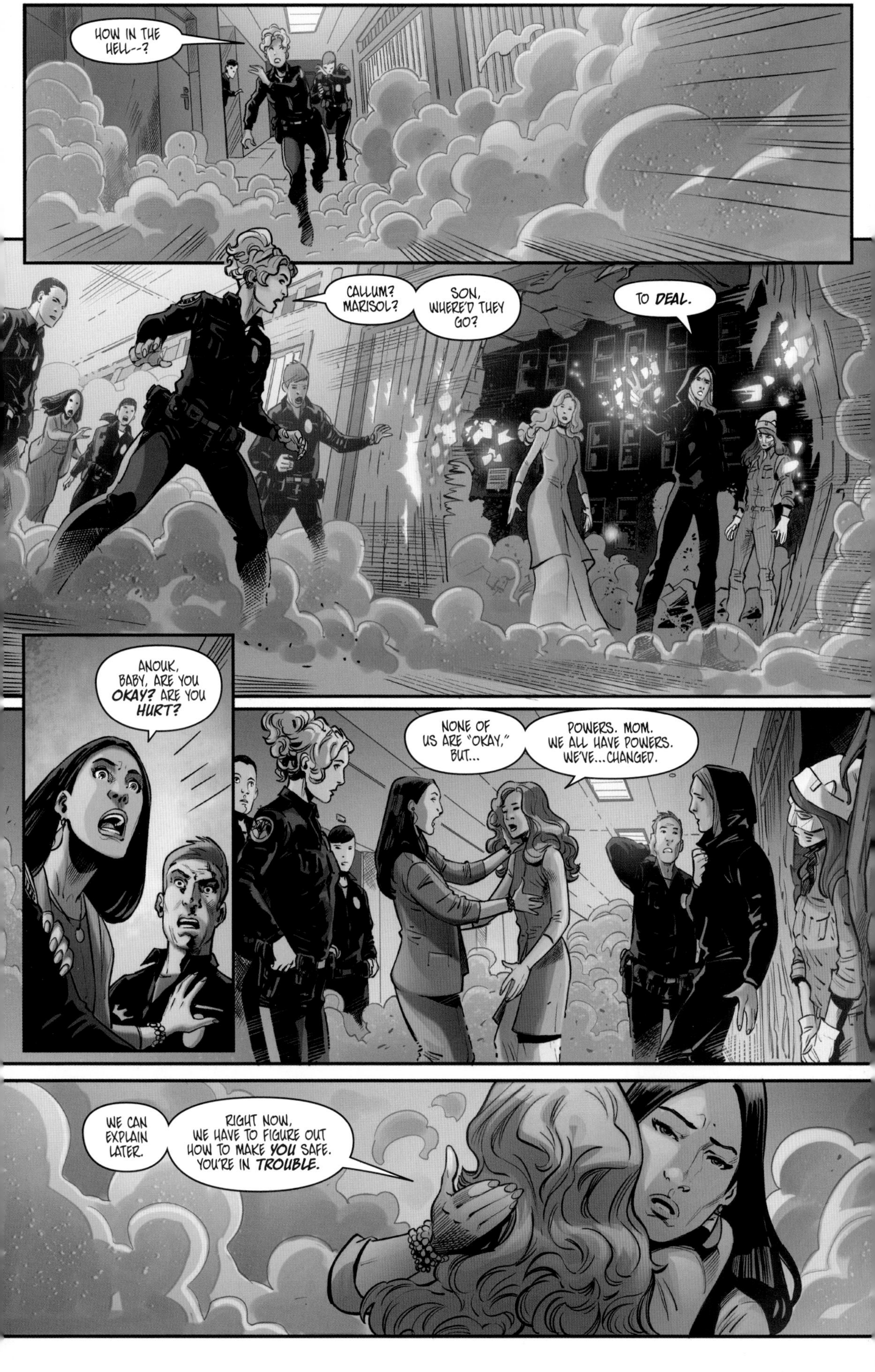
HOW IN THE HELL--?
CALLUM? MARISOL?
SON, WHERE'D THEY GO?
TO DEAL.
ANOUK, BABY, ARE YOU OKAY? ARE YOU HURT?
NONE OF US ARE "OKAY," BUT...
POWERS. MOM. WE ALL HAVE POWERS. WE'VE...CHANGED.
WE CAN EXPLAIN LATER.
RIGHT NOW, WE HAVE TO FIGURE OUT HOW TO MAKE YOU SAFE. YOU'RE IN TROUBLE.

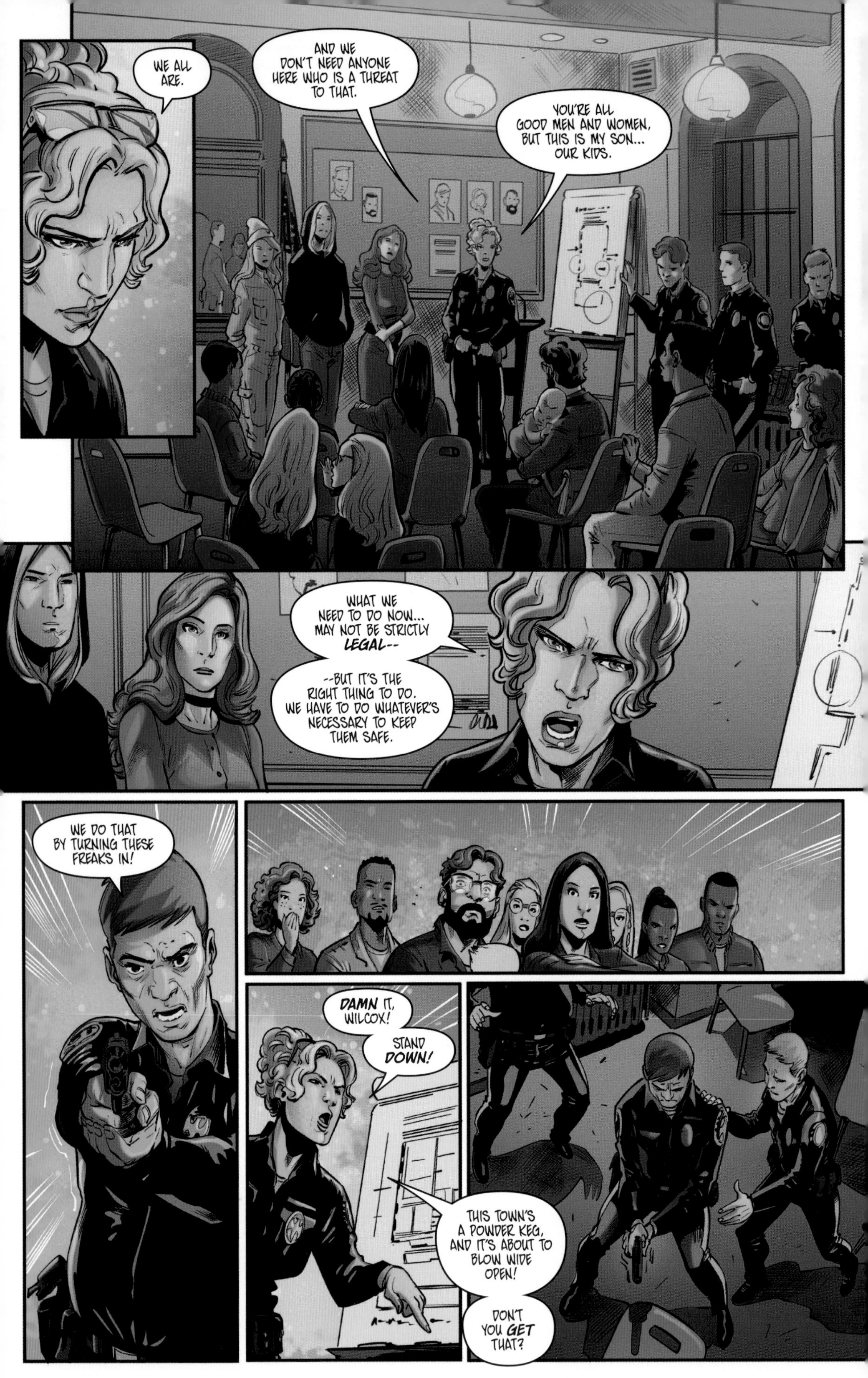
WE ALL ARE.
AND WE DON'T NEED ANYONE HERE WHO IS A THREAT TO THAT.
YOU'RE ALL GOOD MEN AND WOMEN, BUT THIS IS MY SON... OUR KIDS.
WHAT WE NEED TO DO NOW... MAY NOT BE STRICTLY **LEGAL**--
--BUT IT'S THE RIGHT THING TO DO. WE HAVE TO DO WHATEVER'S NECESSARY TO KEEP THEM SAFE.
WE DO THAT BY TURNING THESE FREAKS IN!
DAMN IT, WILCOX!
STAND **DOWN!**
THIS TOWN'S A POWDER KEG, AND IT'S ABOUT TO BLOW WIDE OPEN!
DON'T YOU **GET** THAT?

HOW MUCH FURTHER, MATE?

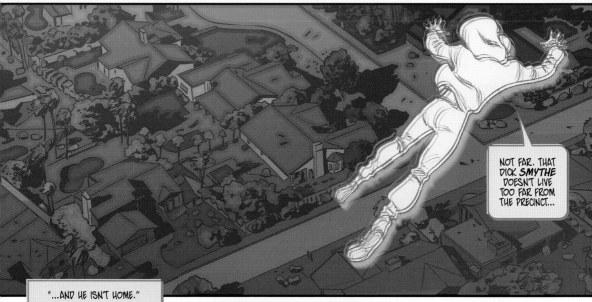

NOT FAR. THAT DICK *SMYTHE* DOESN'T LIVE TOO FAR FROM THE PRECINCT...

"...AND HE ISN'T HOME."

I'M GETTING THREE TIMES OUR AVERAGE SUBSCRIBERS--

--SINCE LOCAL NEWS PICKED UP MY *EXCLUSIVE* ON THESE KIDS.

BREAK OUT THE CHAMPAGNE, FOLKS.

BRRRNG

THIS IS SMYTHE.

⟫SNIFF⟪

THIS IS *DOXXHUND.*

I DIDN'T SHARE THAT INFO WITH YOU TO RELEASE IN TOTAL TO THE PUBLIC, SMYTHE.

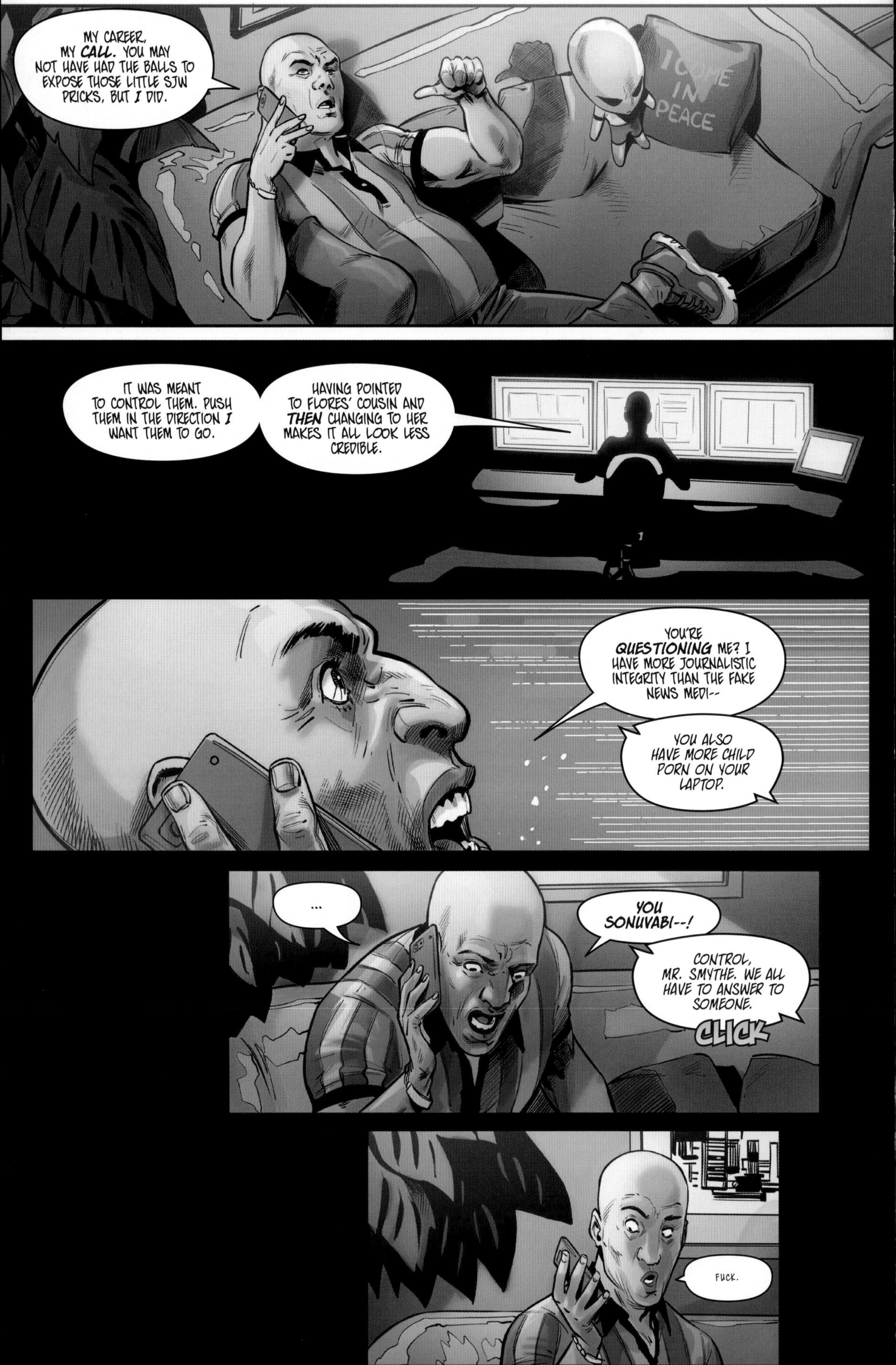

MY CAREER, MY CALL. YOU MAY NOT HAVE HAD THE BALLS TO EXPOSE THOSE LITTLE SJW PRICKS, BUT I DID.
I COME IN PEACE
IT WAS MEANT TO CONTROL THEM. PUSH THEM IN THE DIRECTION I WANT THEM TO GO.
HAVING POINTED TO FLORES' COUSIN AND THEN CHANGING TO HER MAKES IT ALL LOOK LESS CREDIBLE.
YOU'RE QUESTIONING ME? I HAVE MORE JOURNALISTIC INTEGRITY THAN THE FAKE NEWS MEDI--
YOU ALSO HAVE MORE CHILD PORN ON YOUR LAPTOP.
...
YOU SONUVABI--!
CONTROL, MR. SMYTHE. WE ALL HAVE TO ANSWER TO SOMEONE.
CLICK
FUCK.

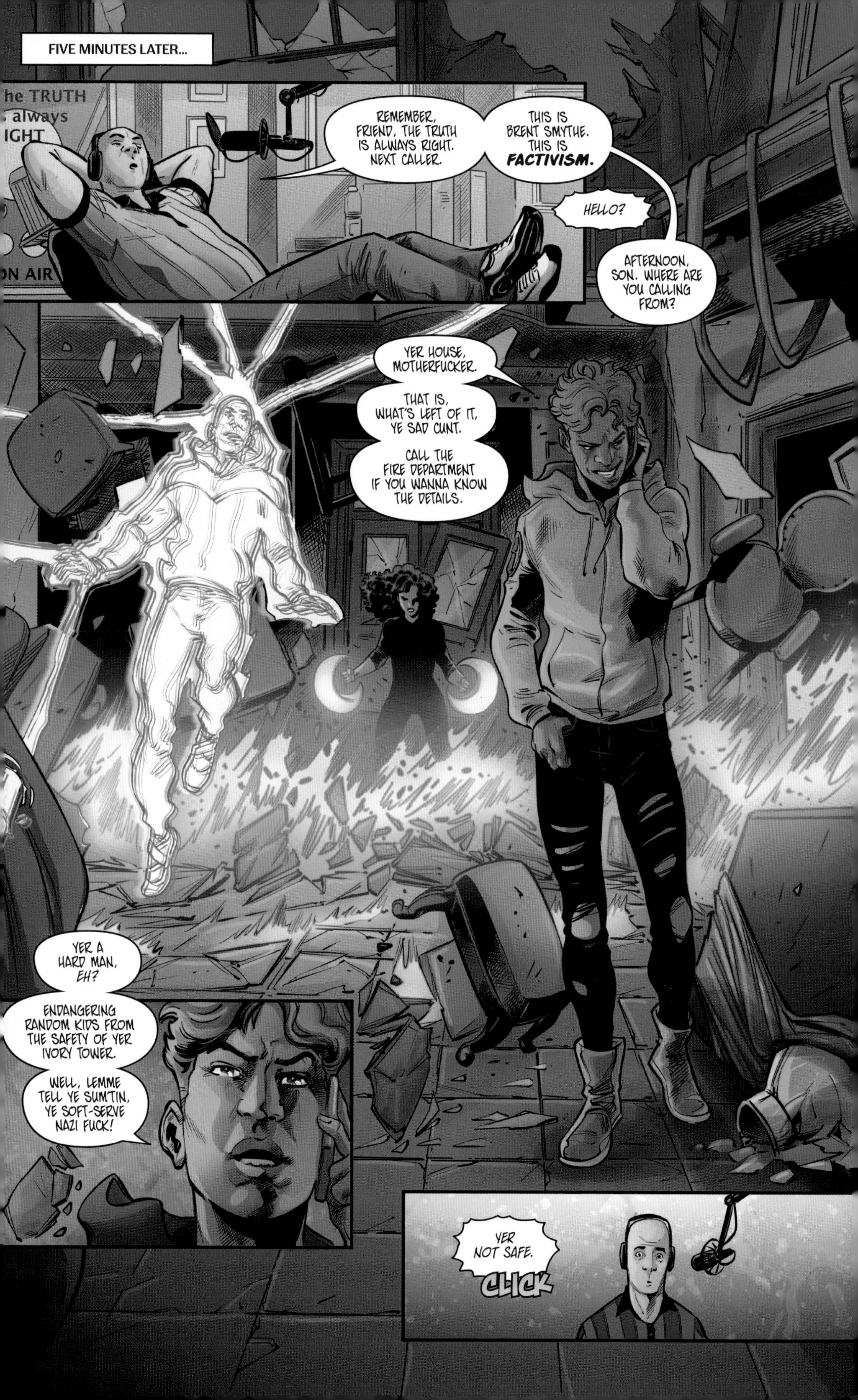
FIVE MINUTES LATER...
The TRUTH
s always
IGHT
ON AIR
REMEMBER, FRIEND, THE TRUTH IS ALWAYS RIGHT. NEXT CALLER.
THIS IS BRENT SMYTHE. THIS IS FACTIVISM.
HELLO?
AFTERNOON, SON. WHERE ARE YOU CALLING FROM?
YER HOUSE, MOTHERFUCKER.
THAT IS, WHAT'S LEFT OF IT, YE SAD CUNT.
CALL THE FIRE DEPARTMENT IF YOU WANNA KNOW THE DETAILS.
YER A HARD MAN, EH?
ENDANGERING RANDOM KIDS FROM THE SAFETY OF YER IVORY TOWER.
WELL, LEMME TELL YE SUM'TIN, YE SOFT-SERVE NAZI FUCK!
YER NOT SAFE.
CLICK

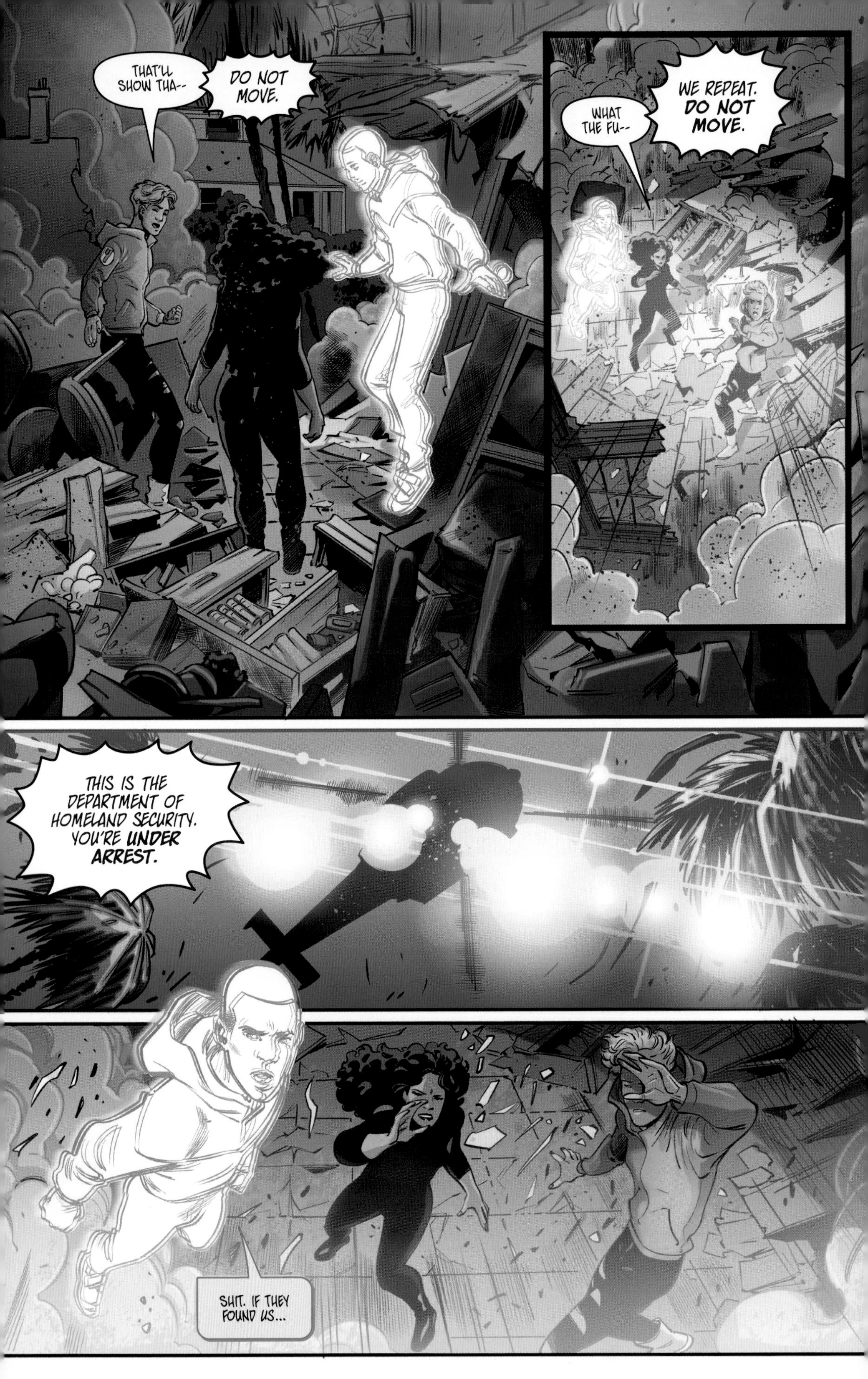
THAT'LL SHOW THA--
DO NOT MOVE.
WHAT THE FU--
WE REPEAT. DO NOT MOVE.
THIS IS THE DEPARTMENT OF HOMELAND SECURITY. YOU'RE UNDER ARREST.
SHIT. IF THEY FOUND US...

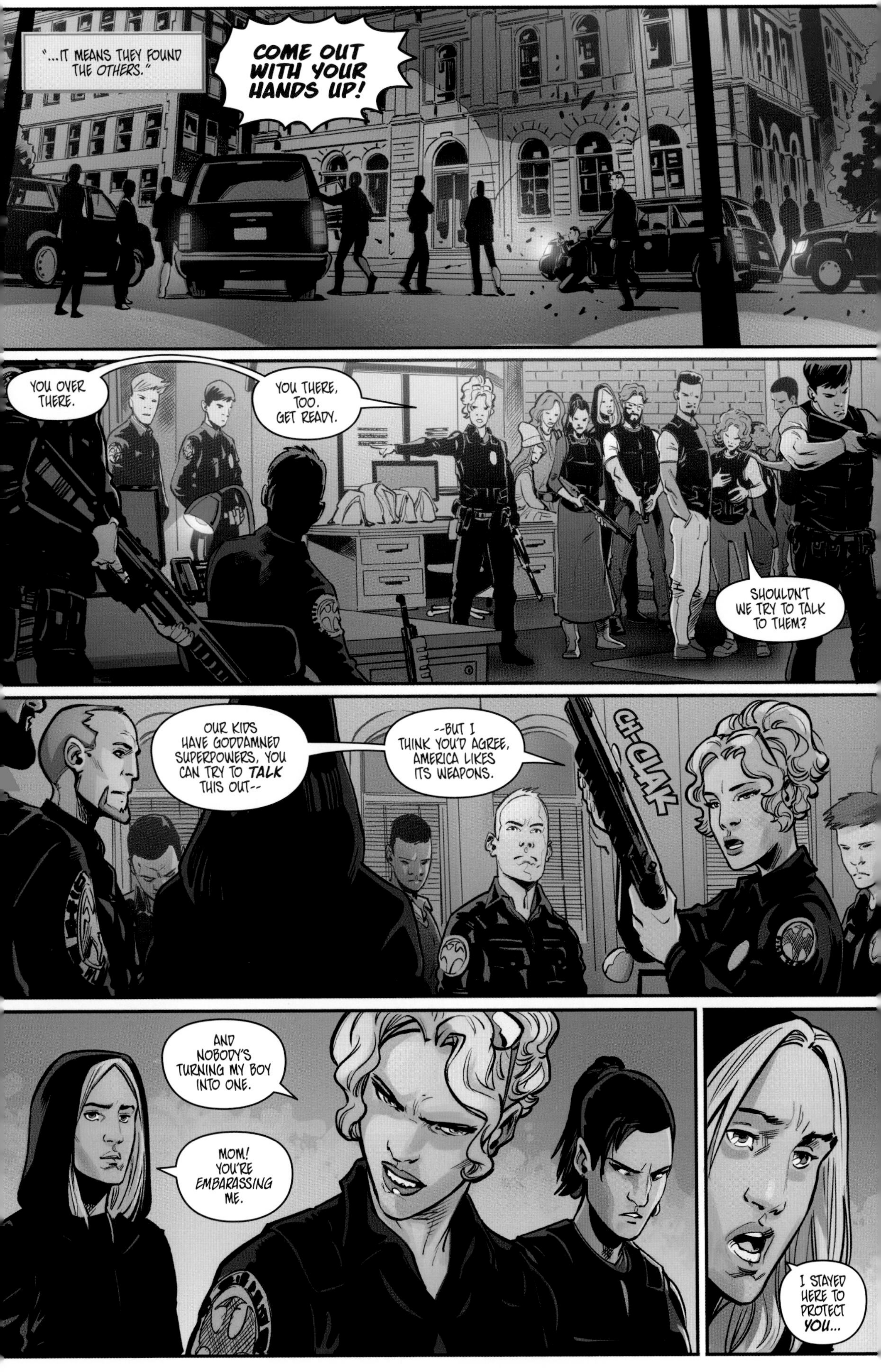
"...IT MEANS THEY FOUND THE OTHERS."
COME OUT WITH YOUR HANDS UP!
YOU OVER THERE.
YOU THERE, TOO. GET READY.
SHOULDN'T WE TRY TO TALK TO THEM?
OUR KIDS HAVE GODDAMNED SUPERPOWERS, YOU CAN TRY TO TALK THIS OUT--
--BUT I THINK YOU'D AGREE, AMERICA LIKES ITS WEAPONS.
CH-CLAK
AND NOBODY'S TURNING MY BOY INTO ONE.
MOM! YOU'RE EMBARASSING ME.
I STAYED HERE TO PROTECT YOU...

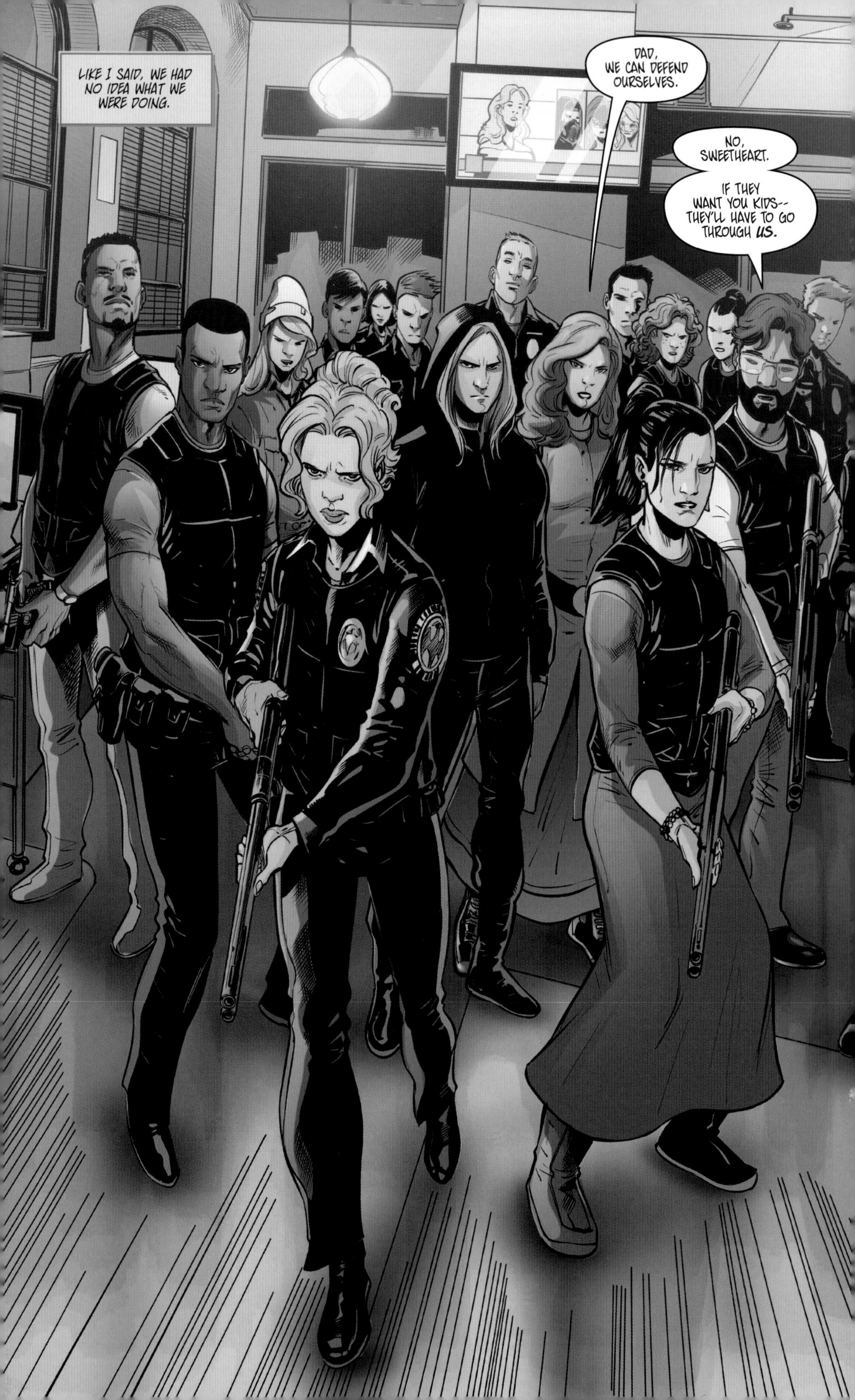
LIKE I SAID, WE HAD NO IDEA WHAT WE WERE DOING.
DAD, WE CAN DEFEND OURSELVES.
NO, SWEETHEART.
IF THEY WANT YOU KIDS-- THEY'LL HAVE TO GO THROUGH US.

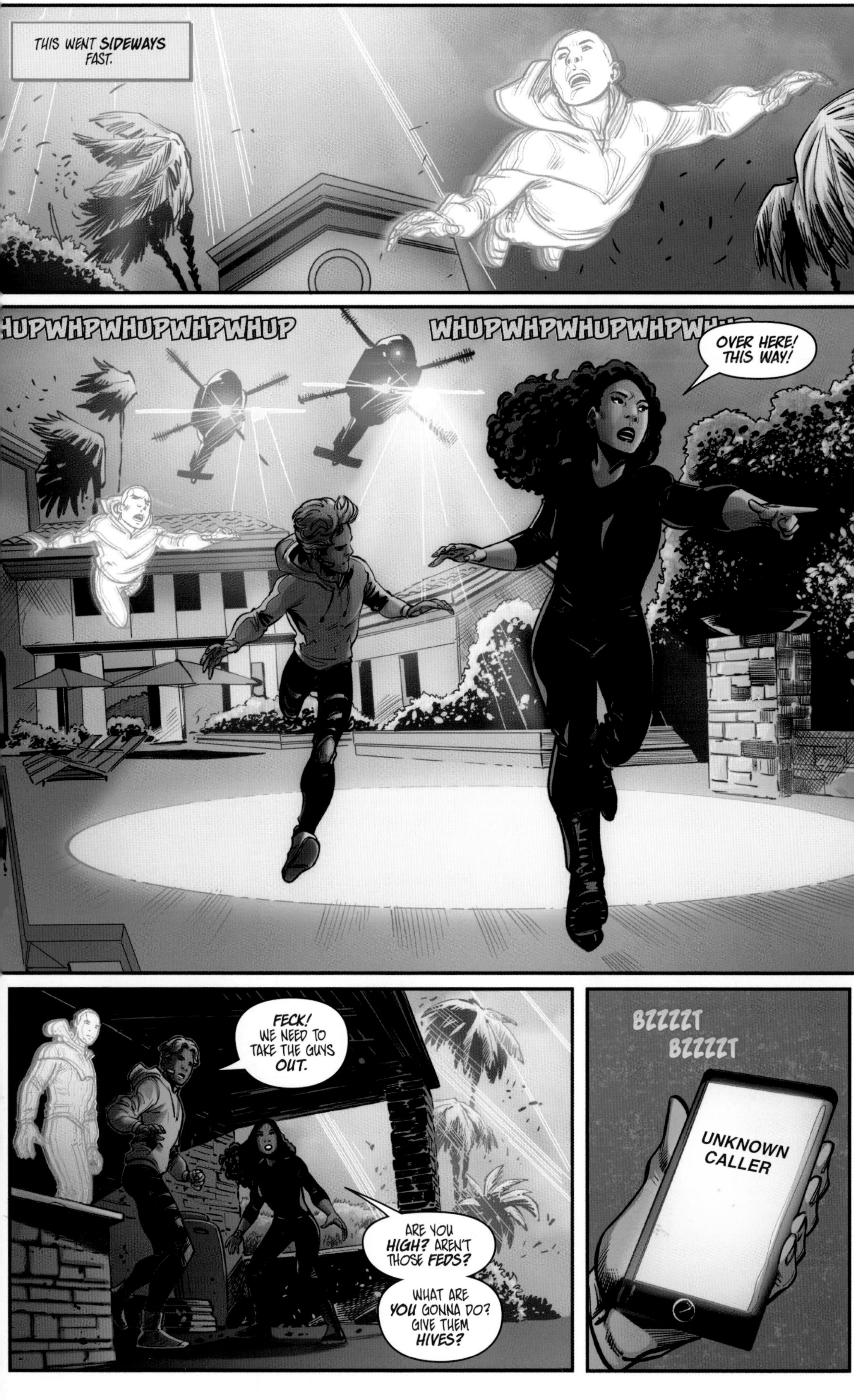
THIS WENT SIDEWAYS FAST.
HUPWHPWHUPWHPWHUP
WHUPWHPWHUPWHPWHU
OVER HERE! THIS WAY!
FECK! WE NEED TO TAKE THE GUYS OUT.
ARE YOU HIGH? AREN'T THOSE FEDS?
WHAT ARE YOU GONNA DO? GIVE THEM HIVES?
BZZZZT
BZZZZT
UNKNOWN CALLER

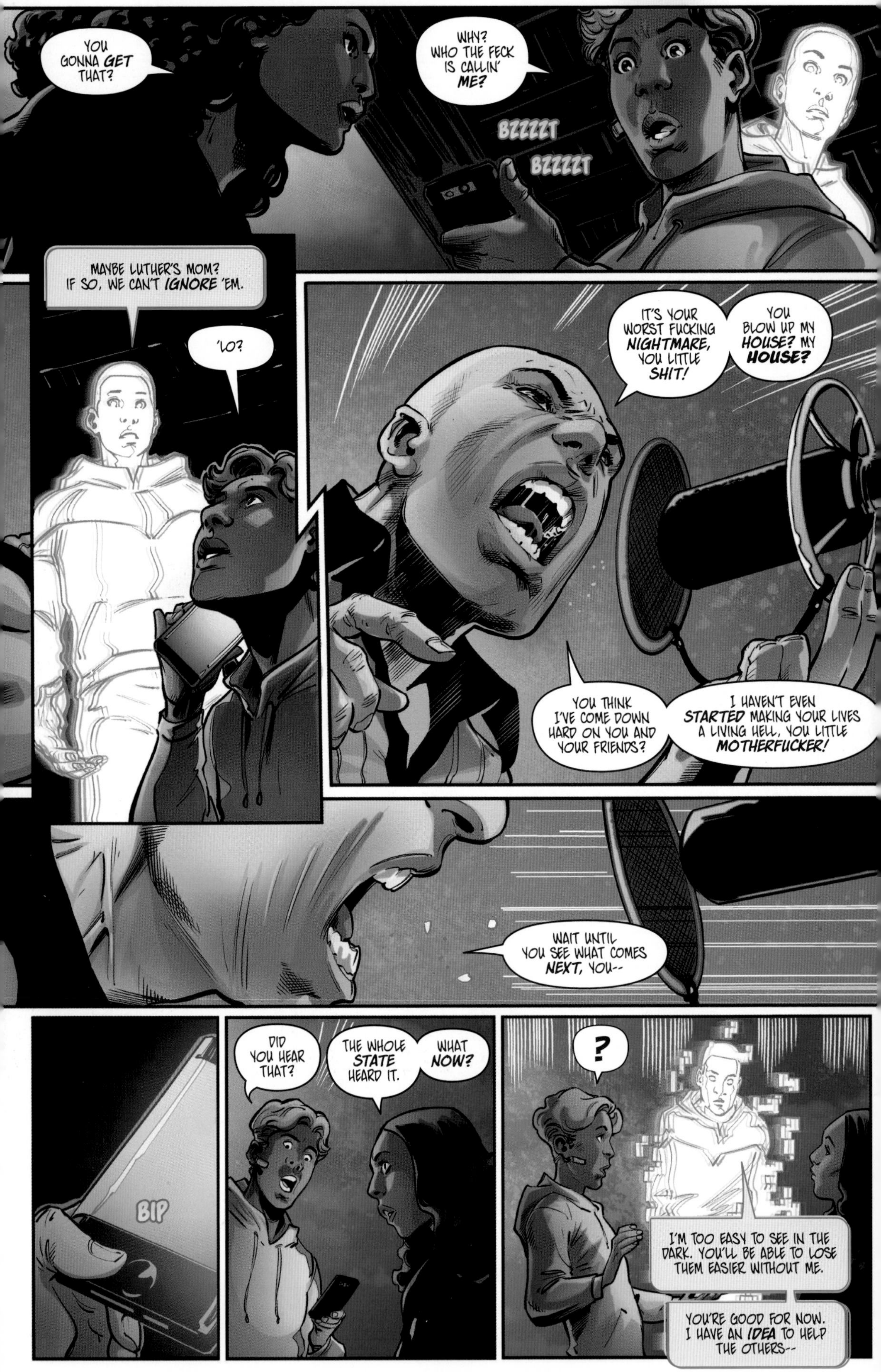

YOU GONNA GET THAT?
WHY? WHO THE FECK IS CALLIN' ME?
BZZZZT
BZZZZT
MAYBE LUTHER'S MOM? IF SO, WE CAN'T IGNORE 'EM.
'LO?
IT'S YOUR WORST FUCKING NIGHTMARE, YOU LITTLE SHIT!
YOU BLOW UP MY HOUSE? MY HOUSE?
YOU THINK I'VE COME DOWN HARD ON YOU AND YOUR FRIENDS?
I HAVEN'T EVEN STARTED MAKING YOUR LIVES A LIVING HELL, YOU LITTLE MOTHERFUCKER!
WAIT UNTIL YOU SEE WHAT COMES NEXT, YOU--
BIP
DID YOU HEAR THAT?
THE WHOLE STATE HEARD IT.
WHAT NOW?
?
I'M TOO EASY TO SEE IN THE DARK. YOU'LL BE ABLE TO LOSE THEM EASIER WITHOUT ME.
YOU'RE GOOD FOR NOW. I HAVE AN IDEA TO HELP THE OTHERS--

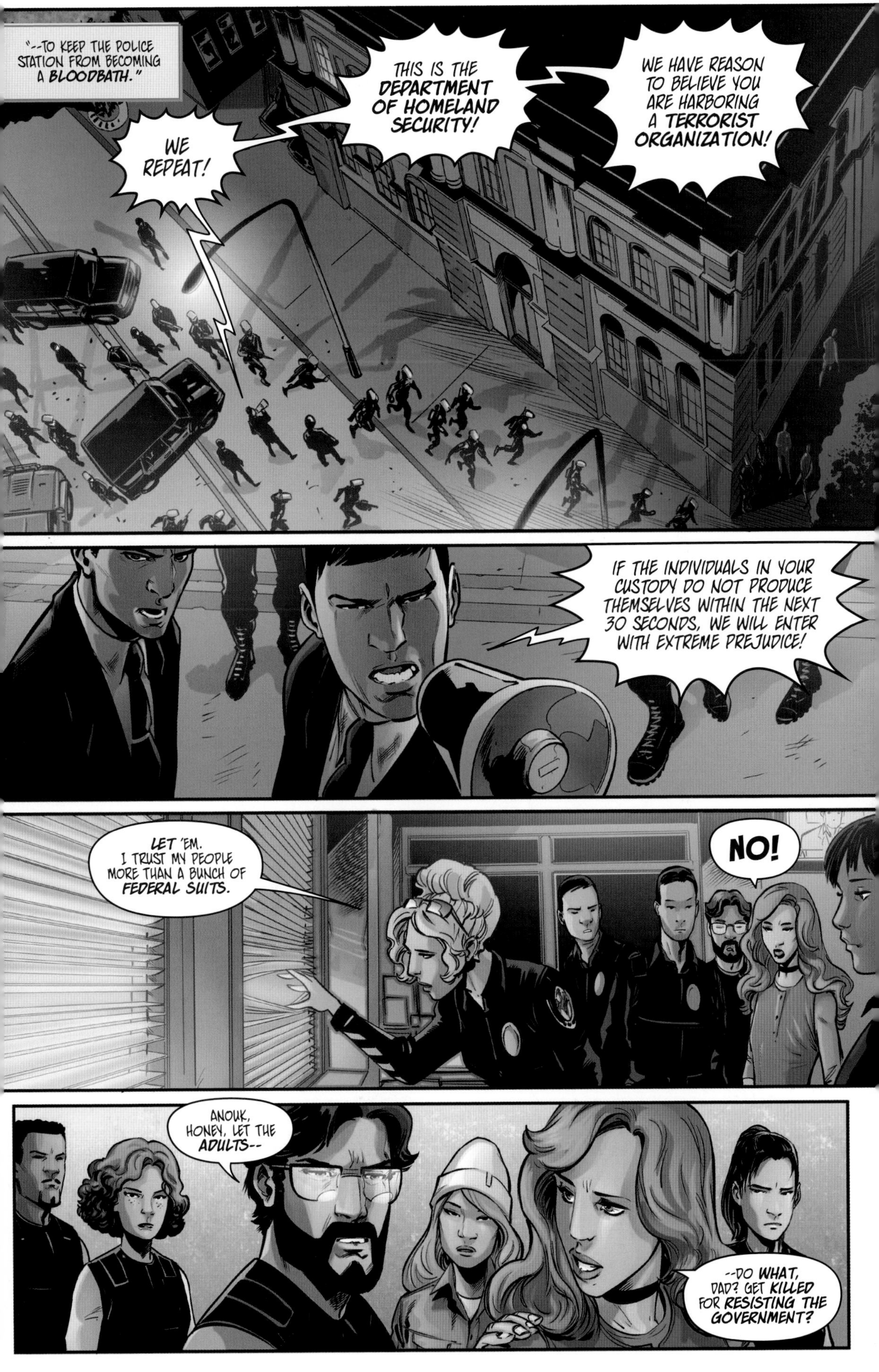
"--TO KEEP THE POLICE STATION FROM BECOMING A BLOODBATH."
WE REPEAT!
THIS IS THE DEPARTMENT OF HOMELAND SECURITY!
WE HAVE REASON TO BELIEVE YOU ARE HARBORING A TERRORIST ORGANIZATION!
IF THE INDIVIDUALS IN YOUR CUSTODY DO NOT PRODUCE THEMSELVES WITHIN THE NEXT 30 SECONDS, WE WILL ENTER WITH EXTREME PREJUDICE!
LET 'EM. I TRUST MY PEOPLE MORE THAN A BUNCH OF FEDERAL SUITS.
NO!
ANOUK, HONEY, LET THE ADULTS--
--DO WHAT, DAD? GET KILLED FOR RESISTING THE GOVERNMENT?

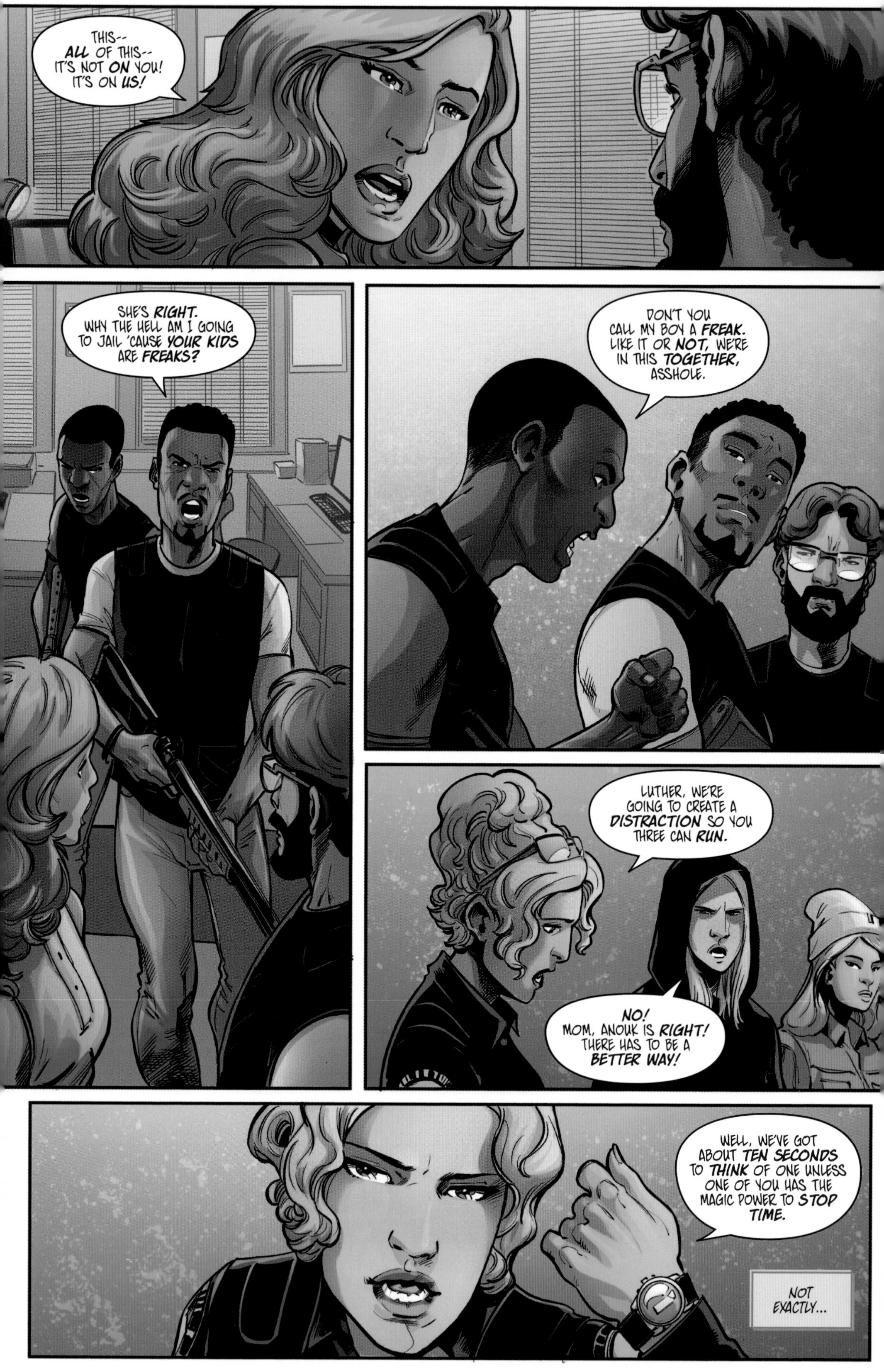
THIS-- ALL OF THIS-- IT'S NOT ON YOU! IT'S ON US!
SHE'S RIGHT. WHY THE HELL AM I GOING TO JAIL 'CAUSE YOUR KIDS ARE FREAKS?
DON'T YOU CALL MY BOY A FREAK. LIKE IT OR NOT, WE'RE IN THIS TOGETHER, ASSHOLE.
LUTHER, WE'RE GOING TO CREATE A DISTRACTION SO YOU THREE CAN RUN.
NO! MOM, ANOUK IS RIGHT! THERE HAS TO BE A BETTER WAY!
WELL, WE'VE GOT ABOUT TEN SECONDS TO THINK OF ONE UNLESS ONE OF YOU HAS THE MAGIC POWER TO STOP TIME.
NOT EXACTLY...

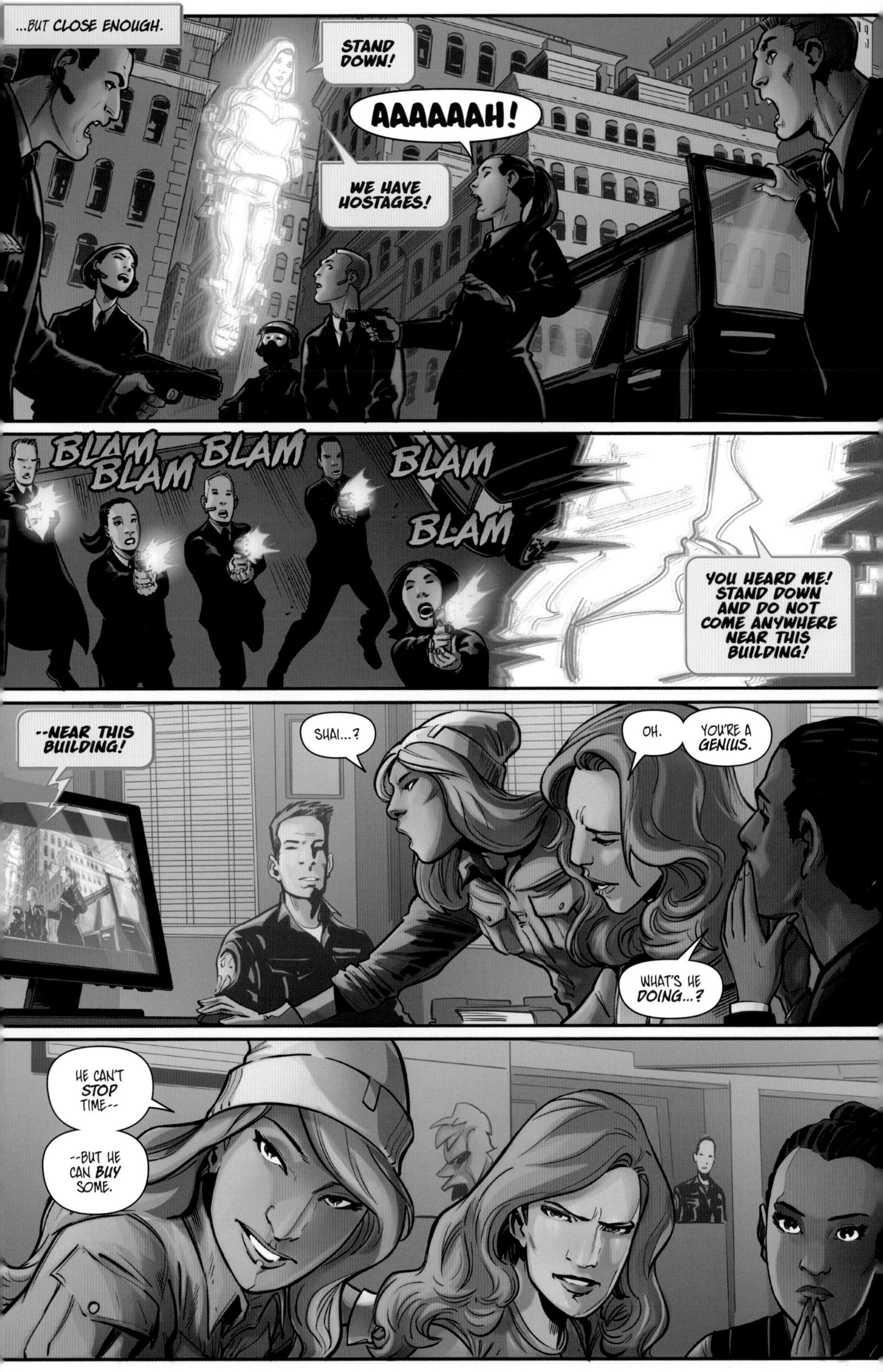
...BUT CLOSE ENOUGH.
STAND DOWN!
AAAAAAH!
WE HAVE HOSTAGES!
BLAM BLAM BLAM
BLAM
BLAM
YOU HEARD ME! STAND DOWN AND DO NOT COME ANYWHERE NEAR THIS BUILDING!
--NEAR THIS BUILDING!
SHAI...?
OH.
YOU'RE A GENIUS.
WHAT'S HE DOING...?
HE CAN'T STOP TIME--
--BUT HE CAN BUY SOME.

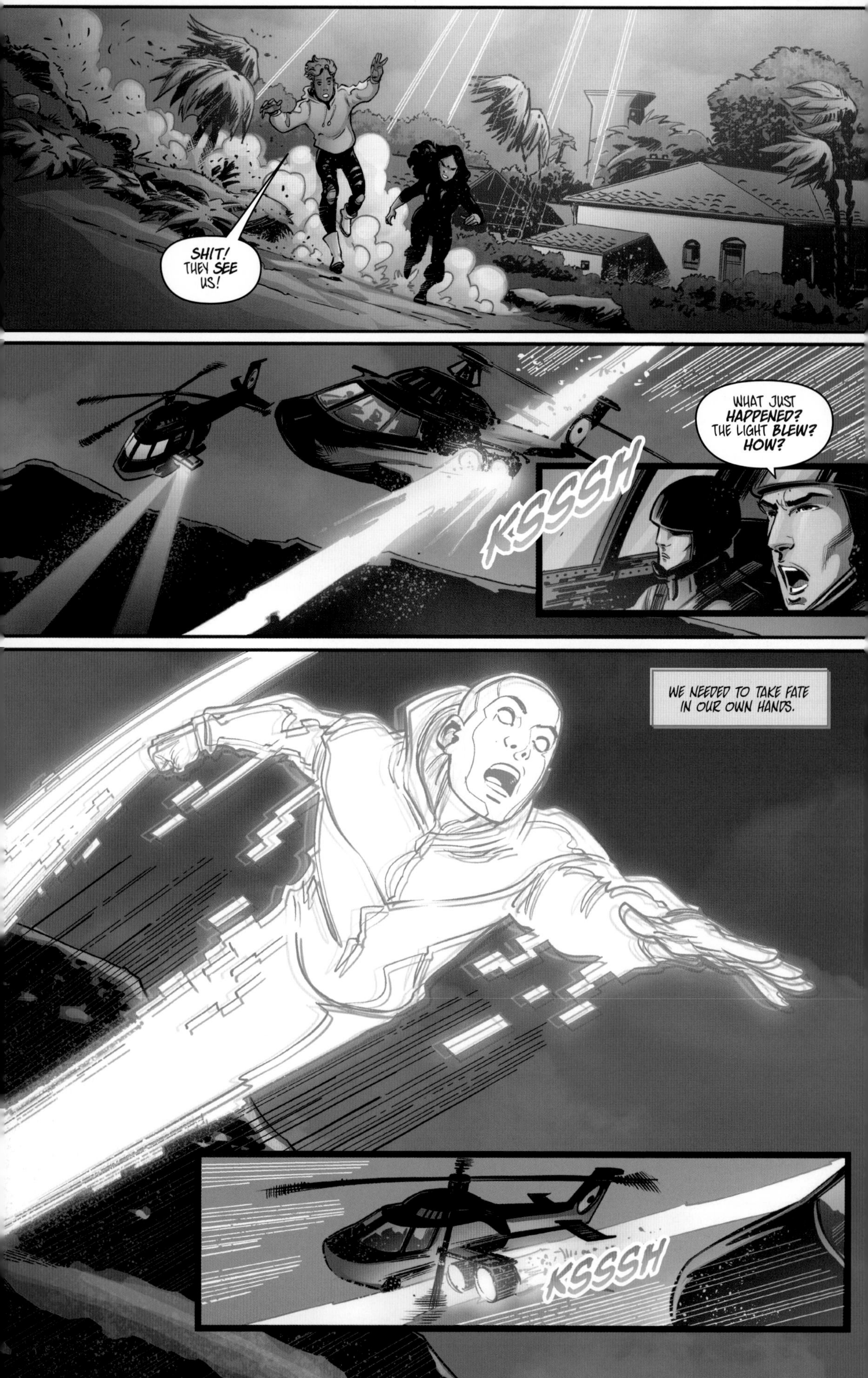
SHIT! THEY SEE US!
WHAT JUST HAPPENED? THE LIGHT BLEW? HOW?
KSSSH
WE NEEDED TO TAKE FATE IN OUR OWN HANDS.
KSSSH

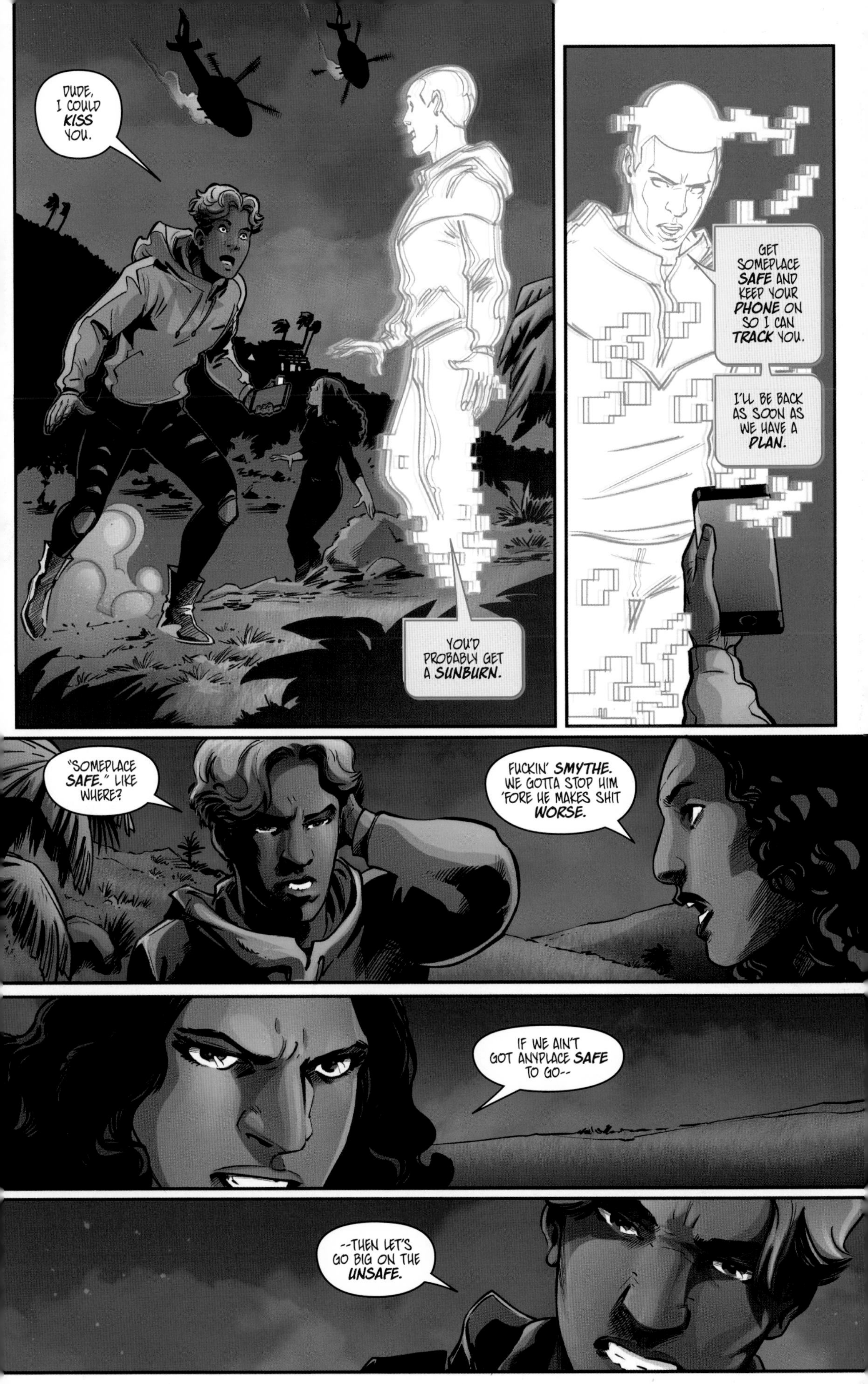
DUDE, I COULD KISS YOU.
YOU'D PROBABLY GET A SUNBURN.
GET SOMEPLACE SAFE AND KEEP YOUR PHONE ON SO I CAN TRACK YOU.
I'LL BE BACK AS SOON AS WE HAVE A PLAN.
"SOMEPLACE SAFE." LIKE WHERE?
FUCKIN' SMYTHE. WE GOTTA STOP HIM 'FORE HE MAKES SHIT WORSE.
IF WE AIN'T GOT ANYPLACE SAFE TO GO--
--THEN LET'S GO BIG ON THE UNSAFE.

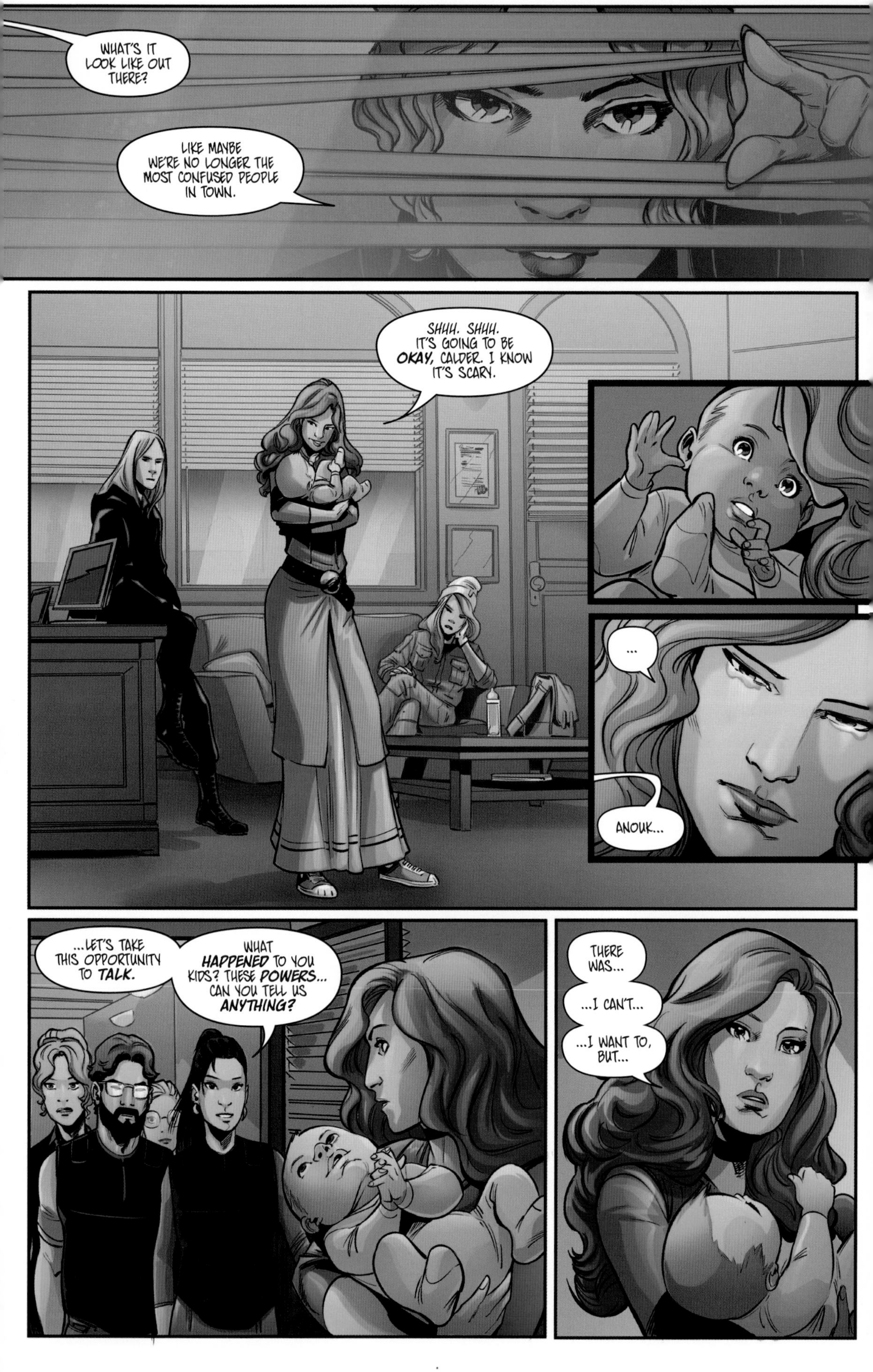
WHAT'S IT LOOK LIKE OUT THERE?
LIKE MAYBE WE'RE NO LONGER THE MOST CONFUSED PEOPLE IN TOWN.
SHHH. SHHH. IT'S GOING TO BE OKAY, CALDER. I KNOW IT'S SCARY.
...
ANOUK...
...LET'S TAKE THIS OPPORTUNITY TO TALK.
WHAT HAPPENED TO YOU KIDS? THESE POWERS... CAN YOU TELL US ANYTHING?
THERE WAS...
...I CAN'T...
...I WANT TO, BUT...

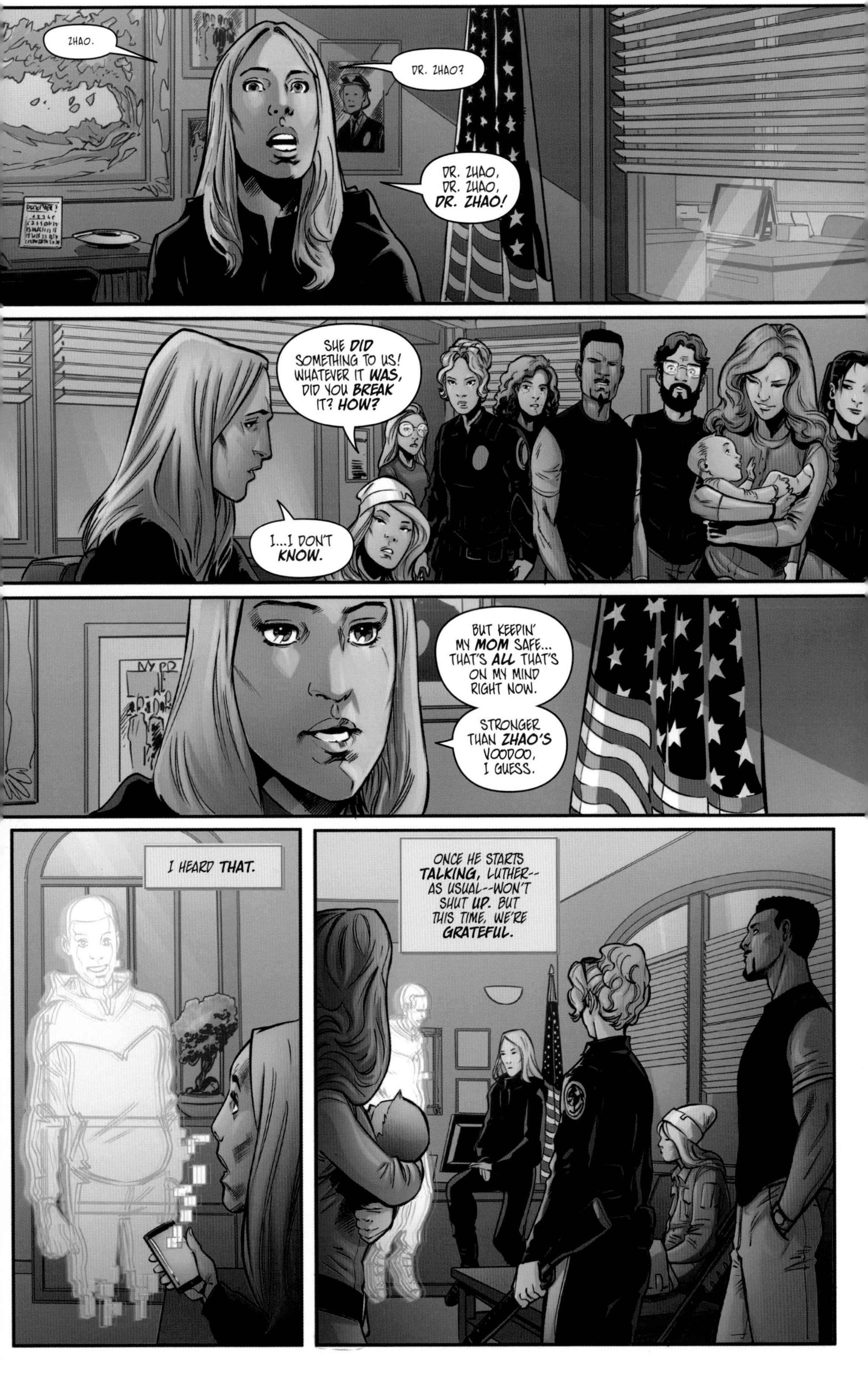
ZHAO.
DR. ZHAO?
DR. ZHAO,
DR. ZHAO,
DR. ZHAO!
SHE DID SOMETHING TO US! WHATEVER IT WAS, DID YOU BREAK IT? HOW?
I...I DON'T KNOW.
BUT KEEPIN' MY MOM SAFE... THAT'S ALL THAT'S ON MY MIND RIGHT NOW.
STRONGER THAN ZHAO'S VOODOO, I GUESS.
I HEARD THAT.
ONCE HE STARTS TALKING, LUTHER-- AS USUAL--WON'T SHUT UP. BUT THIS TIME, WE'RE GRATEFUL.

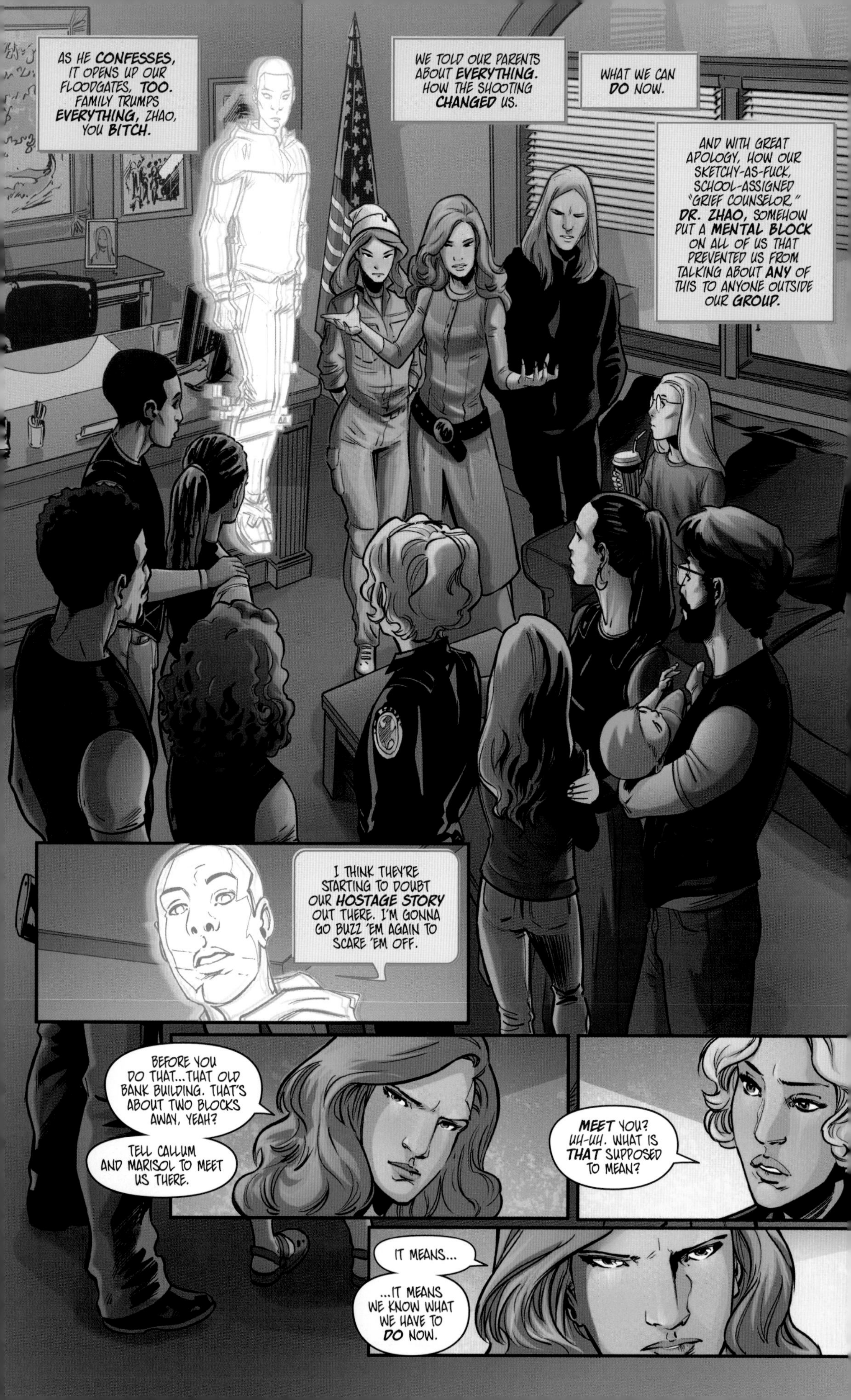
AS HE **CONFESSES,** IT OPENS UP OUR FLOODGATES, **TOO.** FAMILY TRUMPS **EVERYTHING,** ZHAO, YOU **BITCH.**
WE TOLD OUR PARENTS ABOUT **EVERYTHING.** HOW THE SHOOTING **CHANGED** US.
WHAT WE CAN **DO** NOW.
AND WITH GREAT APOLOGY, HOW OUR SKETCHY-AS-FUCK, SCHOOL-ASSIGNED "GRIEF COUNSELOR," **DR. ZHAO,** SOMEHOW PUT A **MENTAL BLOCK** ON ALL OF US THAT PREVENTED US FROM TALKING ABOUT **ANY** OF THIS TO ANYONE OUTSIDE OUR **GROUP.**
I THINK THEY'RE STARTING TO DOUBT OUR ***HOSTAGE STORY*** OUT THERE. I'M GONNA GO BUZZ 'EM AGAIN TO SCARE 'EM OFF.
BEFORE YOU DO THAT...THAT OLD BANK BUILDING. THAT'S ABOUT TWO BLOCKS AWAY, YEAH?
TELL CALLUM AND MARISOL TO MEET US THERE.
MEET YOU? UH-UH. WHAT IS **THAT** SUPPOSED TO MEAN?
IT MEANS...
...IT MEANS WE KNOW WHAT WE HAVE TO ***DO*** NOW.

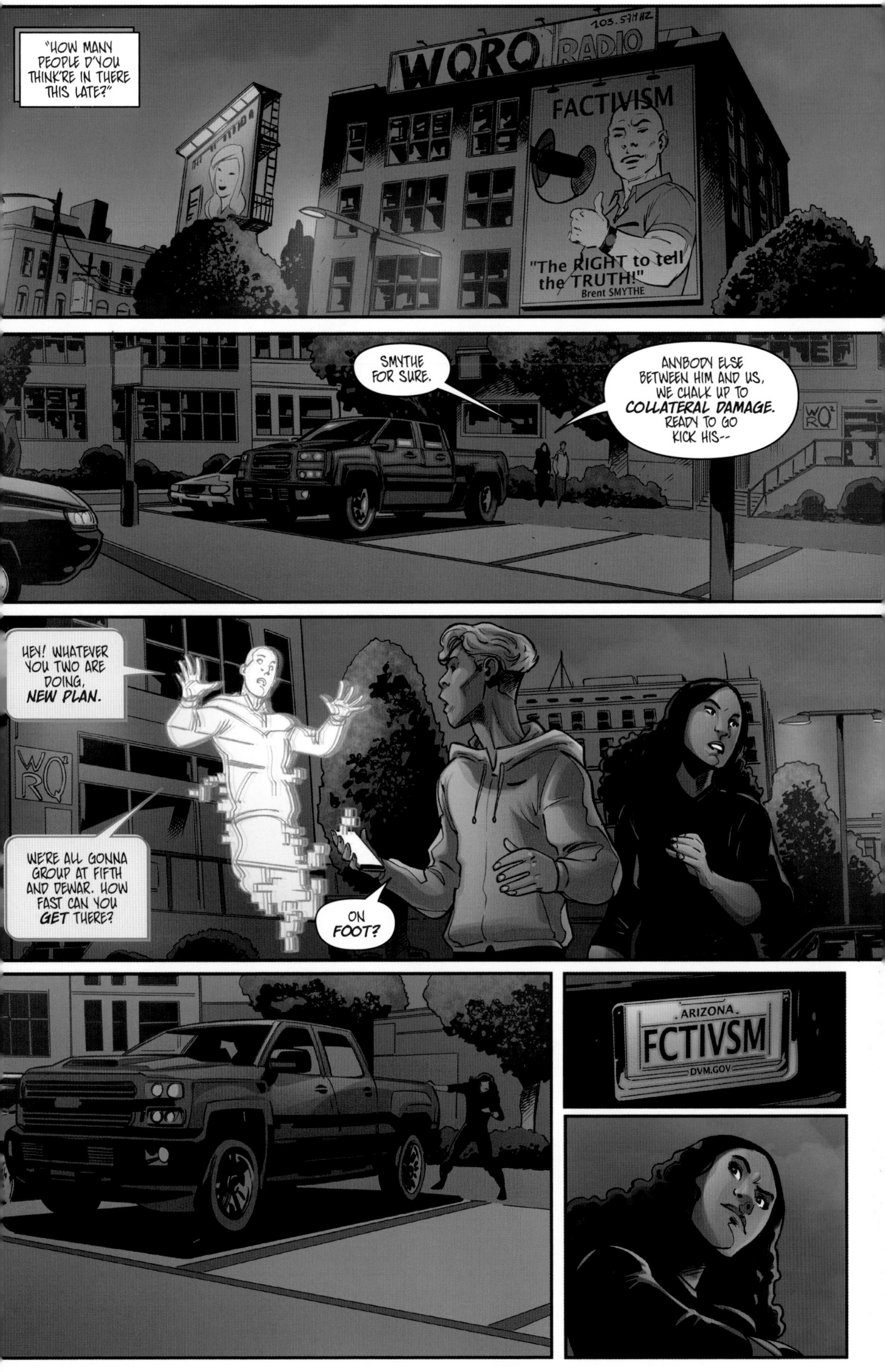
"HOW MANY PEOPLE D'YOU THINK'RE IN THERE THIS LATE?"
103.57MHZ
WQRQ RADIO
FACTIVISM
"The RIGHT to tell the TRUTH!"
Brent SMYTHE
SMYTHE FOR SURE.
ANYBODY ELSE BETWEEN HIM AND US, WE CHALK UP TO COLLATERAL DAMAGE. READY TO GO KICK HIS--
HEY! WHATEVER YOU TWO ARE DOING, NEW PLAN.
WE'RE ALL GONNA GROUP AT FIFTH AND DEWAR. HOW FAST CAN YOU GET THERE?
ON FOOT?
ARIZONA
FCTIVSM
DVM.GOV

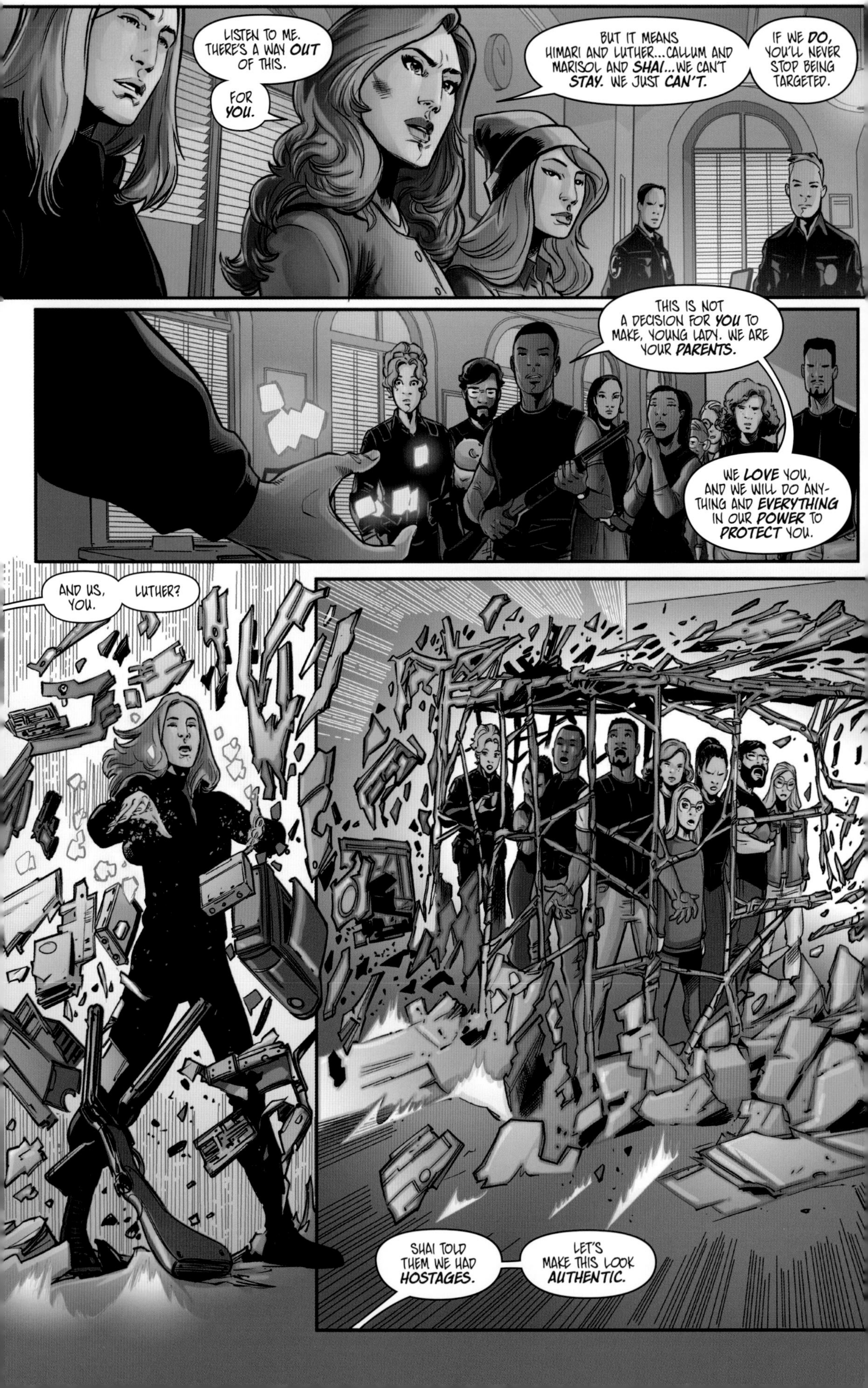
LISTEN TO ME. THERE'S A WAY OUT OF THIS.
FOR YOU.
BUT IT MEANS HIMARI AND LUTHER...CALLUM AND MARISOL AND SHAI...WE CAN'T STAY. WE JUST CAN'T.
IF WE DO, YOU'LL NEVER STOP BEING TARGETED.
THIS IS NOT A DECISION FOR YOU TO MAKE, YOUNG LADY. WE ARE YOUR PARENTS.
WE LOVE YOU, AND WE WILL DO ANYTHING AND EVERYTHING IN OUR POWER TO PROTECT YOU.
AND US, YOU.
LUTHER?
SHAI TOLD THEM WE HAD HOSTAGES.
LET'S MAKE THIS LOOK AUTHENTIC.

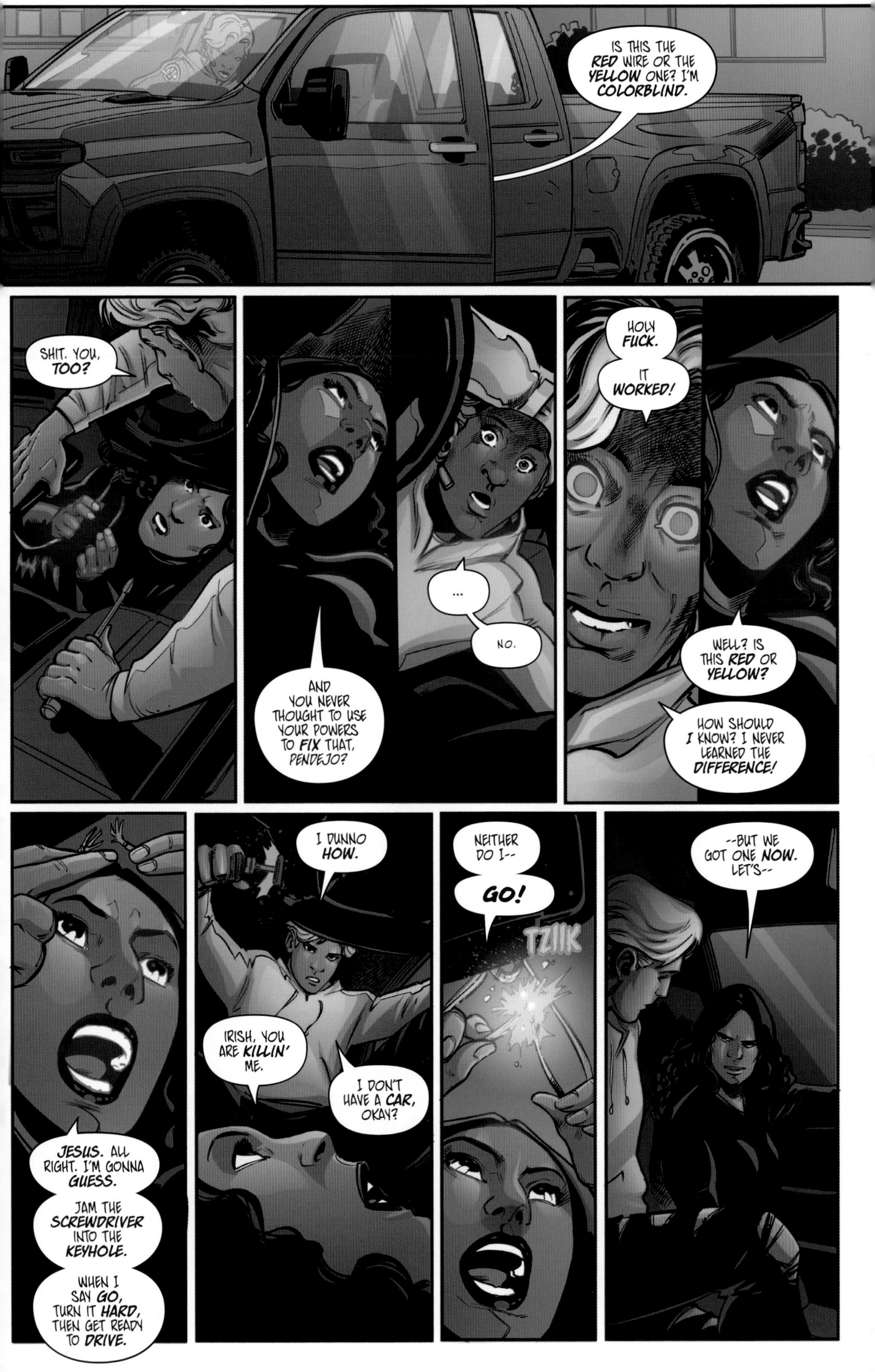
IS THIS THE RED WIRE OR THE YELLOW ONE? I'M COLORBLIND.
SHIT. YOU, TOO?
AND YOU NEVER THOUGHT TO USE YOUR POWERS TO FIX THAT, PENDEJO?
...
NO.
HOLY FUCK.
IT WORKED!
WELL? IS THIS RED OR YELLOW?
HOW SHOULD I KNOW? I NEVER LEARNED THE DIFFERENCE!
JESUS. ALL RIGHT. I'M GONNA GUESS.
JAM THE SCREWDRIVER INTO THE KEYHOLE.
WHEN I SAY GO, TURN IT HARD, THEN GET READY TO DRIVE.
I DUNNO HOW.
IRISH, YOU ARE KILLIN' ME.
I DON'T HAVE A CAR, OKAY?
NEITHER DO I--
GO!
TZIIK
--BUT WE GOT ONE NOW. LET'S--

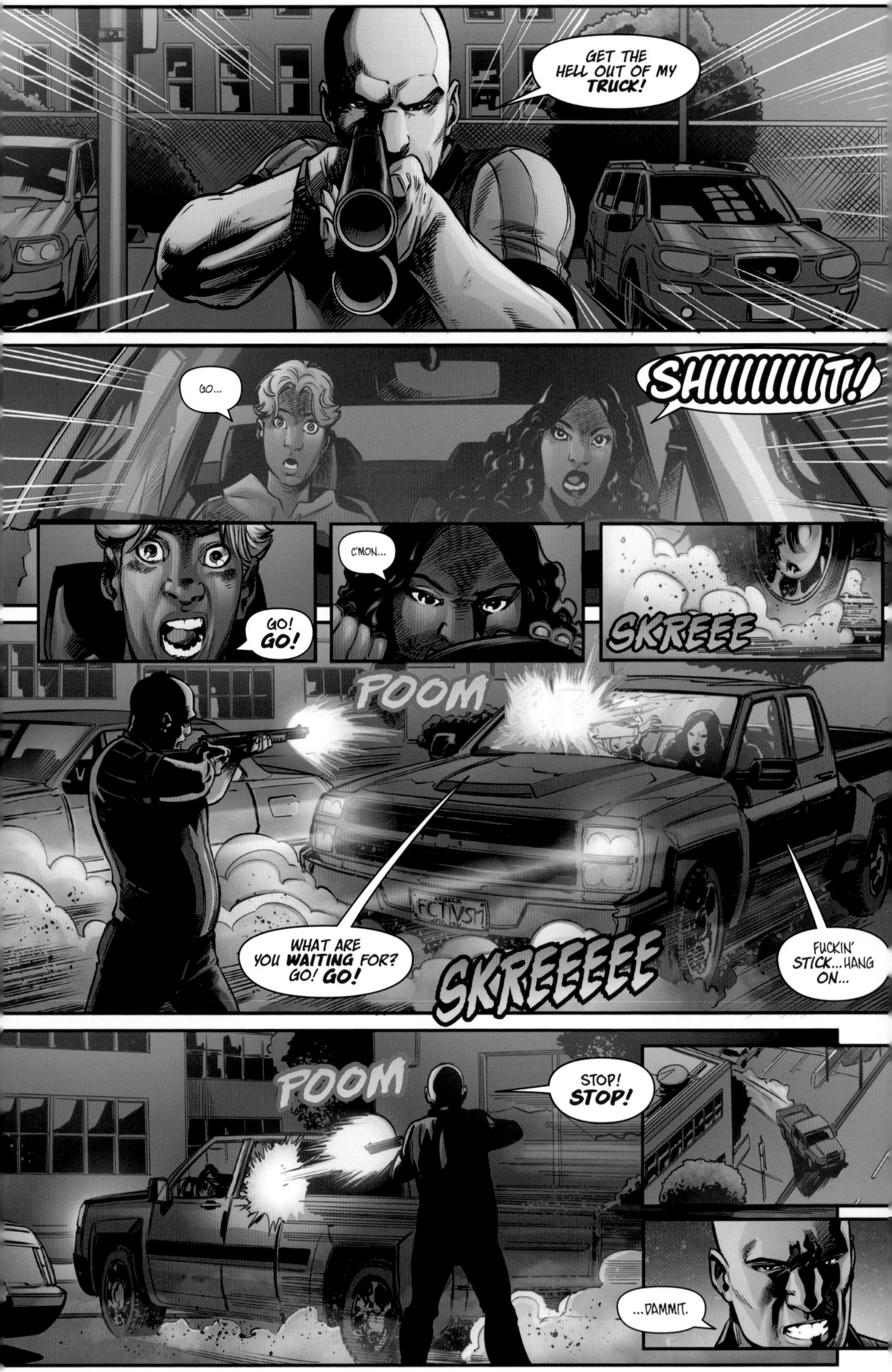
GET THE HELL OUT OF MY TRUCK!
GO...
SHIIIIIIIIT!!
GO! GO!
C'MON...
SKREEE
POOM
WHAT ARE YOU WAITING FOR? GO! GO!
SKREEEEEE
FUCKIN' STICK...HANG ON...
POOM
STOP! STOP!
...DAMMIT.

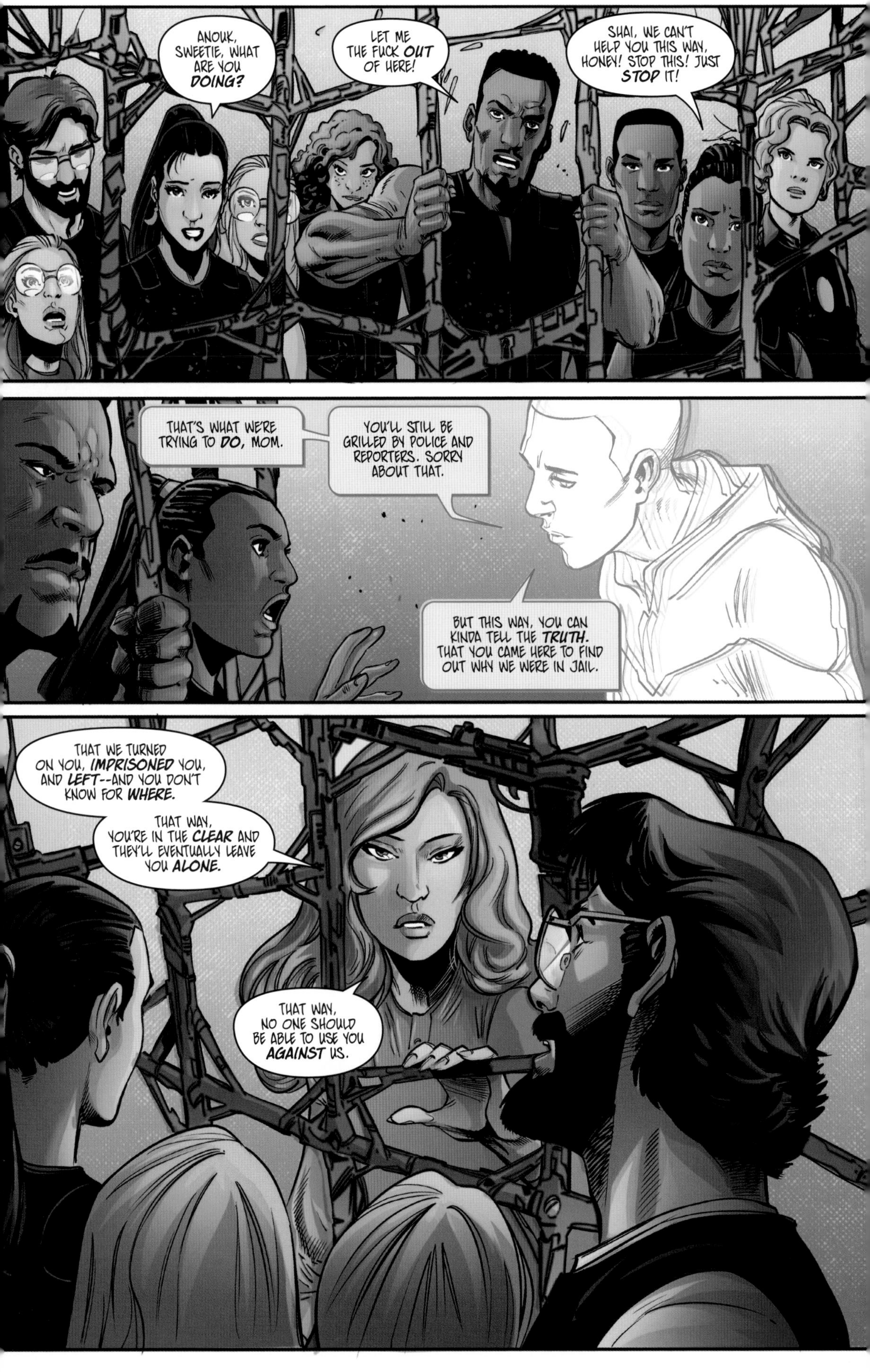
ANOUK, SWEETIE, WHAT ARE YOU DOING?
LET ME THE FUCK OUT OF HERE!
SHAI, WE CAN'T HELP YOU THIS WAY, HONEY! STOP THIS! JUST STOP IT!
THAT'S WHAT WE'RE TRYING TO DO, MOM.
YOU'LL STILL BE GRILLED BY POLICE AND REPORTERS. SORRY ABOUT THAT.
BUT THIS WAY, YOU CAN KINDA TELL THE TRUTH. THAT YOU CAME HERE TO FIND OUT WHY WE WERE IN JAIL.
THAT WE TURNED ON YOU, IMPRISONED YOU, AND LEFT--AND YOU DON'T KNOW FOR WHERE.
THAT WAY, YOU'RE IN THE CLEAR AND THEY'LL EVENTUALLY LEAVE YOU ALONE.
THAT WAY, NO ONE SHOULD BE ABLE TO USE YOU AGAINST US.

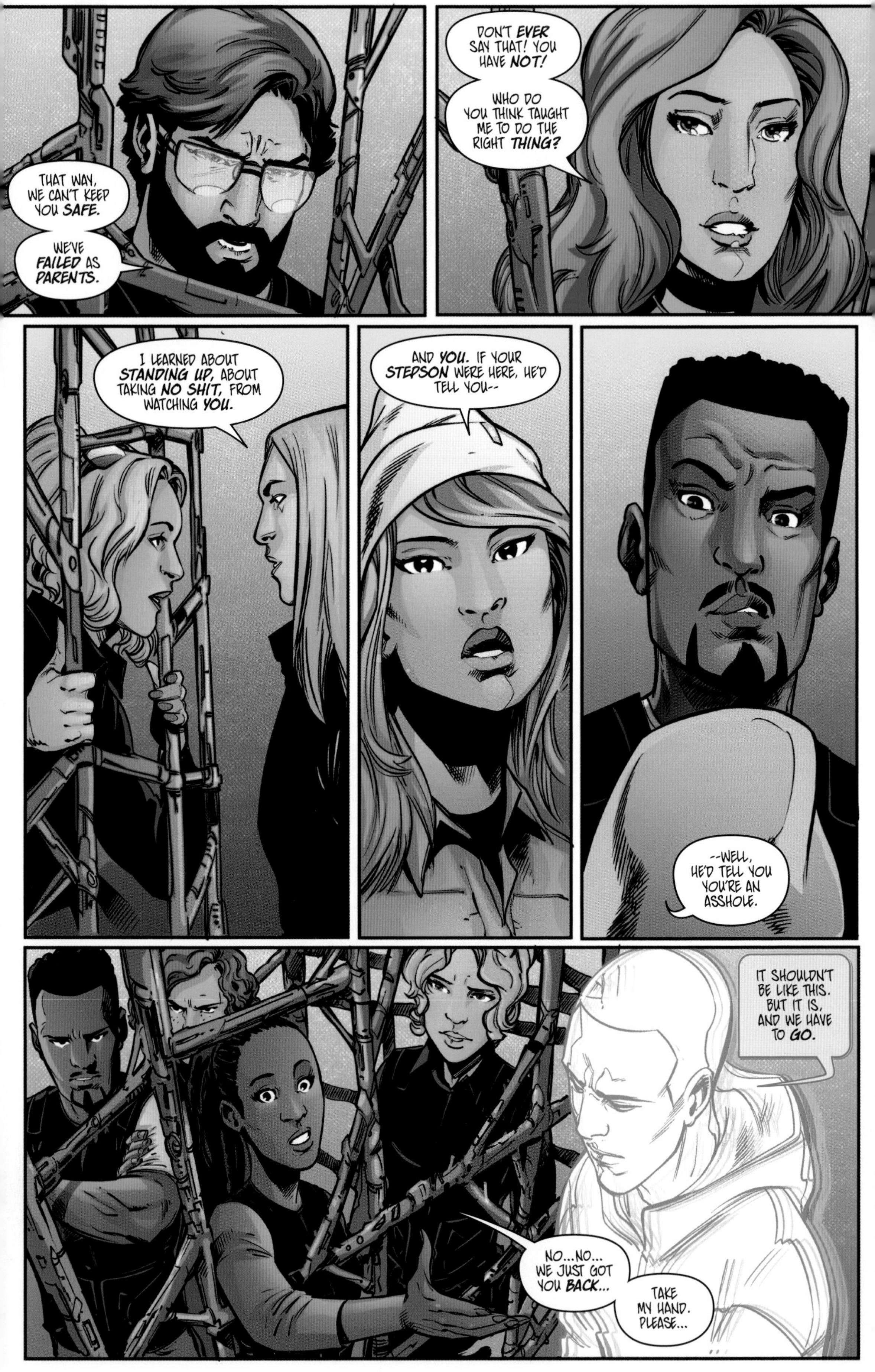
THAT WAY, WE CAN'T KEEP YOU SAFE.
WE'VE FAILED AS PARENTS.
DON'T EVER SAY THAT! YOU HAVE NOT!
WHO DO YOU THINK TAUGHT ME TO DO THE RIGHT THING?
I LEARNED ABOUT STANDING UP, ABOUT TAKING NO SHIT, FROM WATCHING YOU.
AND YOU. IF YOUR STEPSON WERE HERE, HE'D TELL YOU--
--WELL, HE'D TELL YOU YOU'RE AN ASSHOLE.
IT SHOULDN'T BE LIKE THIS. BUT IT IS, AND WE HAVE TO GO.
NO...NO... WE JUST GOT YOU BACK...
TAKE MY HAND. PLEASE...

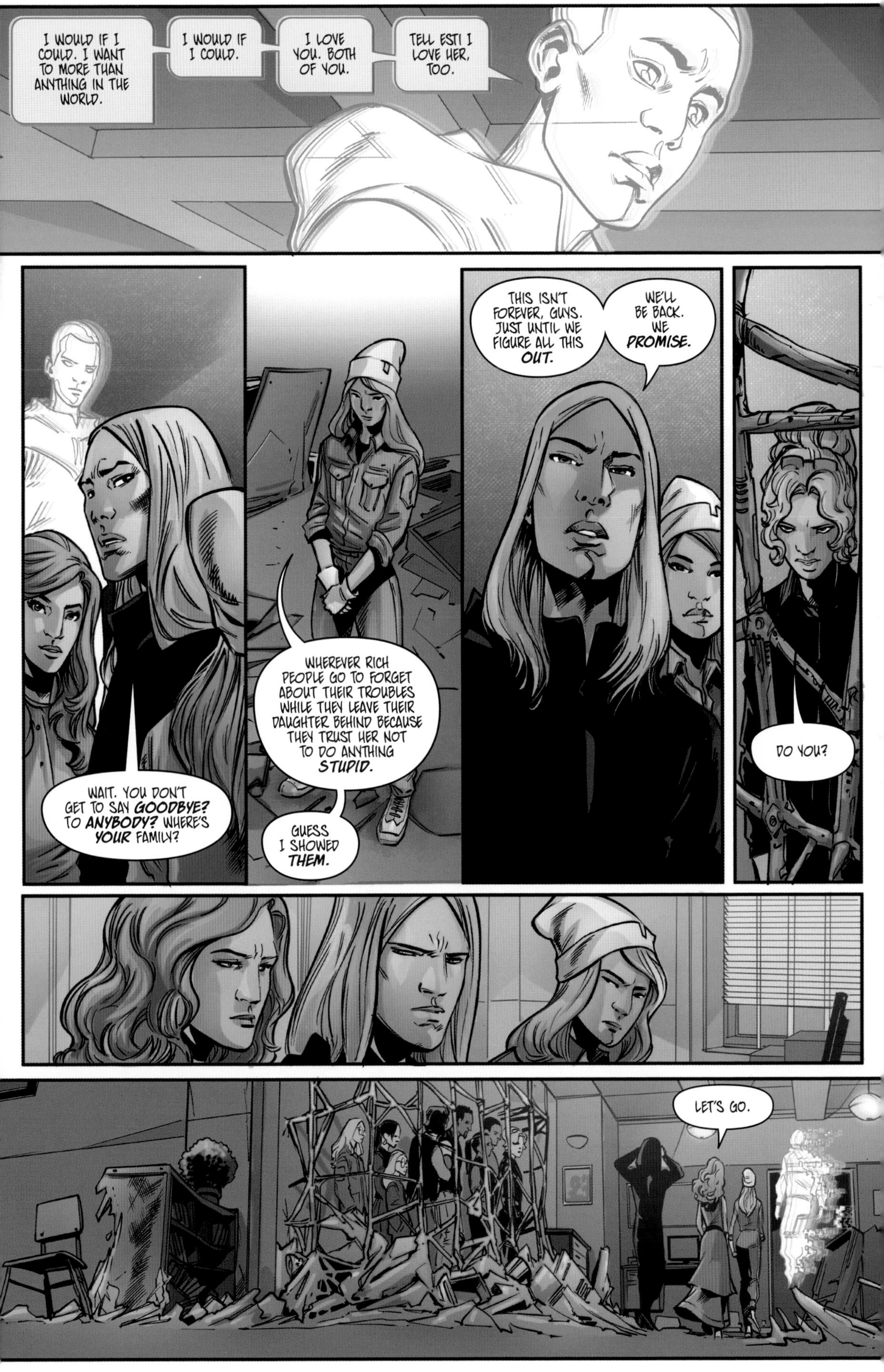
I WOULD IF I COULD. I WANT TO MORE THAN ANYTHING IN THE WORLD.
I WOULD IF I COULD.
I LOVE YOU. BOTH OF YOU.
TELL ESTI I LOVE HER, TOO.
WAIT. YOU DON'T GET TO SAY GOODBYE? TO ANYBODY? WHERE'S YOUR FAMILY?
WHEREVER RICH PEOPLE GO TO FORGET ABOUT THEIR TROUBLES WHILE THEY LEAVE THEIR DAUGHTER BEHIND BECAUSE THEY TRUST HER NOT TO DO ANYTHING STUPID.
GUESS I SHOWED THEM.
THIS ISN'T FOREVER, GUYS. JUST UNTIL WE FIGURE ALL THIS OUT.
WE'LL BE BACK. WE PROMISE.
DO YOU?
LET'S GO.

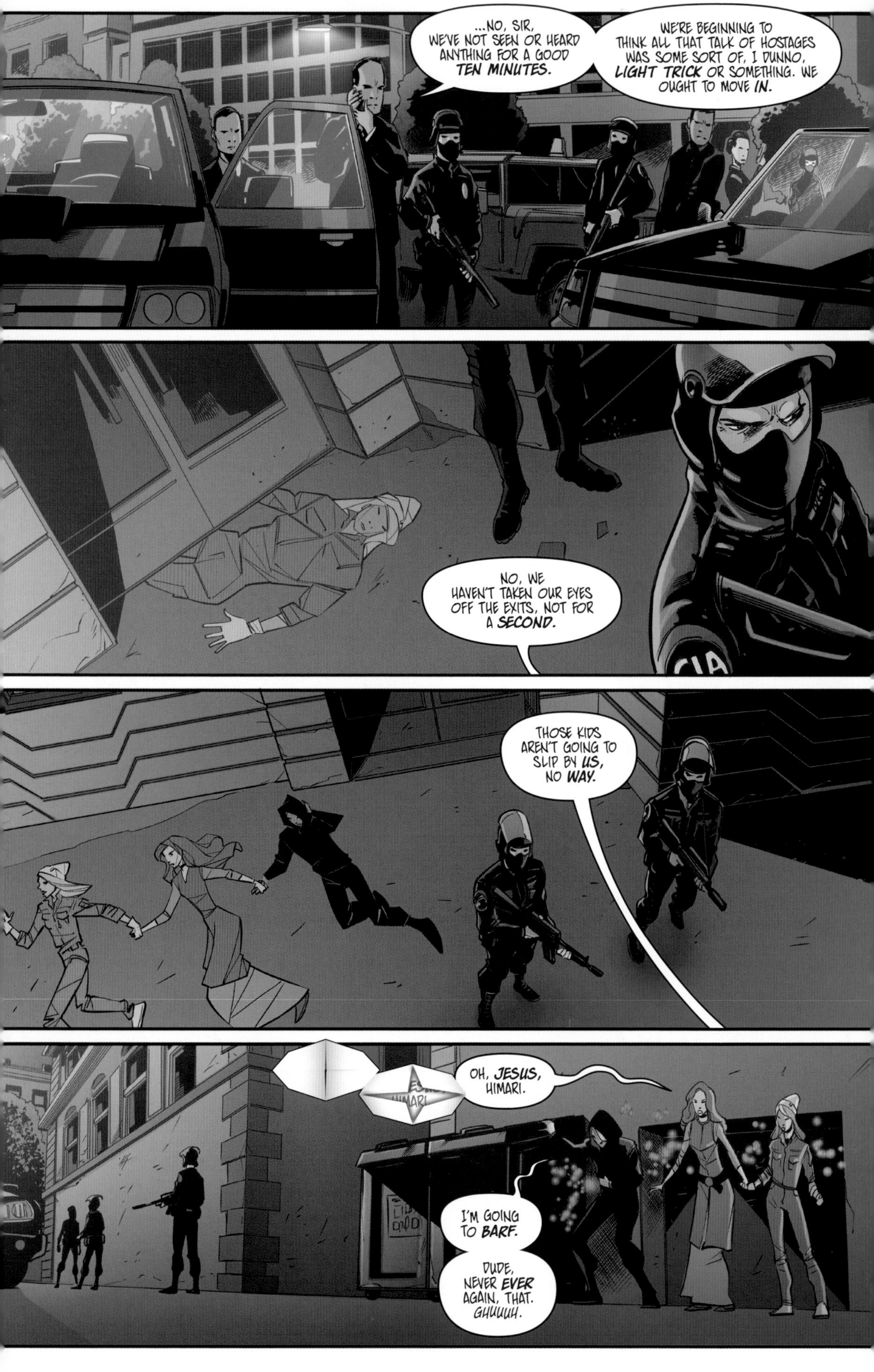
...NO, SIR, WE'VE NOT SEEN OR HEARD ANYTHING FOR A GOOD TEN MINUTES.
WE'RE BEGINNING TO THINK ALL THAT TALK OF HOSTAGES WAS SOME SORT OF, I DUNNO, LIGHT TRICK OR SOMETHING. WE OUGHT TO MOVE IN.
NO, WE HAVEN'T TAKEN OUR EYES OFF THE EXITS, NOT FOR A SECOND.
CIA
THOSE KIDS AREN'T GOING TO SLIP BY US, NO WAY.
OH, JESUS, HIMARI.
I'M GOING TO BARF.
DUDE, NEVER EVER AGAIN, THAT. GHUUUH.

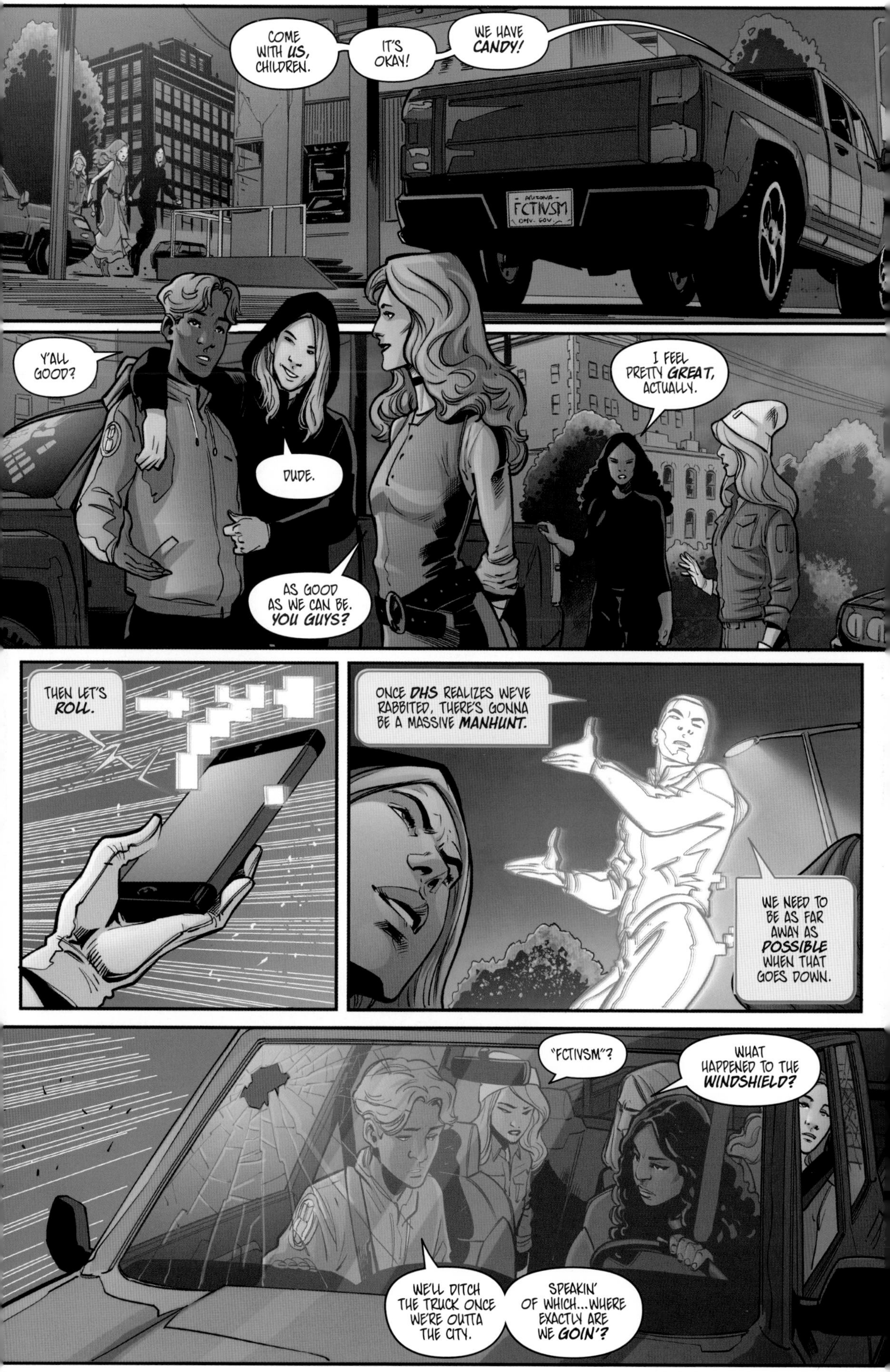
COME WITH US, CHILDREN.
IT'S OKAY!
WE HAVE CANDY!
ARIZONA FCTIVSM DMV. GOV.
Y'ALL GOOD?
DUDE.
AS GOOD AS WE CAN BE. YOU GUYS?
I FEEL PRETTY GREAT, ACTUALLY.
THEN LET'S ROLL.
ONCE DHS REALIZES WE'VE RABBITED, THERE'S GONNA BE A MASSIVE MANHUNT.
WE NEED TO BE AS FAR AWAY AS POSSIBLE WHEN THAT GOES DOWN.
"FCTIVSM"?
WHAT HAPPENED TO THE WINDSHIELD?
WE'LL DITCH THE TRUCK ONCE WE'RE OUTTA THE CITY.
SPEAKIN' OF WHICH...WHERE EXACTLY ARE WE GOIN'?

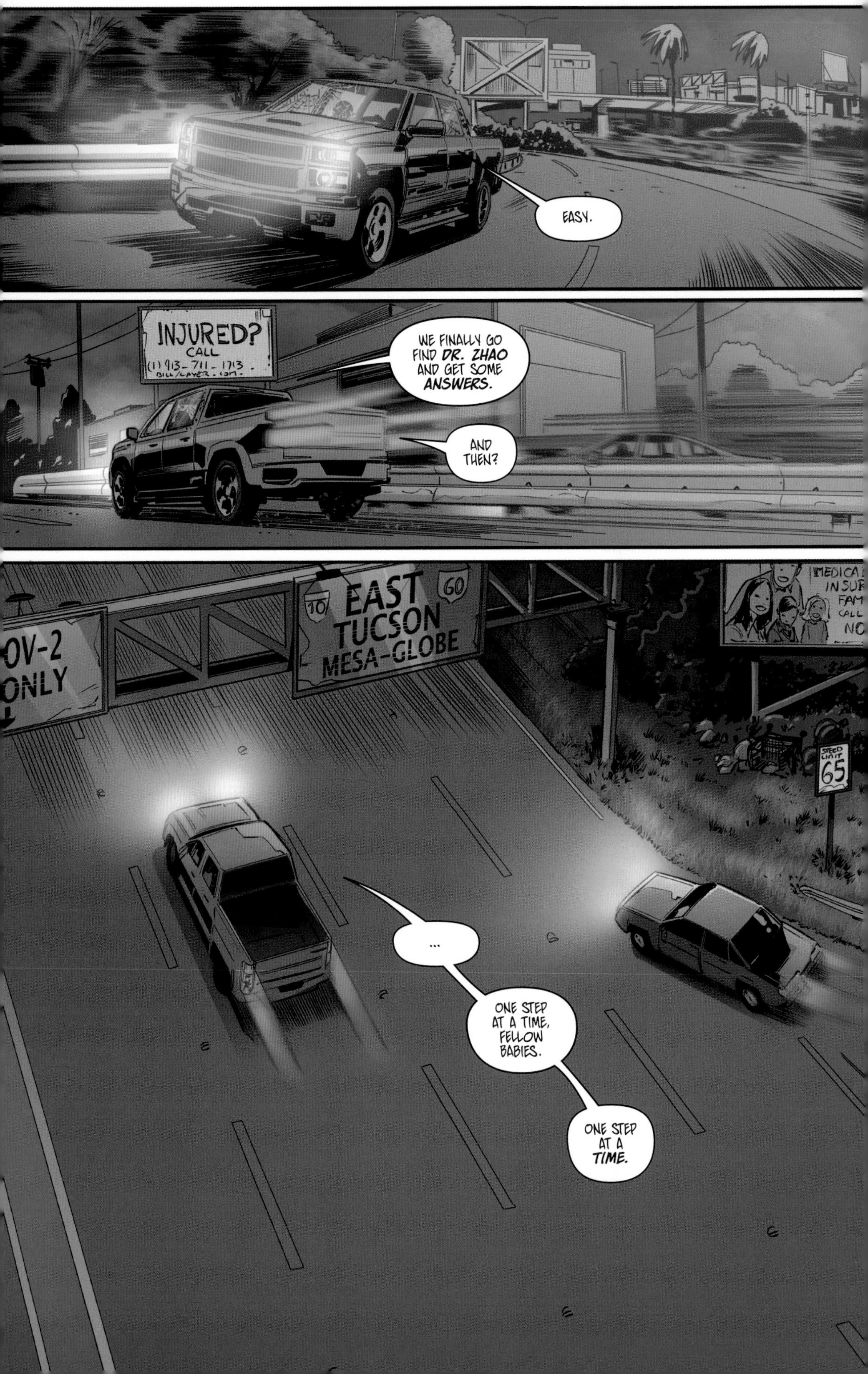

EASY.
INJURED?
CALL
(1) 913-711-1713
WE FINALLY GO FIND DR. ZHAO AND GET SOME ANSWERS.
AND THEN?
OV-2
ONLY
EAST
10
60
TUCSON
MESA-GLOBE
SPEED LIMIT
65
...
ONE STEP AT A TIME, FELLOW BABIES.
ONE STEP AT A TIME.

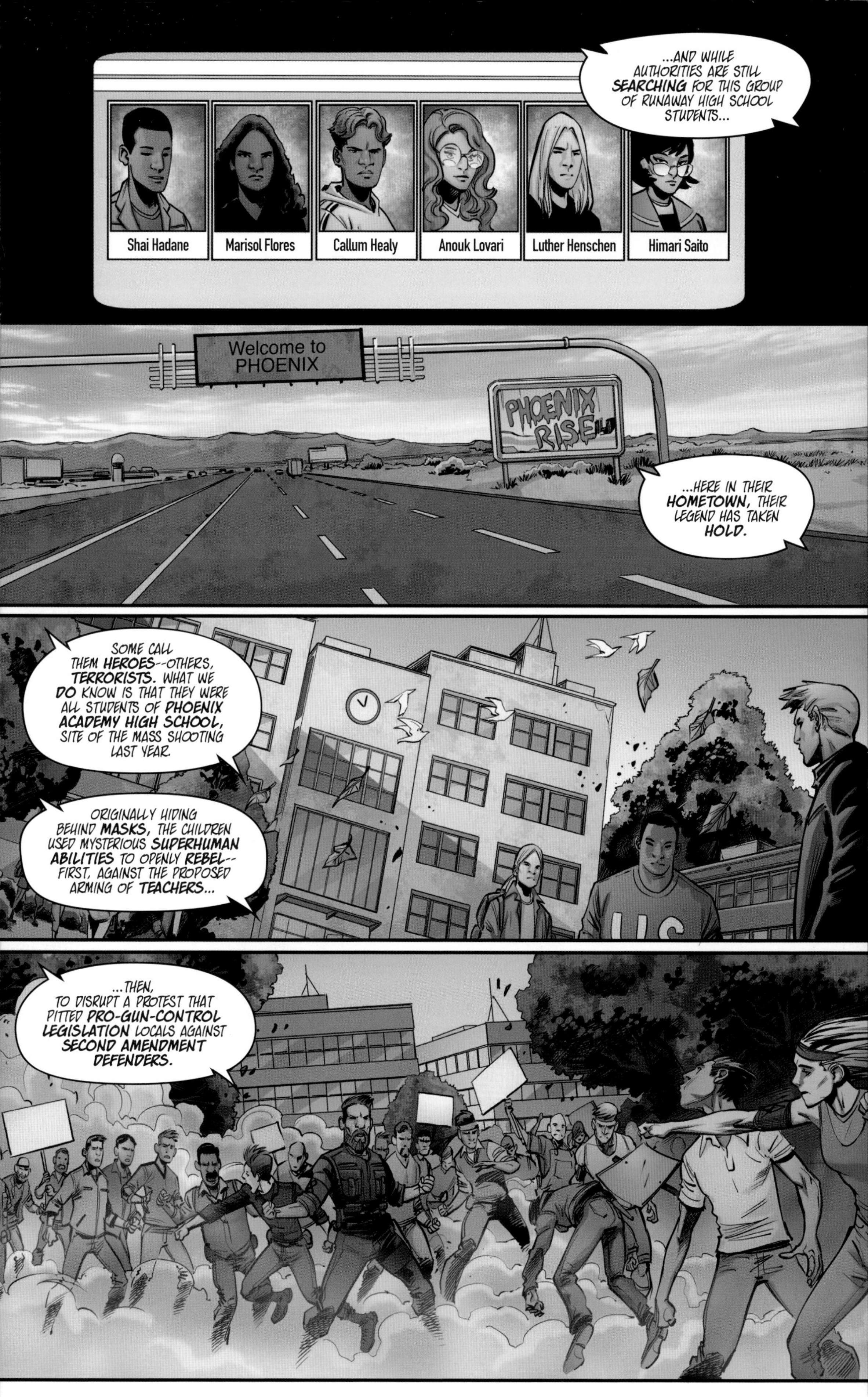
Shai Hadane
Marisol Flores
Callum Healy
Anouk Lovari
Luther Henschen
Himari Saito
...AND WHILE AUTHORITIES ARE STILL SEARCHING FOR THIS GROUP OF RUNAWAY HIGH SCHOOL STUDENTS...
Welcome to PHOENIX
PHOENIX RISE
...HERE IN THEIR HOMETOWN, THEIR LEGEND HAS TAKEN HOLD.
SOME CALL THEM HEROES--OTHERS, TERRORISTS. WHAT WE DO KNOW IS THAT THEY WERE ALL STUDENTS OF PHOENIX ACADEMY HIGH SCHOOL, SITE OF THE MASS SHOOTING LAST YEAR.
ORIGINALLY HIDING BEHIND MASKS, THE CHILDREN USED MYSTERIOUS SUPERHUMAN ABILITIES TO OPENLY REBEL--FIRST, AGAINST THE PROPOSED ARMING OF TEACHERS...
...THEN, TO DISRUPT A PROTEST THAT PITTED PRO-GUN-CONTROL LEGISLATION LOCALS AGAINST SECOND AMENDMENT DEFENDERS.

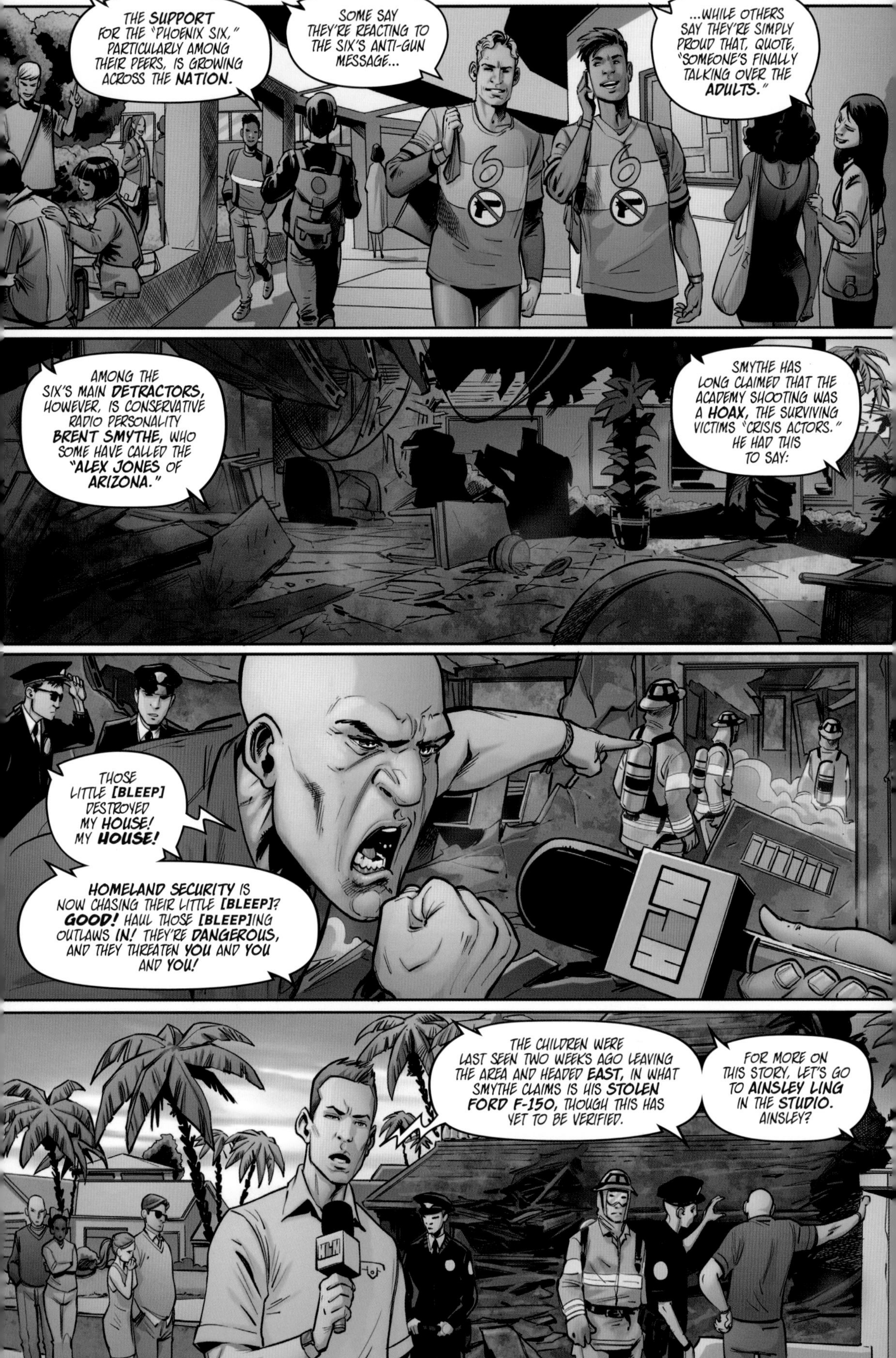
THE SUPPORT FOR THE "PHOENIX SIX," PARTICULARLY AMONG THEIR PEERS, IS GROWING ACROSS THE NATION.
SOME SAY THEY'RE REACTING TO THE SIX'S ANTI-GUN MESSAGE...
...WHILE OTHERS SAY THEY'RE SIMPLY PROUD THAT, QUOTE, "SOMEONE'S FINALLY TALKING OVER THE ADULTS."
AMONG THE SIX'S MAIN DETRACTORS, HOWEVER, IS CONSERVATIVE RADIO PERSONALITY BRENT SMYTHE, WHO SOME HAVE CALLED THE "ALEX JONES OF ARIZONA."
SMYTHE HAS LONG CLAIMED THAT THE ACADEMY SHOOTING WAS A HOAX, THE SURVIVING VICTIMS "CRISIS ACTORS." HE HAD THIS TO SAY:
THOSE LITTLE [BLEEP] DESTROYED MY HOUSE! MY HOUSE!
HOMELAND SECURITY IS NOW CHASING THEIR LITTLE [BLEEP]? GOOD! HAUL THOSE [BLEEP]ING OUTLAWS IN! THEY'RE DANGEROUS, AND THEY THREATEN YOU AND YOU AND YOU!
THE CHILDREN WERE LAST SEEN TWO WEEKS AGO LEAVING THE AREA AND HEADED EAST, IN WHAT SMYTHE CLAIMS IS HIS STOLEN FORD F-150, THOUGH THIS HAS YET TO BE VERIFIED.
FOR MORE ON THIS STORY, LET'S GO TO AINSLEY LING IN THE STUDIO. AINSLEY?

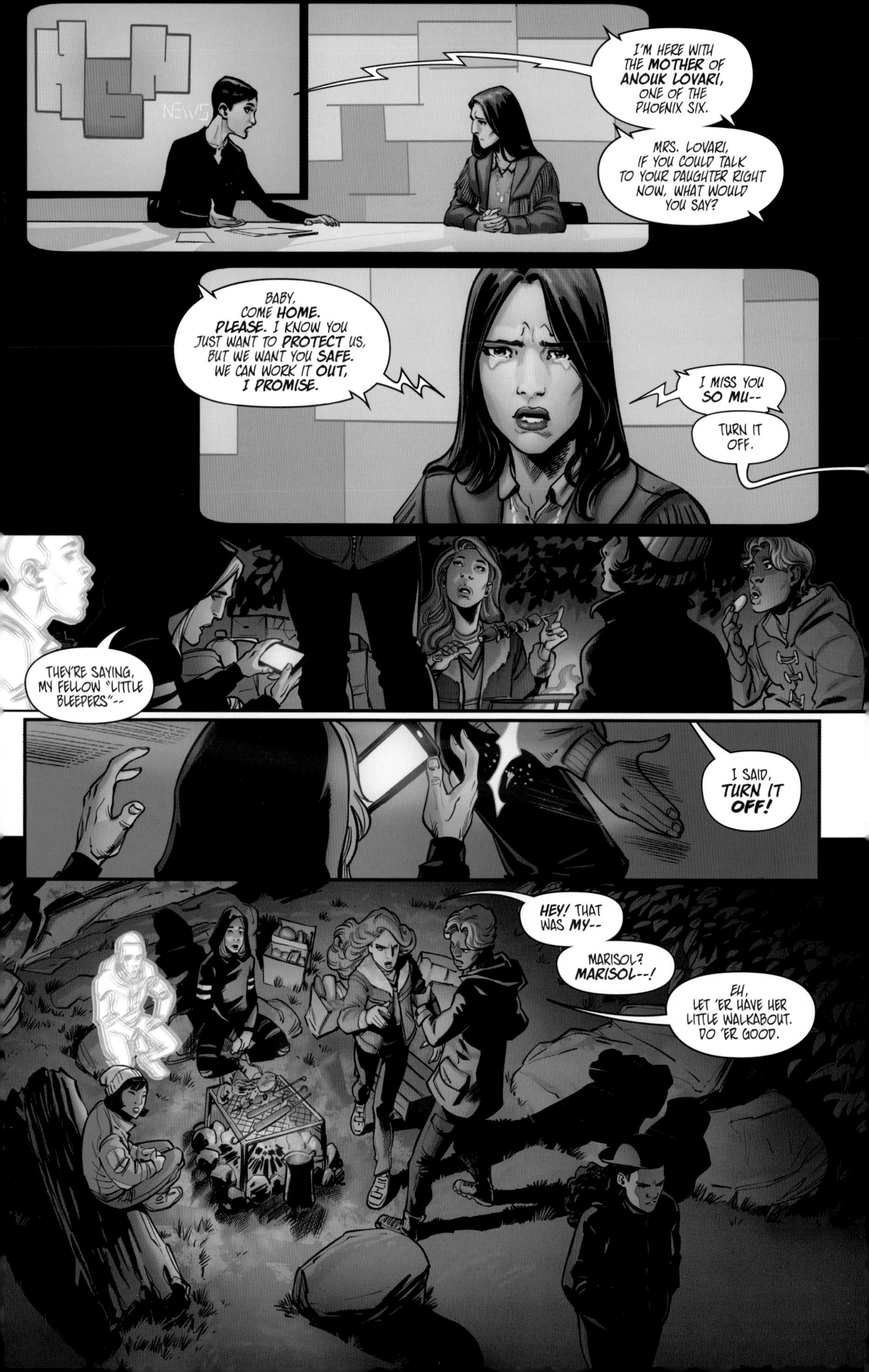
I'M HERE WITH THE **MOTHER** OF **ANOUK LOVARI,** ONE OF THE PHOENIX SIX.
MRS. LOVARI, IF YOU COULD TALK TO YOUR DAUGHTER RIGHT NOW, WHAT WOULD YOU SAY?
BABY, COME **HOME. PLEASE.** I KNOW YOU JUST WANT TO **PROTECT** US, BUT WE WANT YOU **SAFE.** WE CAN WORK IT **OUT, I PROMISE.**
I MISS YOU **SO MU--**
TURN IT OFF.
THEY'RE SAYING, MY FELLOW "LITTLE BLEEPERS"--
I SAID, **TURN IT OFF!**
HEY! THAT WAS **MY--**
MARISOL? **MARISOL--!**
EH, LET 'ER HAVE HER LITTLE WALKABOUT. DO 'ER GOOD.

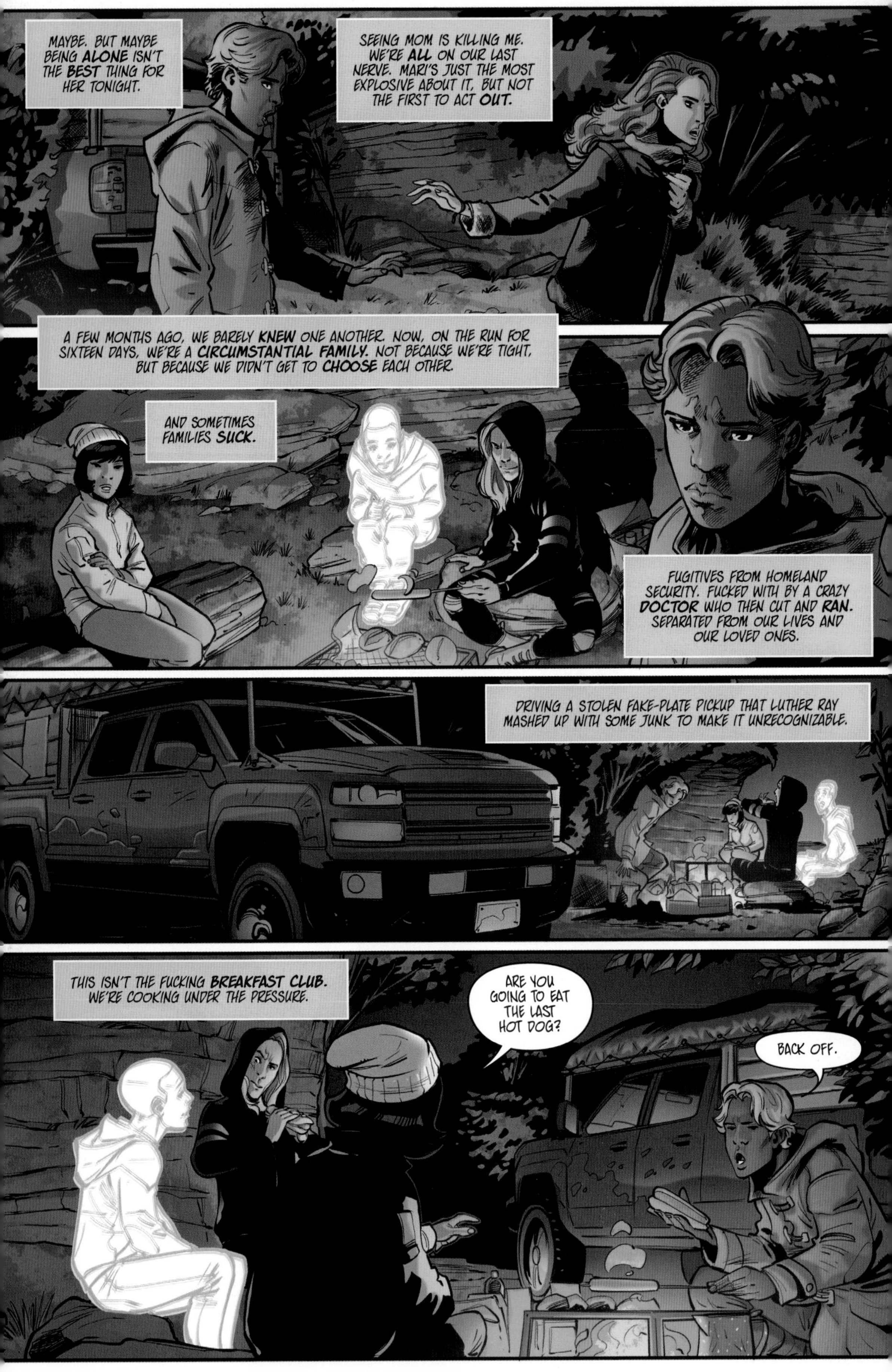
MAYBE. BUT MAYBE BEING ALONE ISN'T THE BEST THING FOR HER TONIGHT.
SEEING MOM IS KILLING ME. WE'RE ALL ON OUR LAST NERVE. MARI'S JUST THE MOST EXPLOSIVE ABOUT IT, BUT NOT THE FIRST TO ACT OUT.
A FEW MONTHS AGO, WE BARELY KNEW ONE ANOTHER. NOW, ON THE RUN FOR SIXTEEN DAYS, WE'RE A CIRCUMSTANTIAL FAMILY. NOT BECAUSE WE'RE TIGHT, BUT BECAUSE WE DIDN'T GET TO CHOOSE EACH OTHER.
AND SOMETIMES FAMILIES SUCK.
FUGITIVES FROM HOMELAND SECURITY. FUCKED WITH BY A CRAZY DOCTOR WHO THEN CUT AND RAN. SEPARATED FROM OUR LIVES AND OUR LOVED ONES.
DRIVING A STOLEN FAKE-PLATE PICKUP THAT LUTHER RAY MASHED UP WITH SOME JUNK TO MAKE IT UNRECOGNIZABLE.
THIS ISN'T THE FUCKING BREAKFAST CLUB. WE'RE COOKING UNDER THE PRESSURE.
ARE YOU GOING TO EAT THE LAST HOT DOG?
BACK OFF.

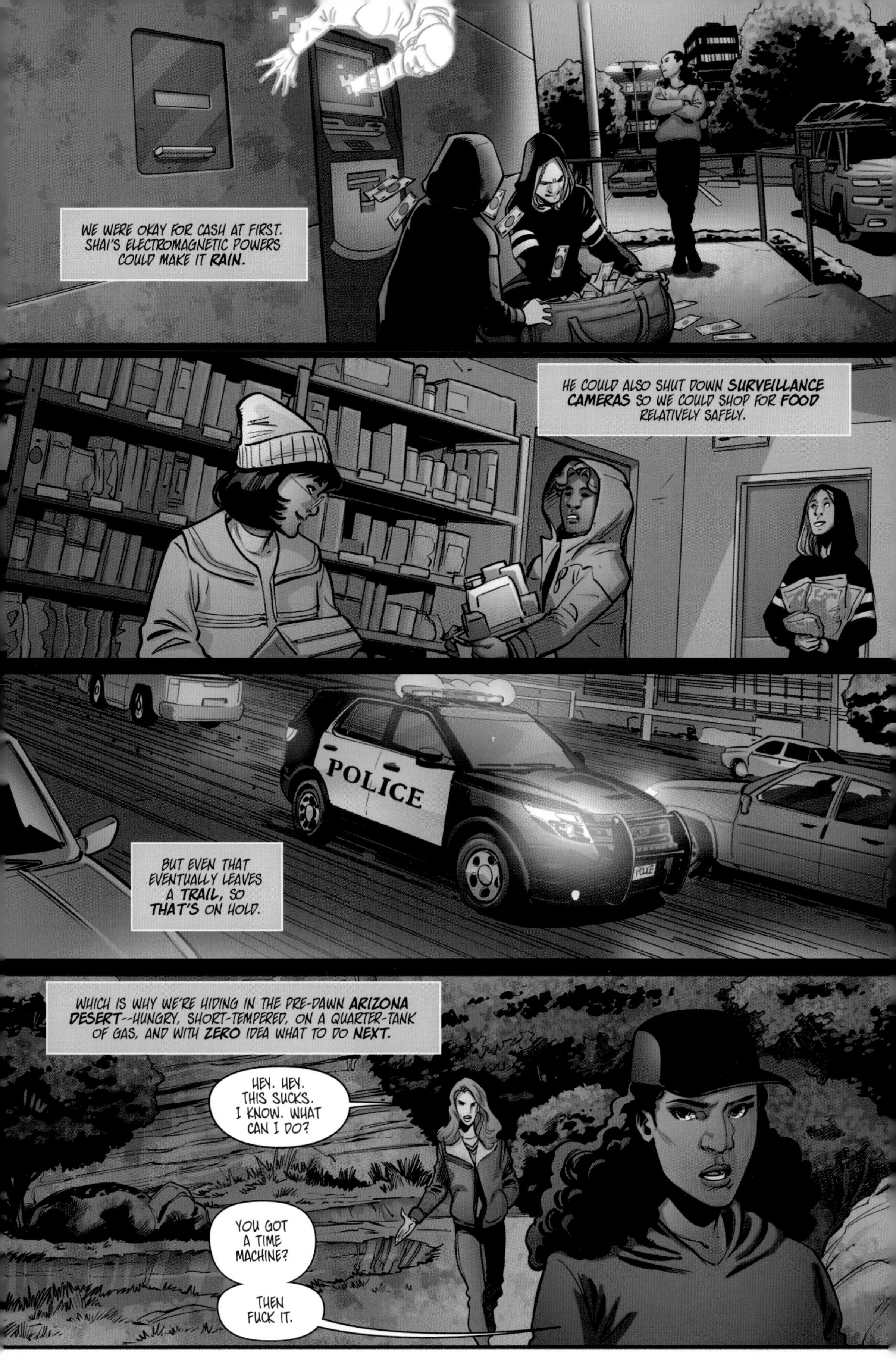
WE WERE OKAY FOR CASH AT FIRST. SHAI'S ELECTROMAGNETIC POWERS COULD MAKE IT **RAIN.**
HE COULD ALSO SHUT DOWN **SURVEILLANCE CAMERAS** SO WE COULD SHOP FOR **FOOD** RELATIVELY SAFELY.
POLICE
BUT EVEN THAT EVENTUALLY LEAVES A **TRAIL,** SO **THAT'S** ON HOLD.
WHICH IS WHY WE'RE HIDING IN THE PRE-DAWN **ARIZONA DESERT**--HUNGRY, SHORT-TEMPERED, ON A QUARTER-TANK OF GAS, AND WITH **ZERO** IDEA WHAT TO DO **NEXT.**
HEY. HEY. THIS SUCKS. I KNOW. WHAT CAN I DO?
YOU GOT A TIME MACHINE?
THEN FUCK IT.

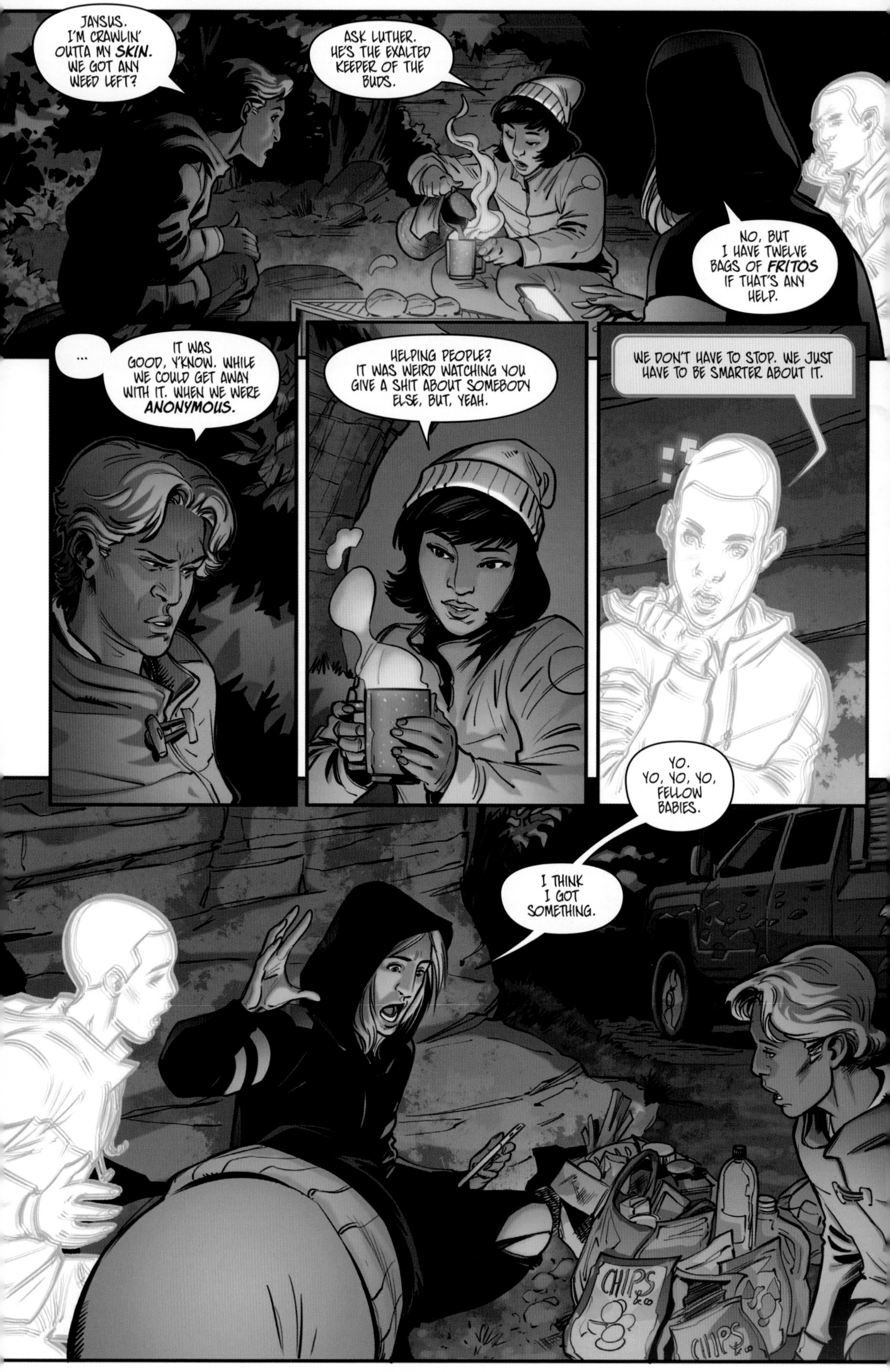
JAYSUS. I'M CRAWLIN' OUTTA MY **SKIN**. WE GOT ANY WEED LEFT?
ASK LUTHER. HE'S THE EXALTED KEEPER OF THE BUDS.
NO, BUT I HAVE TWELVE BAGS OF **FRITOS** IF THAT'S ANY HELP.
...
IT WAS GOOD, Y'KNOW. WHILE WE COULD GET AWAY WITH IT. WHEN WE WERE **ANONYMOUS**.
HELPING PEOPLE? IT WAS WEIRD WATCHING YOU GIVE A SHIT ABOUT SOMEBODY ELSE, BUT, YEAH.
WE DON'T HAVE TO STOP. WE JUST HAVE TO BE SMARTER ABOUT IT.
YO. YO, YO, YO, FELLOW BABIES.
I THINK I GOT SOMETHING.
CHIPS & CO
CHIPS & CO

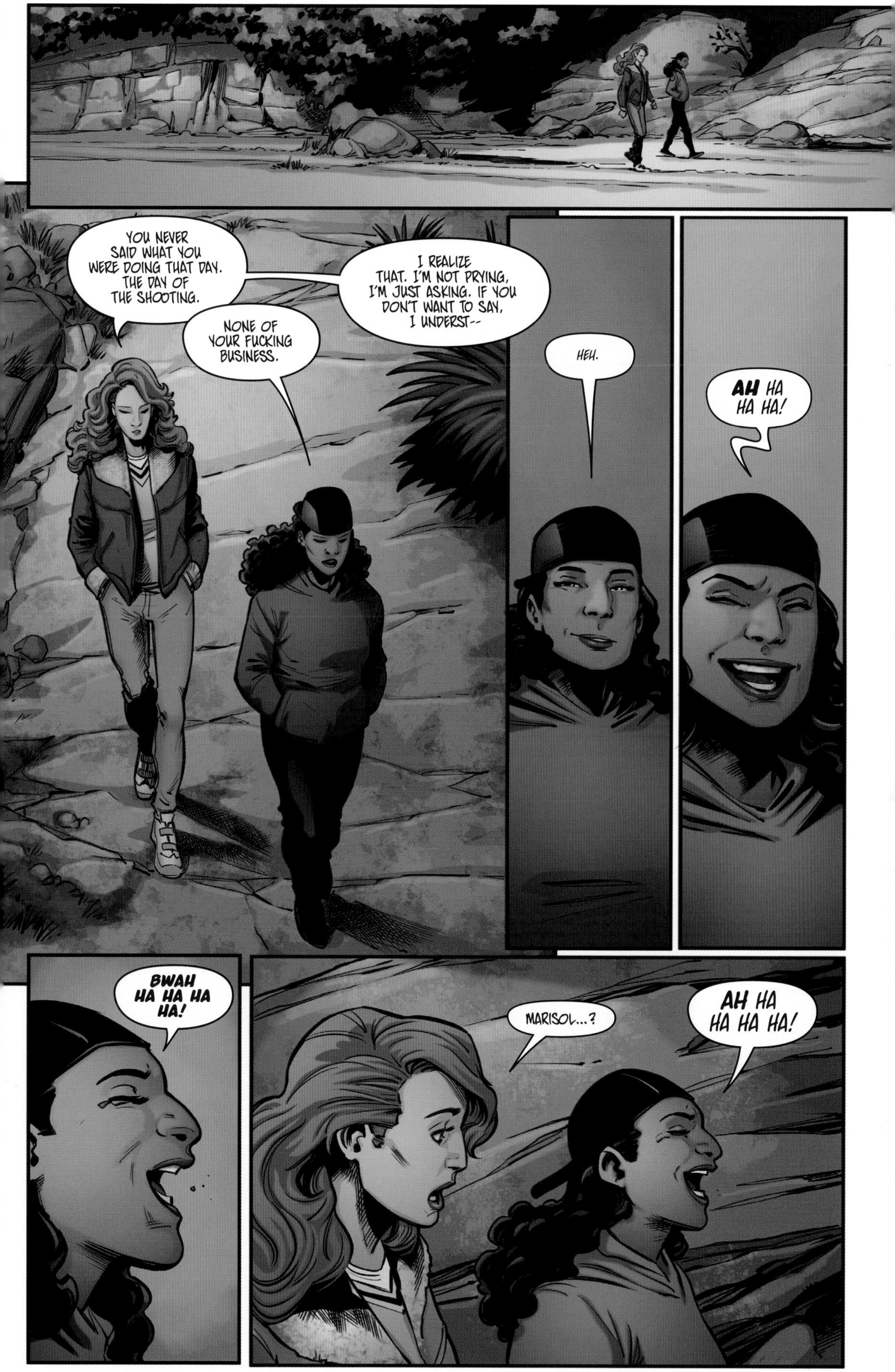
YOU NEVER SAID WHAT YOU WERE DOING THAT DAY. THE DAY OF THE SHOOTING.
NONE OF YOUR FUCKING BUSINESS.
I REALIZE THAT. I'M NOT PRYING, I'M JUST ASKING. IF YOU DON'T WANT TO SAY, I UNDERST--
HEH.
AH HA HA HA!
BWAH HA HA HA HA!
MARISOL...?
AH HA HA HA HA!

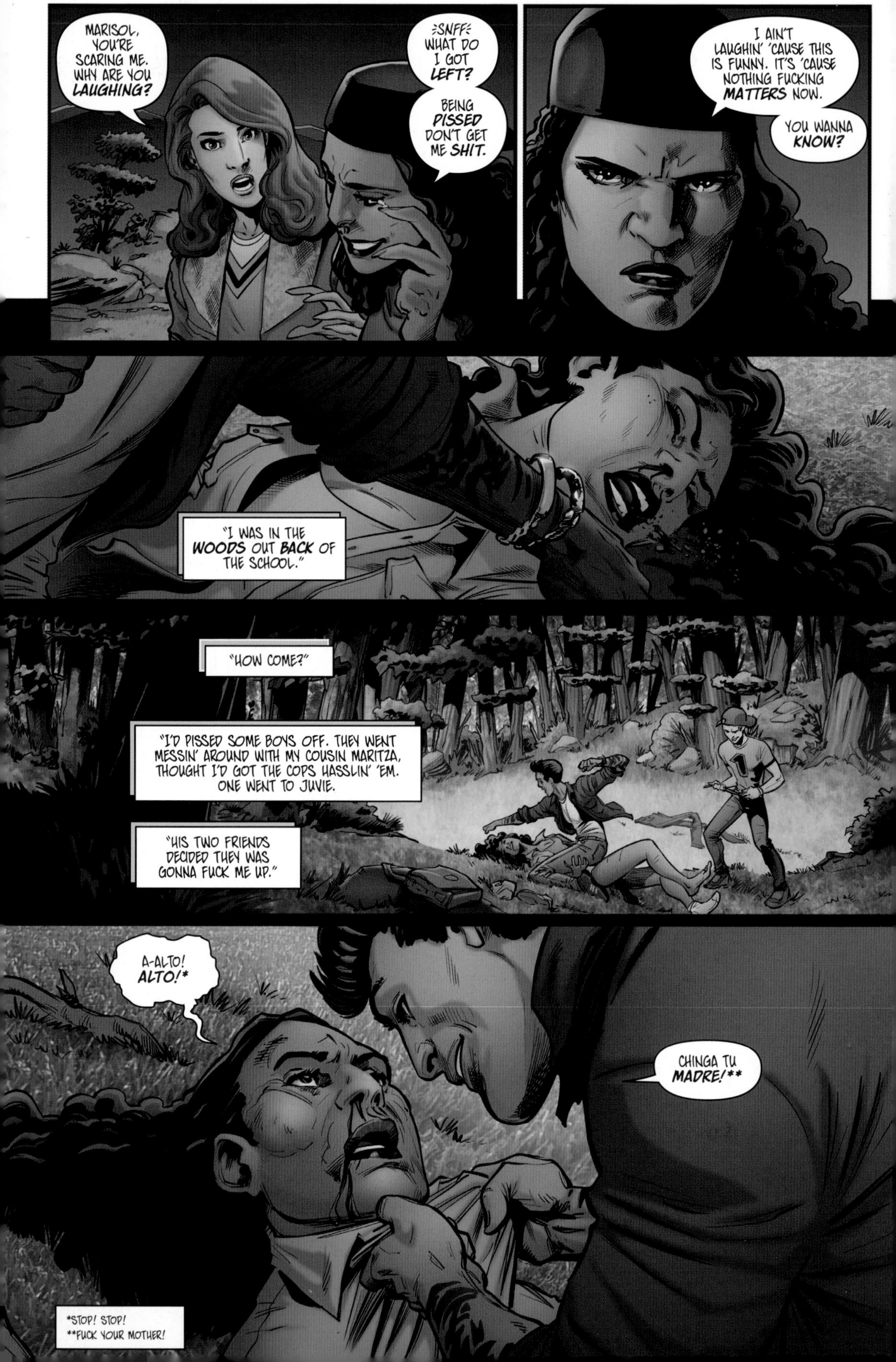
MARISOL, YOU'RE SCARING ME. WHY ARE YOU **LAUGHING?**
SNFF WHAT DO I GOT **LEFT?**
BEING **PISSED** DON'T GET ME **SHIT**.
I AIN'T LAUGHIN' 'CAUSE THIS IS FUNNY. IT'S 'CAUSE NOTHING FUCKING **MATTERS** NOW.
YOU WANNA **KNOW?**
"I WAS IN THE **WOODS** OUT **BACK** OF THE SCHOOL."
"HOW COME?"
"I'D PISSED SOME BOYS OFF. THEY WENT MESSIN' AROUND WITH MY COUSIN MARITZA, THOUGHT I'D GOT THE COPS HASSLIN' 'EM. ONE WENT TO JUVIE.
"HIS TWO FRIENDS DECIDED THEY WAS GONNA FUCK ME UP."
A-ALTO! **ALTO!***
CHINGA TU **MADRE!****
*STOP! STOP!
**FUCK YOUR MOTHER!

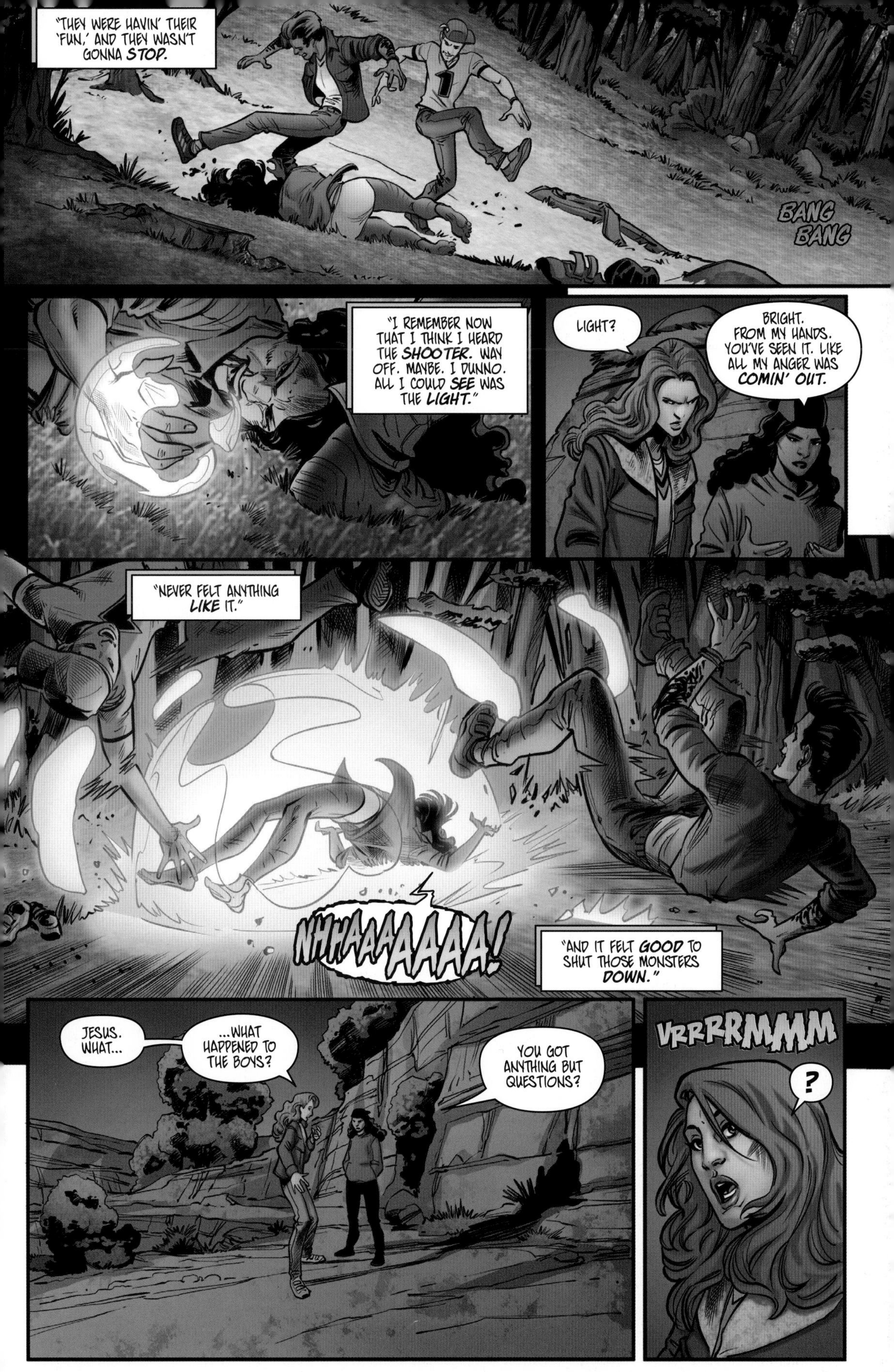

"THEY WERE HAVIN' THEIR 'FUN,' AND THEY WASN'T GONNA STOP.
BANG BANG
"I REMEMBER NOW THAT I THINK I HEARD THE SHOOTER. WAY OFF. MAYBE. I DUNNO. ALL I COULD SEE WAS THE LIGHT."
LIGHT?
BRIGHT. FROM MY HANDS. YOU'VE SEEN IT. LIKE ALL MY ANGER WAS COMIN' OUT.
"NEVER FELT ANYTHING LIKE IT."
NHHAAAAAAAA!
"AND IT FELT GOOD TO SHUT THOSE MONSTERS DOWN."
JESUS. WHAT...
...WHAT HAPPENED TO THE BOYS?
YOU GOT ANYTHING BUT QUESTIONS?
VRRRRMMM
?

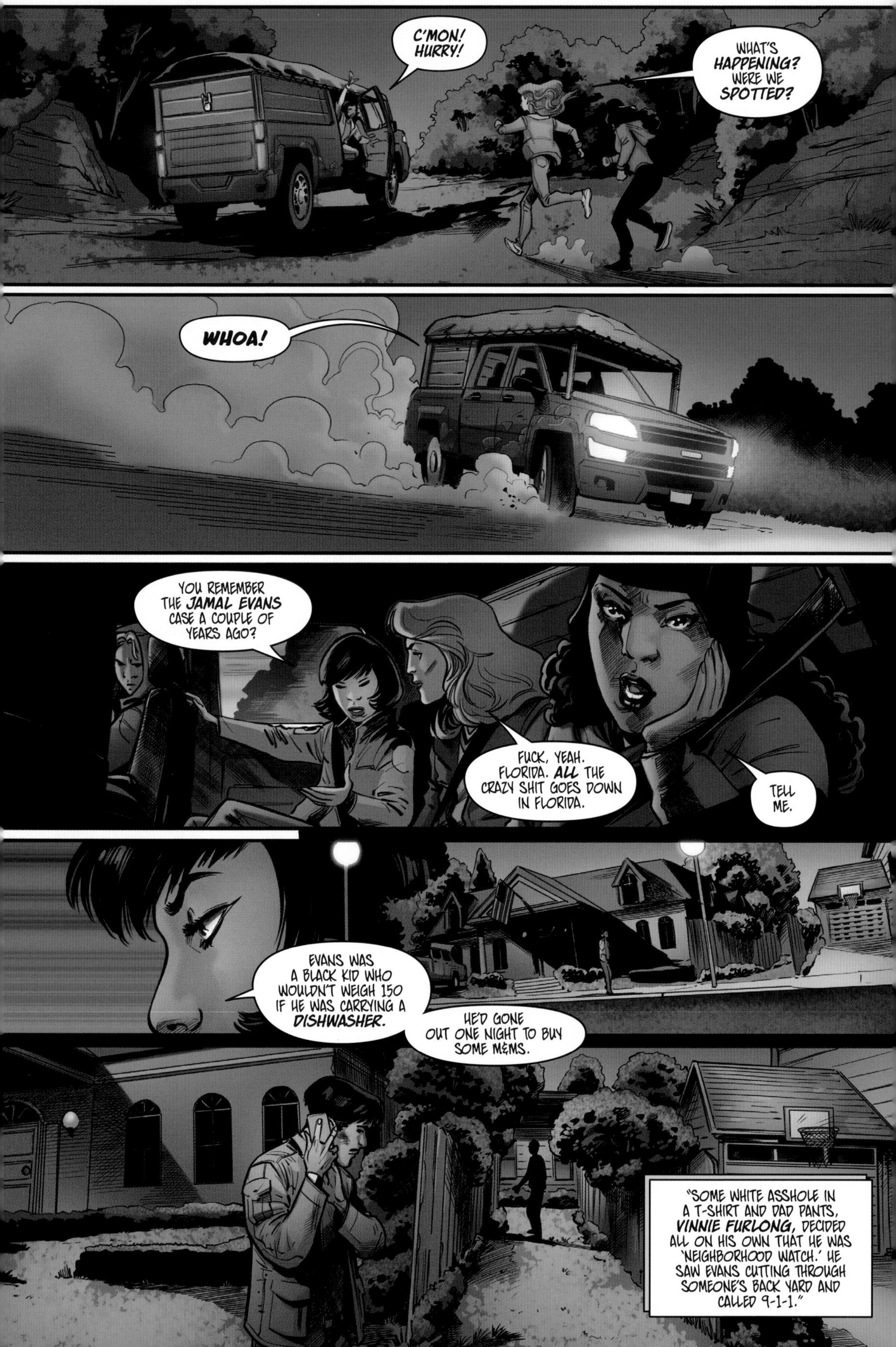
C'MON! HURRY!
WHAT'S HAPPENING? WERE WE SPOTTED?
WHOA!
YOU REMEMBER THE JAMAL EVANS CASE A COUPLE OF YEARS AGO?
FUCK, YEAH. FLORIDA. ALL THE CRAZY SHIT GOES DOWN IN FLORIDA.
TELL ME.
EVANS WAS A BLACK KID WHO WOULDN'T WEIGH 150 IF HE WAS CARRYING A DISHWASHER.
HE'D GONE OUT ONE NIGHT TO BUY SOME M&MS.
"SOME WHITE ASSHOLE IN A T-SHIRT AND DAD PANTS, VINNIE FURLONG, DECIDED ALL ON HIS OWN THAT HE WAS 'NEIGHBORHOOD WATCH.' HE SAW EVANS CUTTING THROUGH SOMEONE'S BACK YARD AND CALLED 9-1-1."

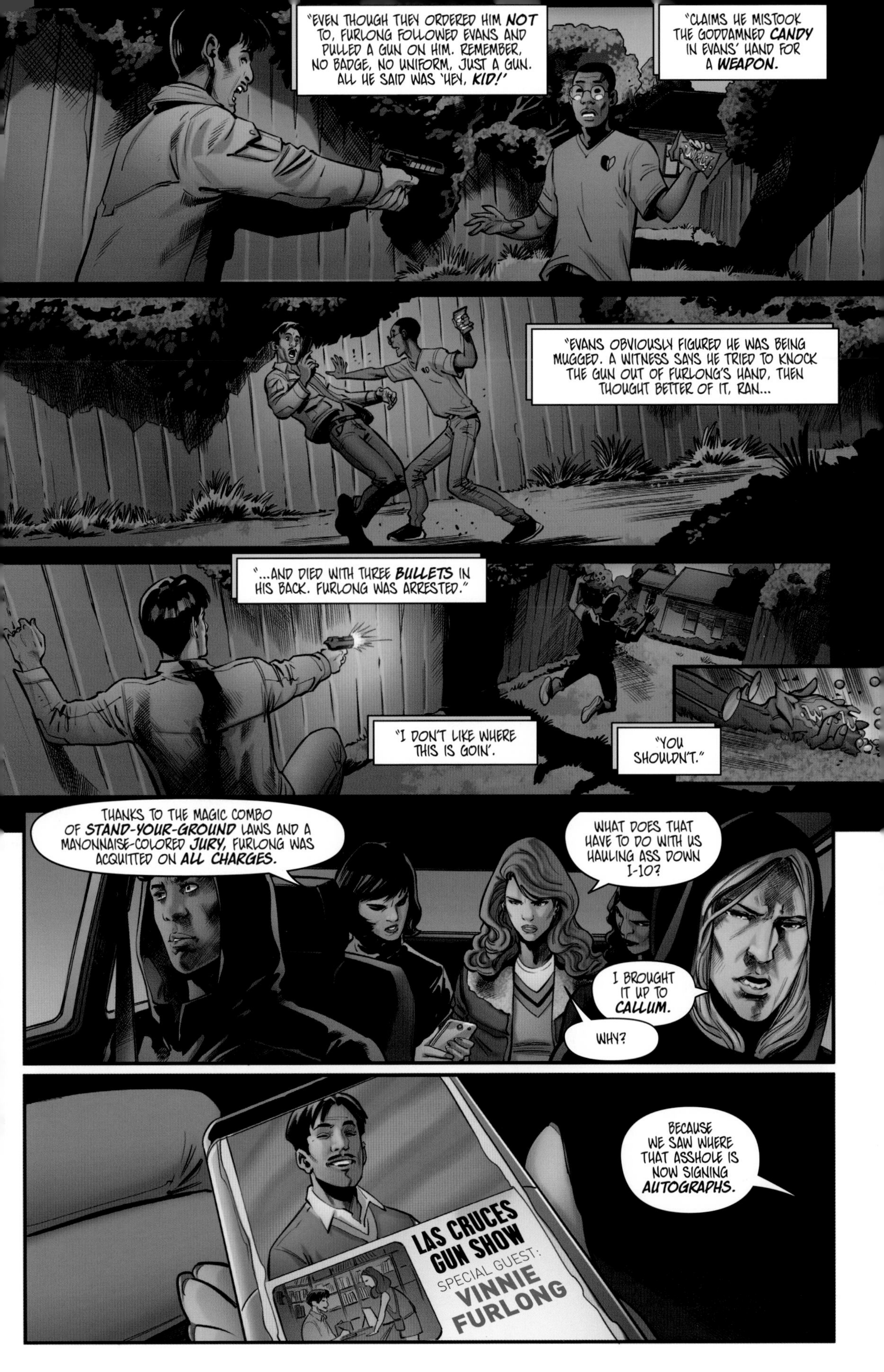
"EVEN THOUGH THEY ORDERED HIM NOT TO, FURLONG FOLLOWED EVANS AND PULLED A GUN ON HIM. REMEMBER, NO BADGE, NO UNIFORM, JUST A GUN. ALL HE SAID WAS 'HEY, KID!'
"CLAIMS HE MISTOOK THE GODDAMNED CANDY IN EVANS' HAND FOR A WEAPON.
"EVANS OBVIOUSLY FIGURED HE WAS BEING MUGGED. A WITNESS SAYS HE TRIED TO KNOCK THE GUN OUT OF FURLONG'S HAND, THEN THOUGHT BETTER OF IT, RAN...
"...AND DIED WITH THREE BULLETS IN HIS BACK. FURLONG WAS ARRESTED."
"I DON'T LIKE WHERE THIS IS GOIN'.
"YOU SHOULDN'T."
THANKS TO THE MAGIC COMBO OF STAND-YOUR-GROUND LAWS AND A MAYONNAISE-COLORED JURY, FURLONG WAS ACQUITTED ON ALL CHARGES.
WHAT DOES THAT HAVE TO DO WITH US HAULING ASS DOWN I-10?
I BROUGHT IT UP TO CALLUM.
WHY?
BECAUSE WE SAW WHERE THAT ASSHOLE IS NOW SIGNING AUTOGRAPHS.
LAS CRUCES GUN SHOW
SPECIAL GUEST:
VINNIE FURLONG

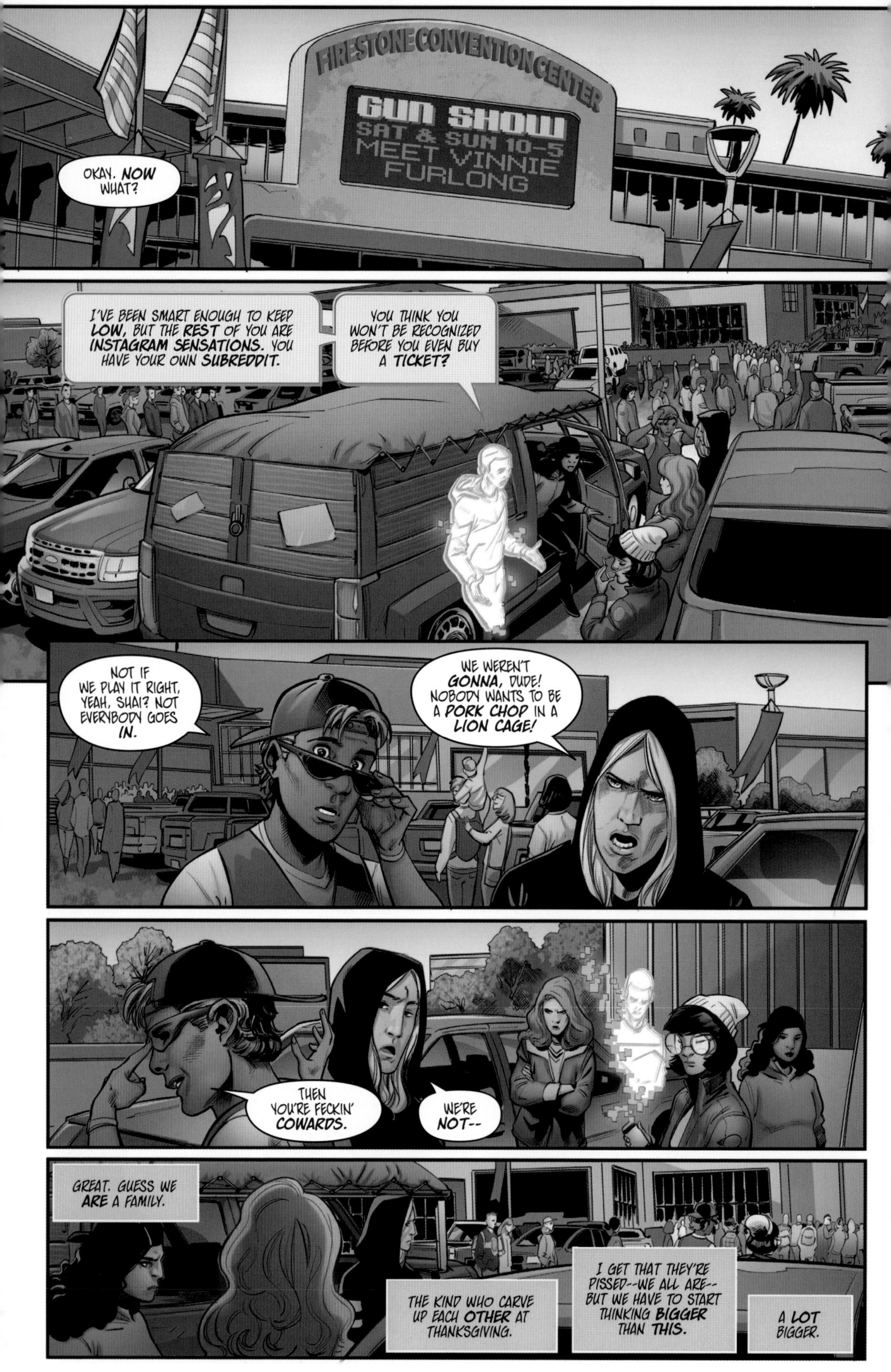
FIRESTONE CONVENTION CENTER
GUN SHOW
SAT & SUN 10-5
MEET VINNIE FURLONG
OKAY. NOW WHAT?
I'VE BEEN SMART ENOUGH TO KEEP LOW, BUT THE REST OF YOU ARE INSTAGRAM SENSATIONS. YOU HAVE YOUR OWN SUBREDDIT.
YOU THINK YOU WON'T BE RECOGNIZED BEFORE YOU EVEN BUY A TICKET?
NOT IF WE PLAY IT RIGHT, YEAH, SHAI? NOT EVERYBODY GOES IN.
WE WEREN'T GONNA, DUDE! NOBODY WANTS TO BE A PORK CHOP IN A LION CAGE!
THEN YOU'RE FECKIN' COWARDS.
WE'RE NOT--
GREAT. GUESS WE ARE A FAMILY.
THE KIND WHO CARVE UP EACH OTHER AT THANKSGIVING.
I GET THAT THEY'RE PISSED--WE ALL ARE--BUT WE HAVE TO START THINKING BIGGER THAN THIS.
A LOT BIGGER.

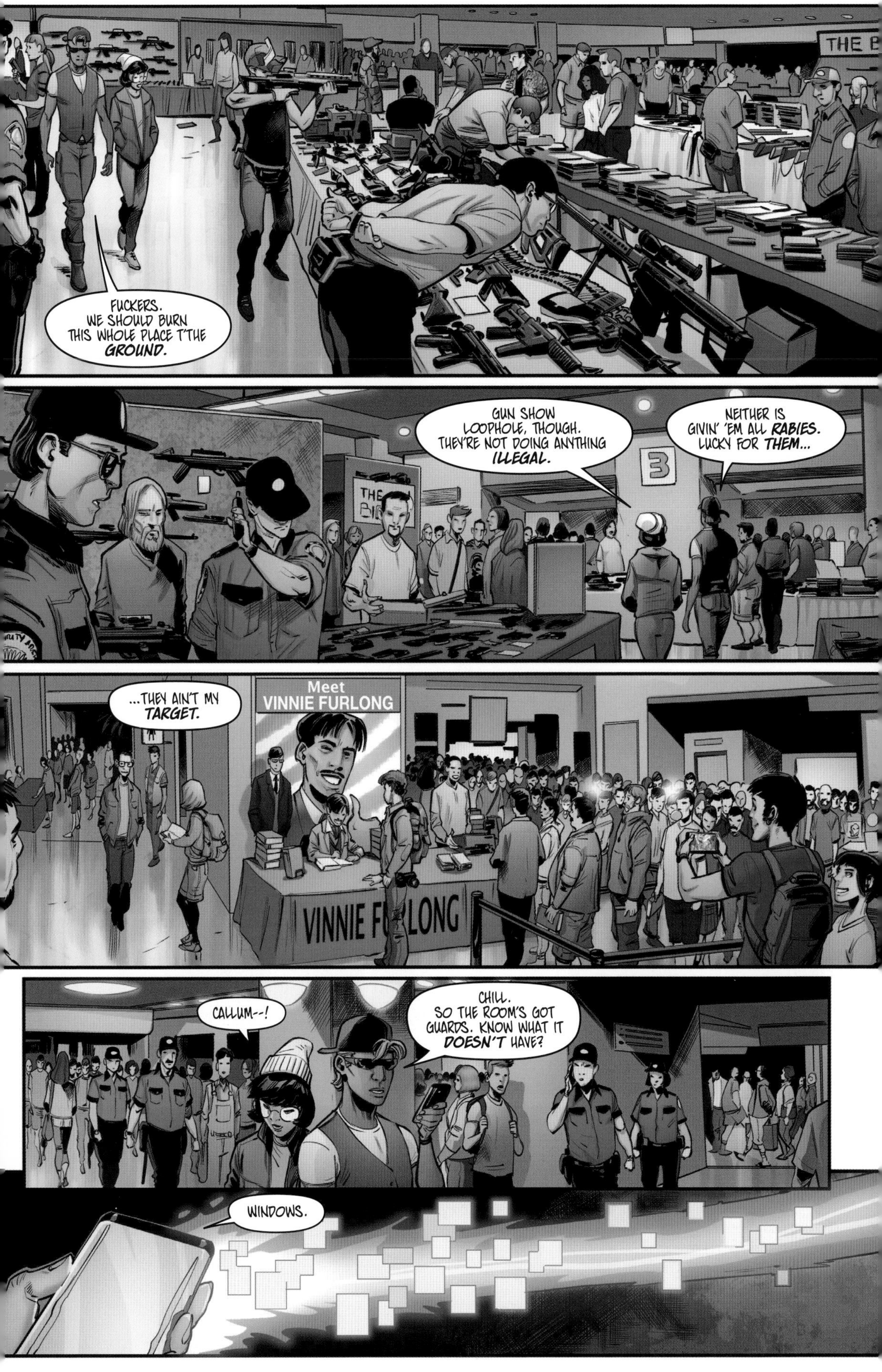
THE B
FUCKERS. WE SHOULD BURN THIS WHOLE PLACE T'THE GROUND.
GUN SHOW LOOPHOLE, THOUGH. THEY'RE NOT DOING ANYTHING ILLEGAL.
NEITHER IS GIVIN' 'EM ALL RABIES. LUCKY FOR THEM...
3
...THEY AIN'T MY TARGET.
Meet VINNIE FURLONG
VINNIE FURLONG
CALLUM--!
CHILL. SO THE ROOM'S GOT GUARDS. KNOW WHAT IT DOESN'T HAVE?
WINDOWS.

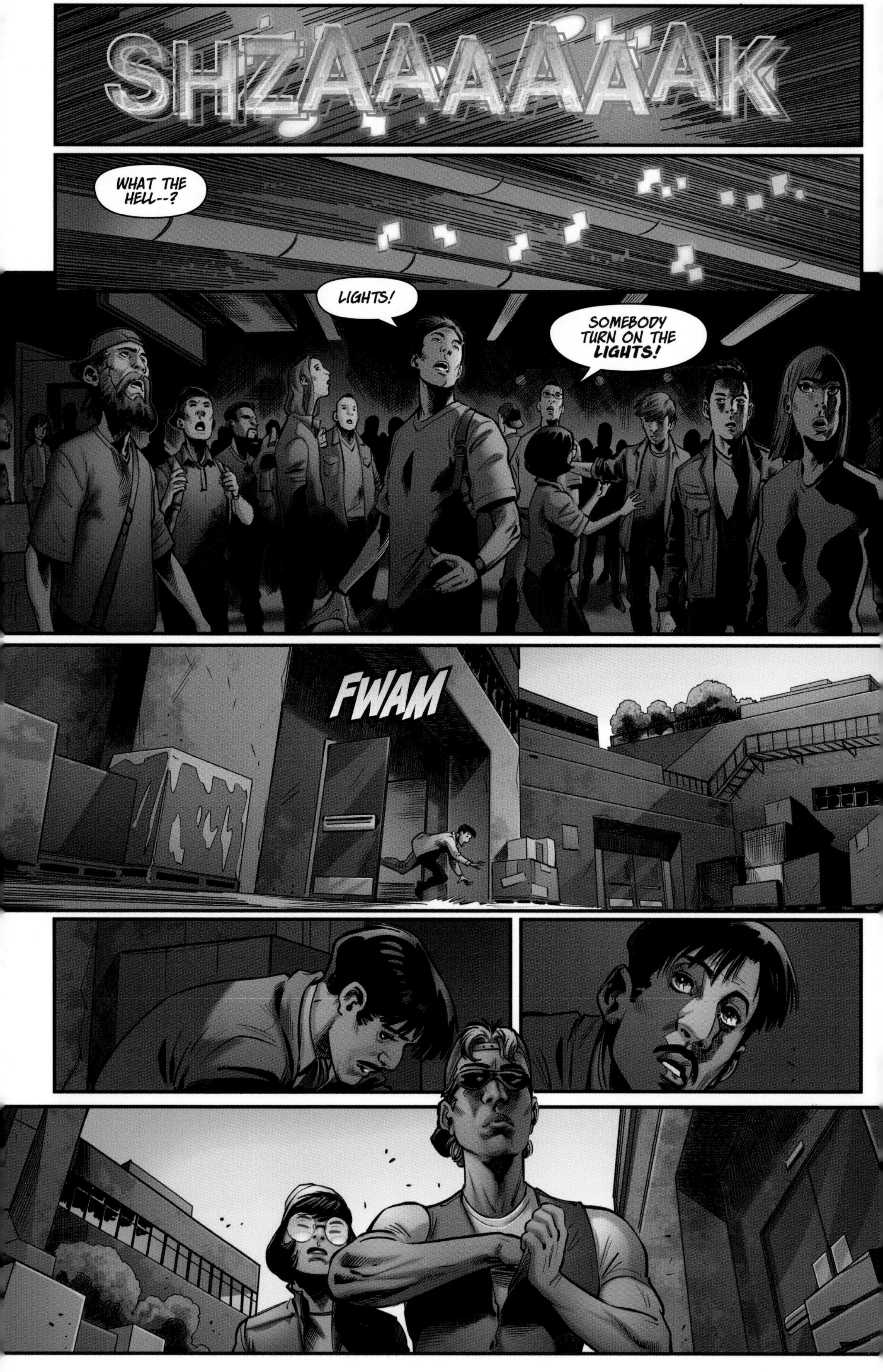
SHZAAAAAK
WHAT THE HELL--?
LIGHTS!
SOMEBODY TURN ON THE LIGHTS!
FWAM

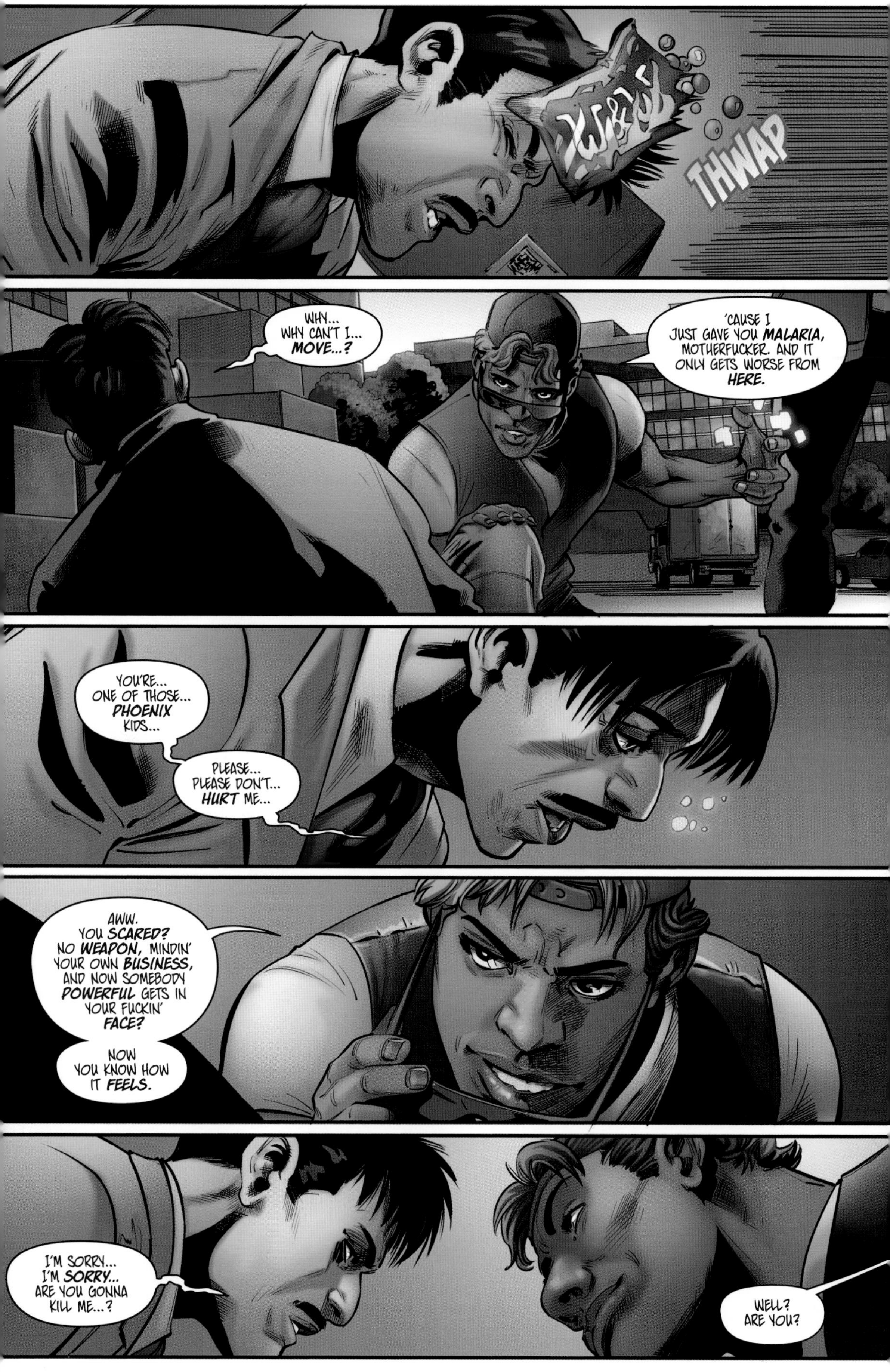
THWAP
WHY... WHY CAN'T I... MOVE...?
'CAUSE I JUST GAVE YOU MALARIA, MOTHERFUCKER. AND IT ONLY GETS WORSE FROM HERE.
YOU'RE... ONE OF THOSE... PHOENIX KIDS...
PLEASE... PLEASE DON'T... HURT ME...
AWW. YOU SCARED? NO WEAPON, MINDIN' YOUR OWN BUSINESS, AND NOW SOMEBODY POWERFUL GETS IN YOUR FUCKIN' FACE?
NOW YOU KNOW HOW IT FEELS.
I'M SORRY... I'M SORRY... ARE YOU GONNA KILL ME...?
WELL? ARE YOU?

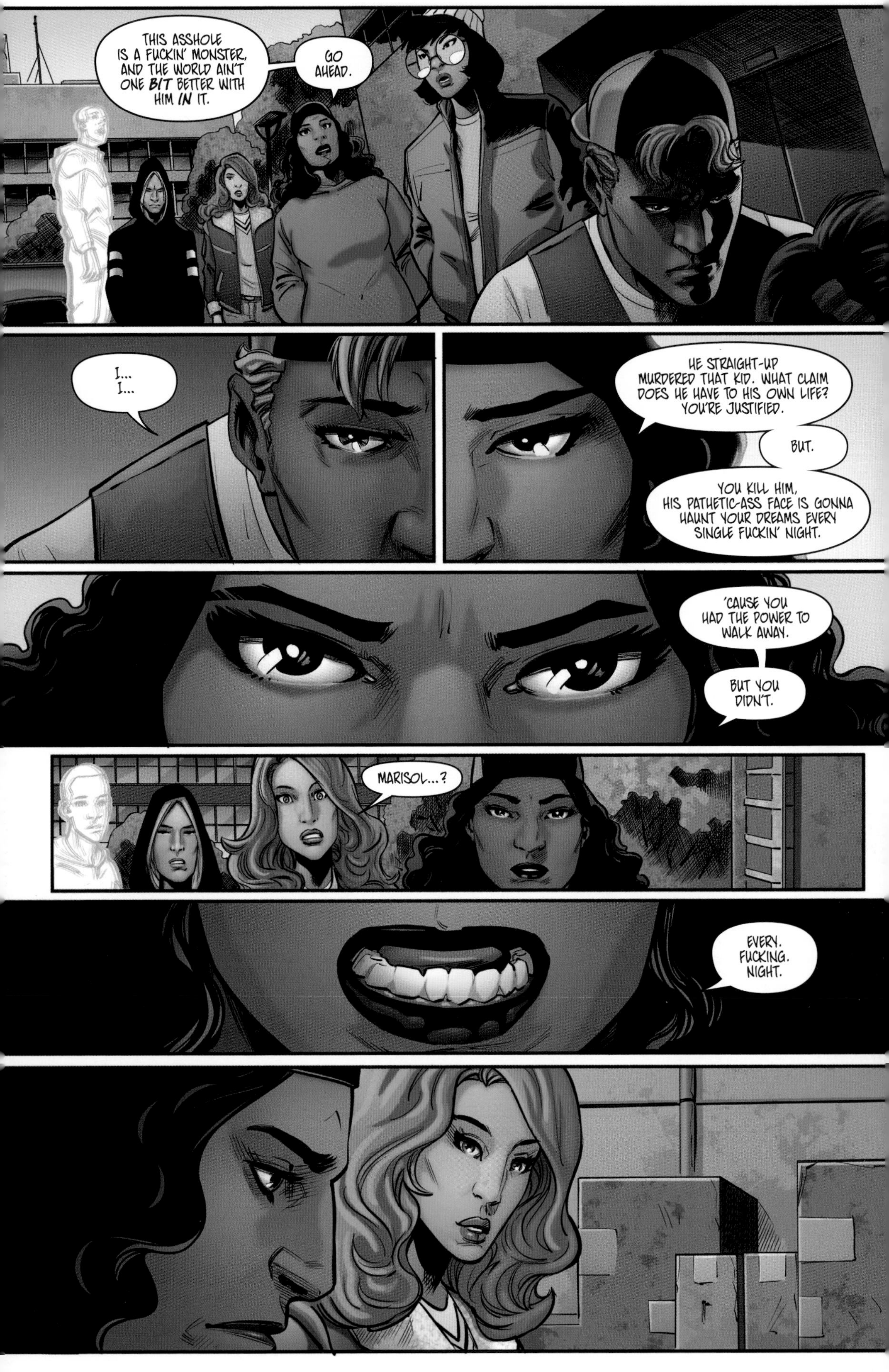
THIS ASSHOLE IS A FUCKIN' MONSTER, AND THE WORLD AIN'T ONE BIT BETTER WITH HIM IN IT.
GO AHEAD.
I... I...
HE STRAIGHT-UP MURDERED THAT KID. WHAT CLAIM DOES HE HAVE TO HIS OWN LIFE? YOU'RE JUSTIFIED.
BUT.
YOU KILL HIM, HIS PATHETIC-ASS FACE IS GONNA HAUNT YOUR DREAMS EVERY SINGLE FUCKIN' NIGHT.
'CAUSE YOU HAD THE POWER TO WALK AWAY.
BUT YOU DIDN'T.
MARISOL...?
EVERY. FUCKING. NIGHT.

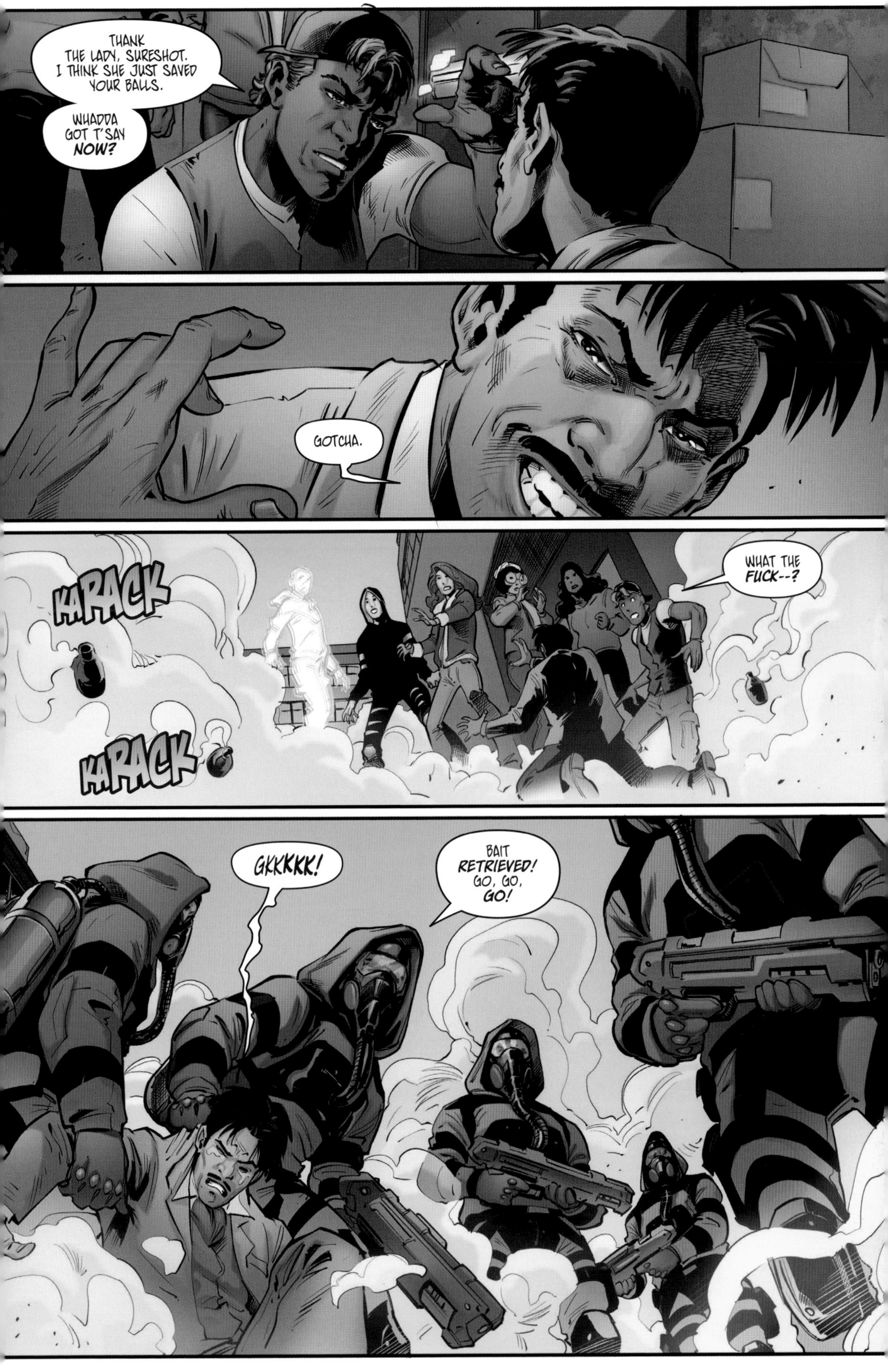
THANK THE LADY, SURESHOT. I THINK SHE JUST SAVED YOUR BALLS.
WHADDA GOT T'SAY NOW?
GOTCHA.
KARACK
KARACK
WHAT THE FUCK--?
GKKKKK!
BAIT RETRIEVED! GO, GO, GO!

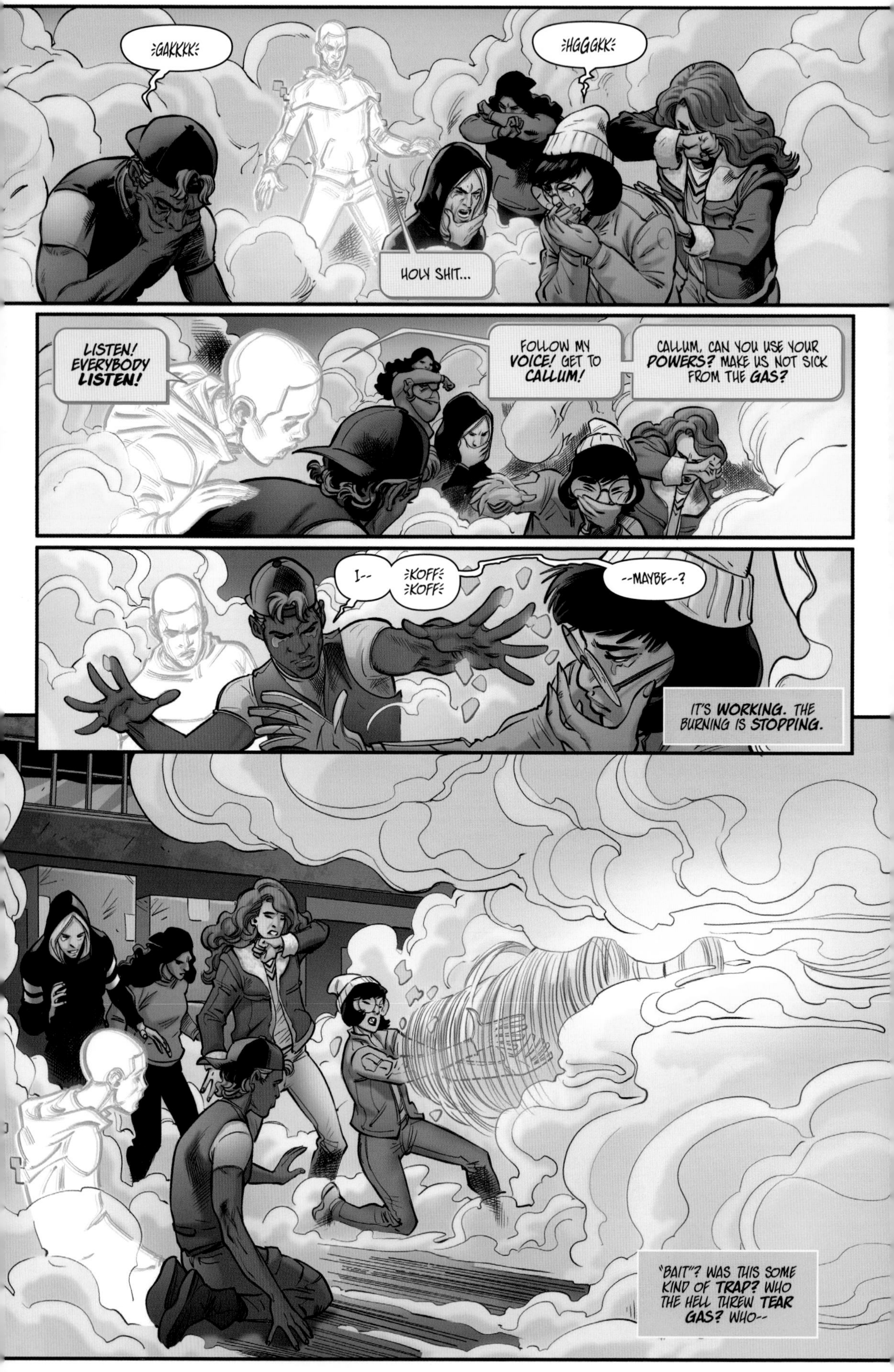

GAKKKK
HGGGKK
HOLY SHIT...
LISTEN! EVERYBODY LISTEN!
FOLLOW MY VOICE! GET TO CALLUM!
CALLUM, CAN YOU USE YOUR POWERS? MAKE US NOT SICK FROM THE GAS?
I--
KOFF KOFF
--MAYBE--?
IT'S WORKING. THE BURNING IS STOPPING.
"BAIT"? WAS THIS SOME KIND OF TRAP? WHO THE HELL THREW TEAR GAS? WHO--

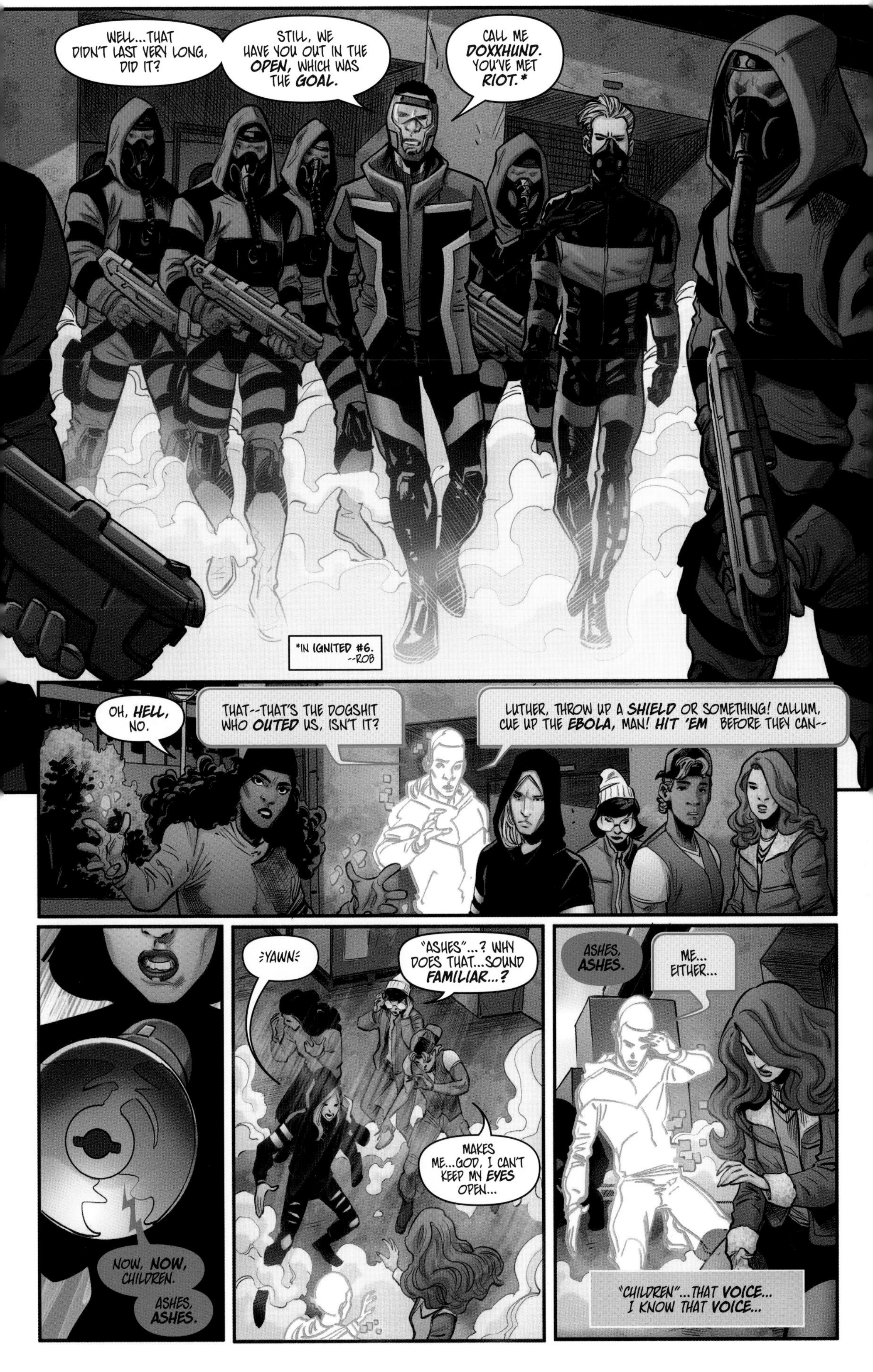
WELL...THAT DIDN'T LAST VERY LONG, DID IT?
STILL, WE HAVE YOU OUT IN THE OPEN, WHICH WAS THE GOAL.
CALL ME DOXXHUND. YOU'VE MET RIOT.*
*IN IGNITED #6. --ROB
OH, HELL, NO.
THAT--THAT'S THE DOGSHIT WHO OUTED US, ISN'T IT?
LUTHER, THROW UP A SHIELD OR SOMETHING! CALLUM, CUE UP THE EBOLA, MAN! HIT 'EM BEFORE THEY CAN--
NOW, NOW, CHILDREN.
ASHES, ASHES.
YAWN
"ASHES"...? WHY DOES THAT...SOUND FAMILIAR...?
MAKES ME...GOD, I CAN'T KEEP MY EYES OPEN...
ASHES, ASHES.
ME... EITHER...
"CHILDREN"...THAT VOICE... I KNOW THAT VOICE...

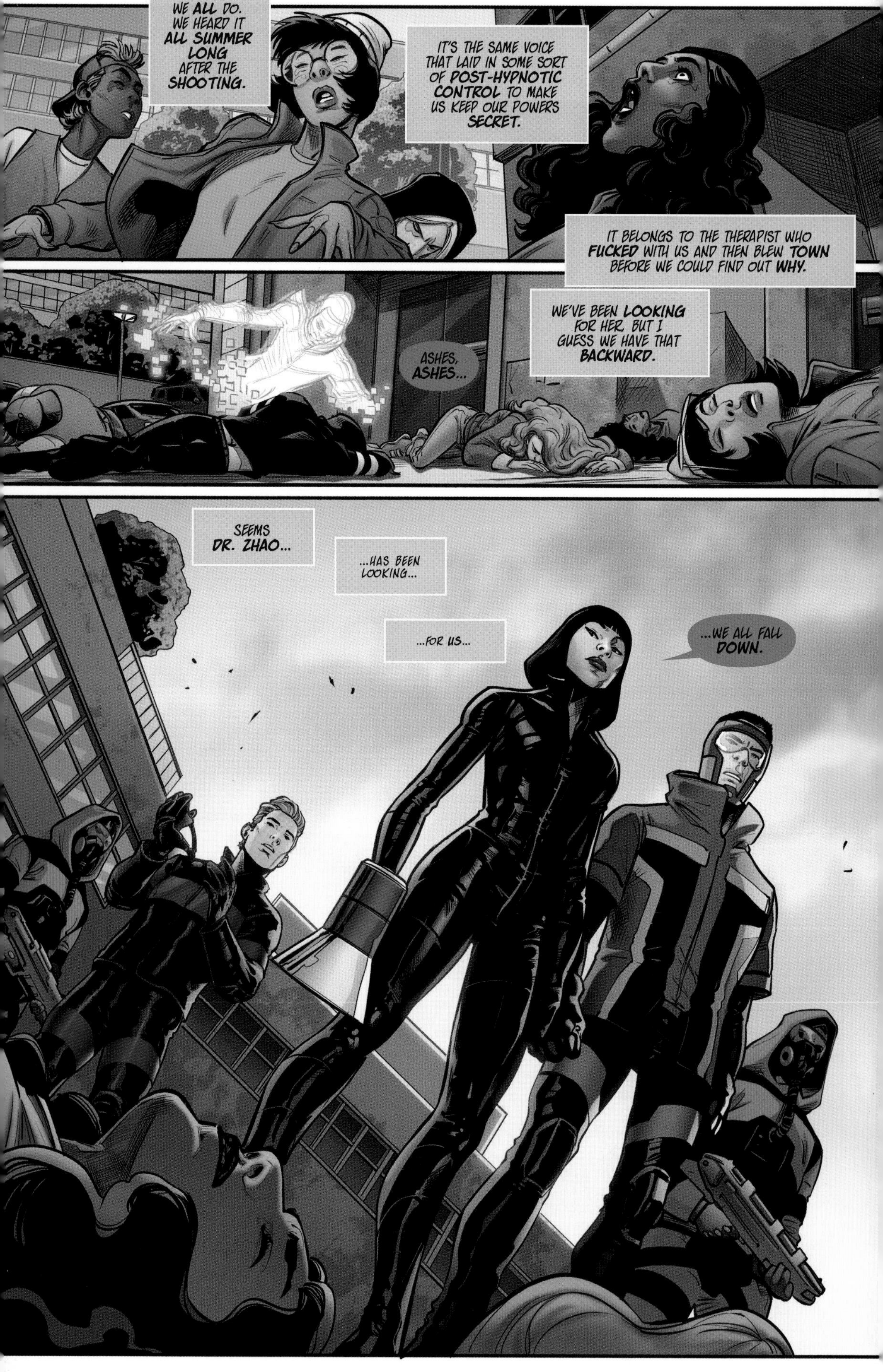
WE ALL DO. WE HEARD IT ALL SUMMER LONG AFTER THE SHOOTING.
IT'S THE SAME VOICE THAT LAID IN SOME SORT OF POST-HYPNOTIC CONTROL TO MAKE US KEEP OUR POWERS SECRET.
IT BELONGS TO THE THERAPIST WHO FUCKED WITH US AND THEN BLEW TOWN BEFORE WE COULD FIND OUT WHY.
ASHES, ASHES...
WE'VE BEEN LOOKING FOR HER, BUT I GUESS WE HAVE THAT BACKWARD.
SEEMS DR. ZHAO...
...HAS BEEN LOOKING...
...FOR US...
...WE ALL FALL DOWN.

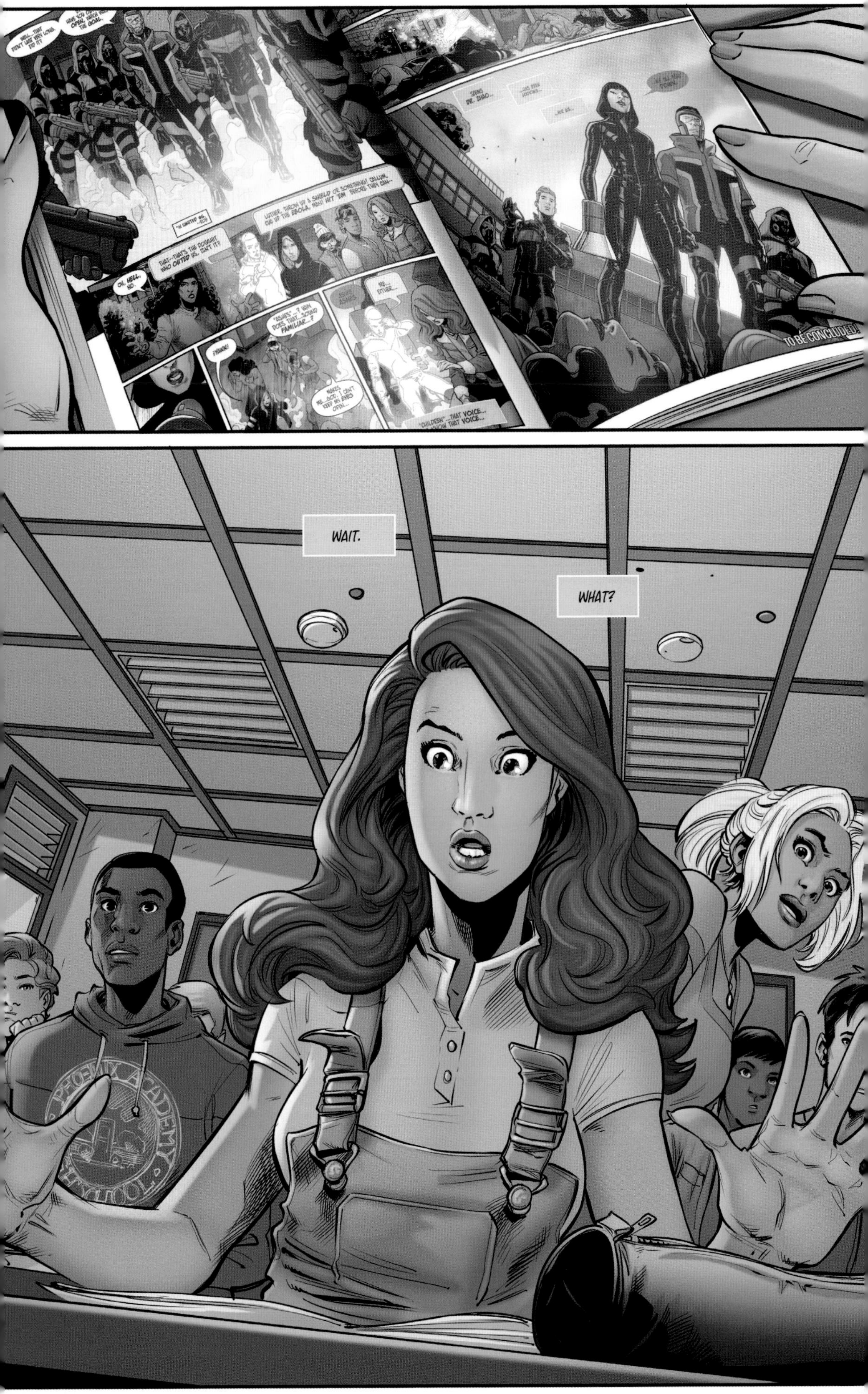
WELL... THAT DIDN'T LAST VERY LONG, DID IT?
THAT--THAT'S THE DOGSHIT WHO OUTED US, ISN'T IT?
OH, HELL, NO.
LUTHER, THROW UP A SHIELD OR SOMETHING! CALLUM, CUE UP THE EBOLA, MAN! HIT 'EM BEFORE THEY CAN--
"ASHES"...? WHY DOES THAT...SOUND FAMILIAR...?
ME... EITHER...
YAWN!
MAKES ME...GOD, I CAN'T KEEP MY EYES OPEN...
"CHILDREN"...THAT VOICE...
SEEMS DR. ZHAO...
...HAS BEEN LOOKING...
...FOR US...
TO BE CONCLUDED!
WAIT.
WHAT?
PHOENIX ACADEMY

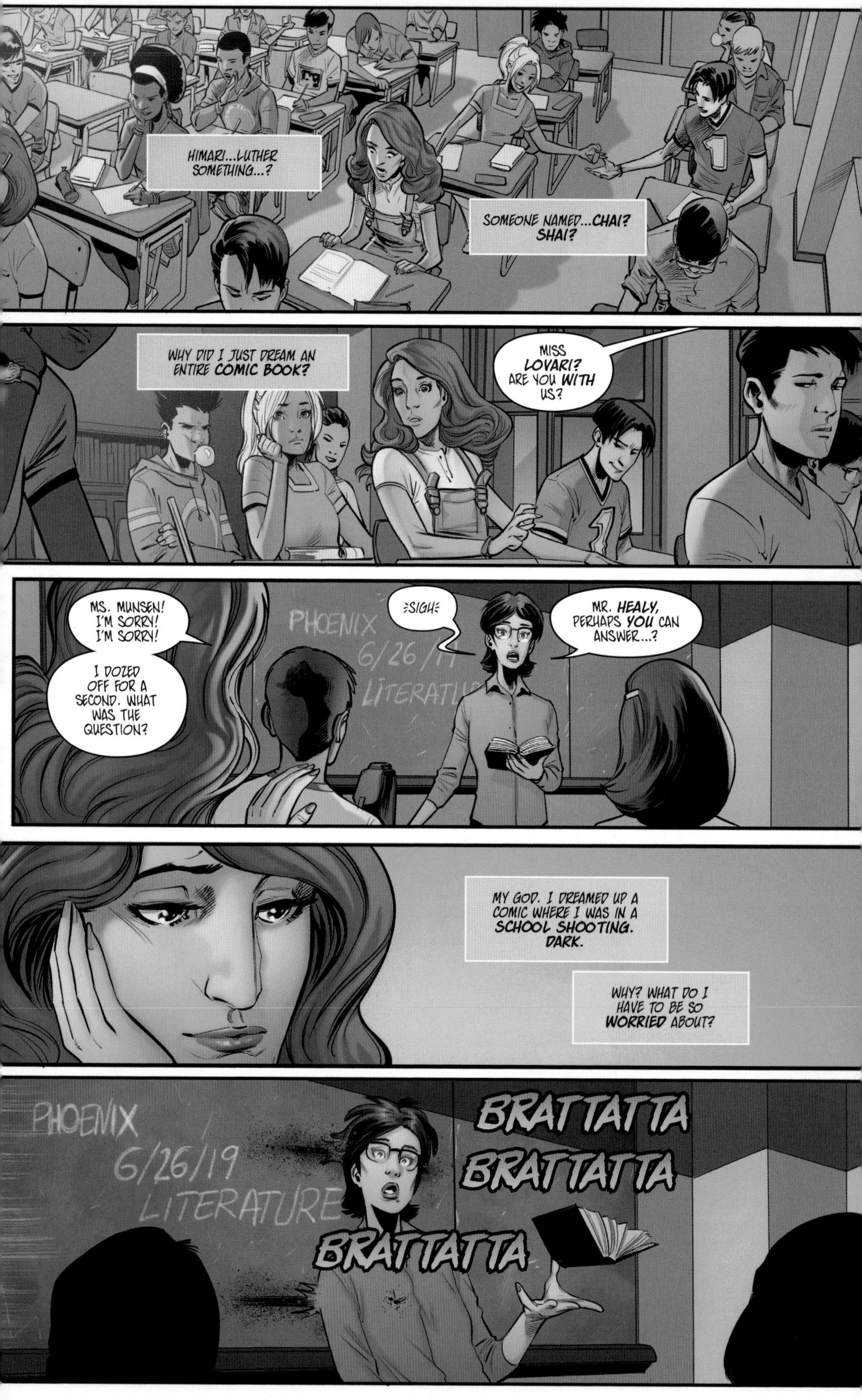
HIMARI...LUTHER SOMETHING...?
SOMEONE NAMED...CHAI? SHAI?
WHY DID I JUST DREAM AN ENTIRE COMIC BOOK?
MISS LOVARI? ARE YOU WITH US?
MS. MUNSEN! I'M SORRY! I'M SORRY!
I DOZED OFF FOR A SECOND. WHAT WAS THE QUESTION?
PHOENIX
SIGH
MR. HEALY, PERHAPS YOU CAN ANSWER...?
MY GOD. I DREAMED UP A COMIC WHERE I WAS IN A SCHOOL SHOOTING. DARK.
WHY? WHAT DO I HAVE TO BE SO WORRIED ABOUT?
PHOENIX
6/26/19
LITERATURE
BRATTATTA
BRATTATTA
BRATTATTA

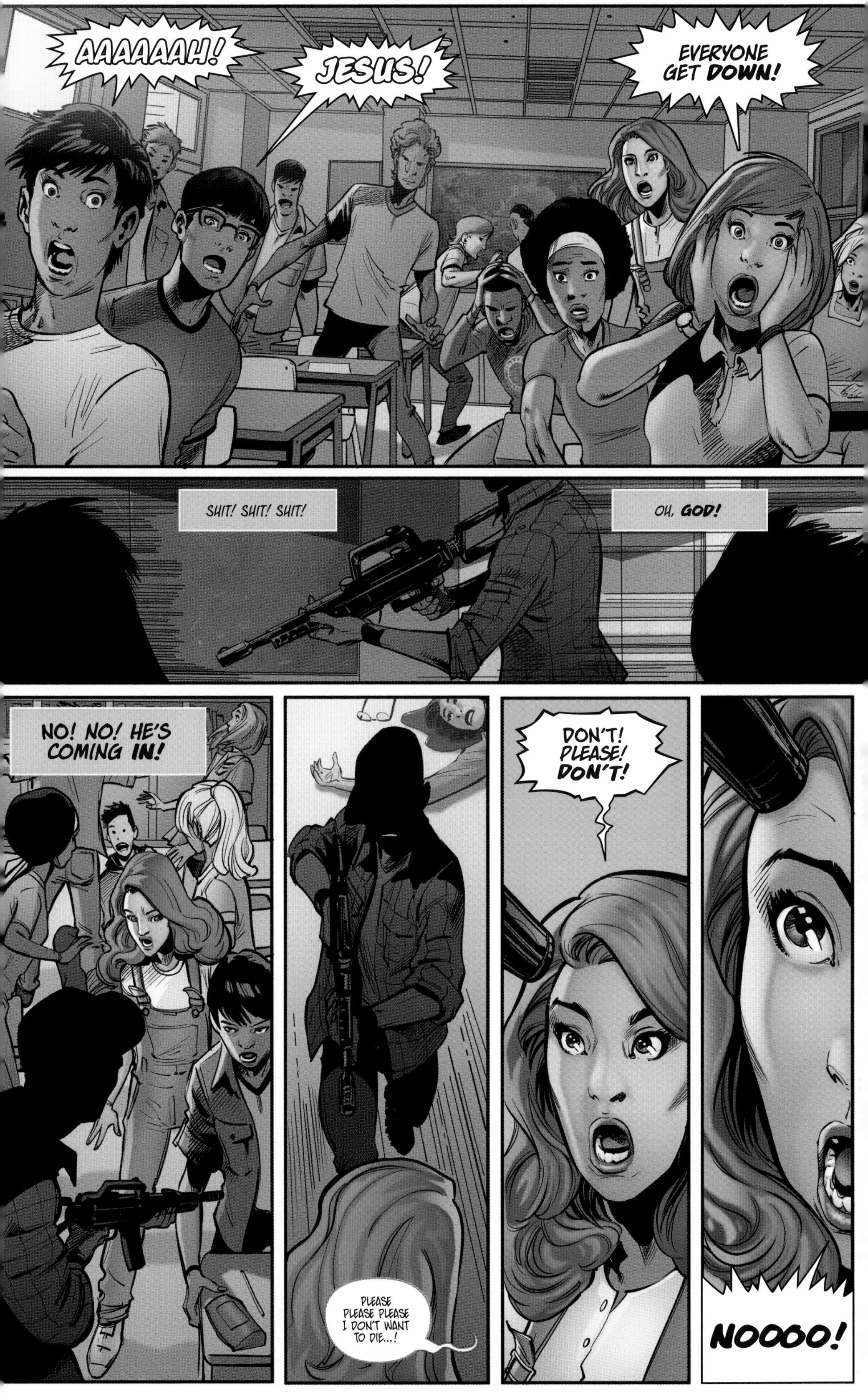
AAAAAAH!
JESUS!
EVERYONE GET DOWN!
SHIT! SHIT! SHIT!
OH, GOD!
NO! NO! HE'S COMING IN!
PLEASE PLEASE PLEASE I DON'T WANT TO DIE...!
DON'T! PLEASE! DON'T!
NOOOO!

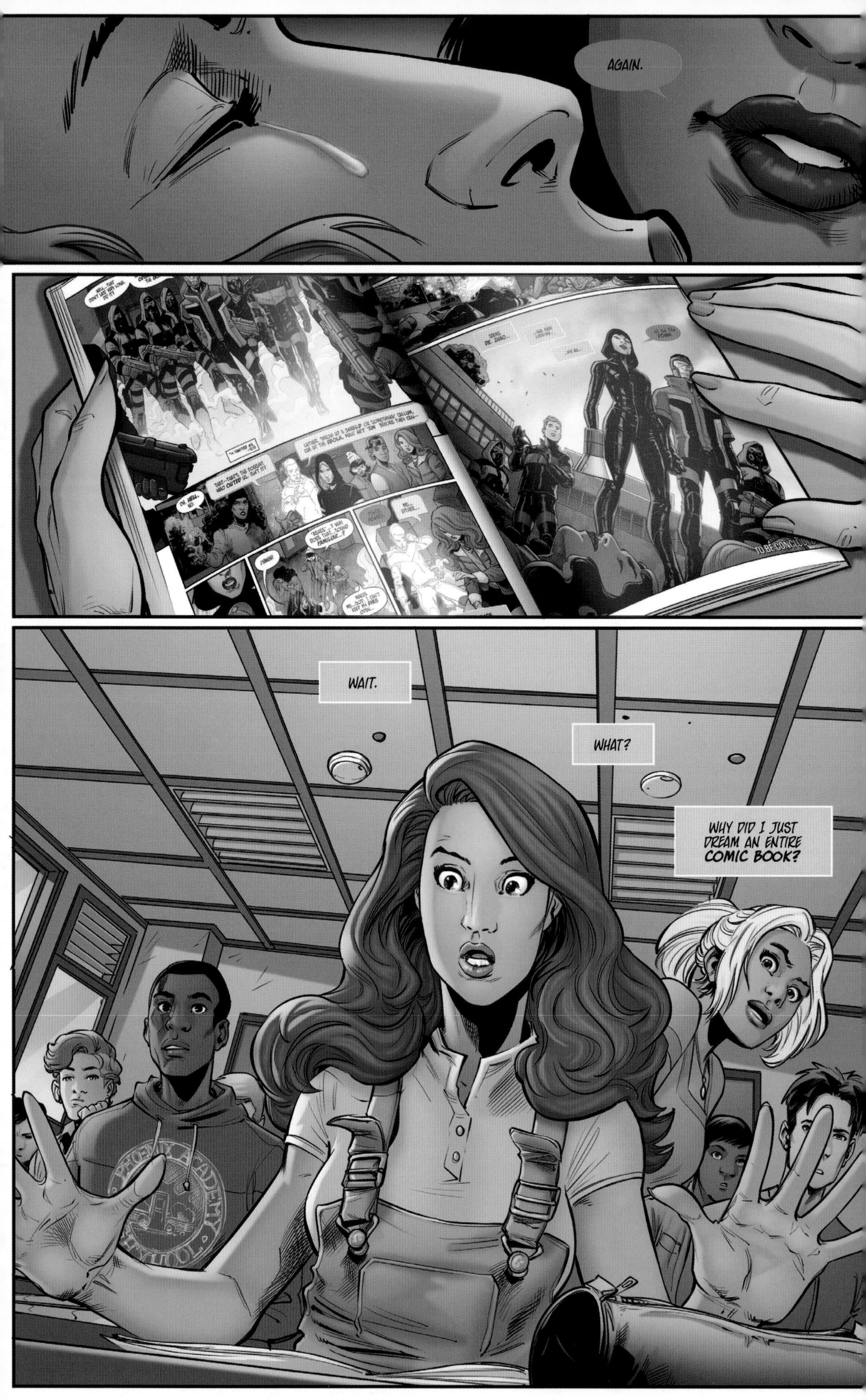
AGAIN.
WAIT.
WHAT?
WHY DID I JUST DREAM AN ENTIRE COMIC BOOK?

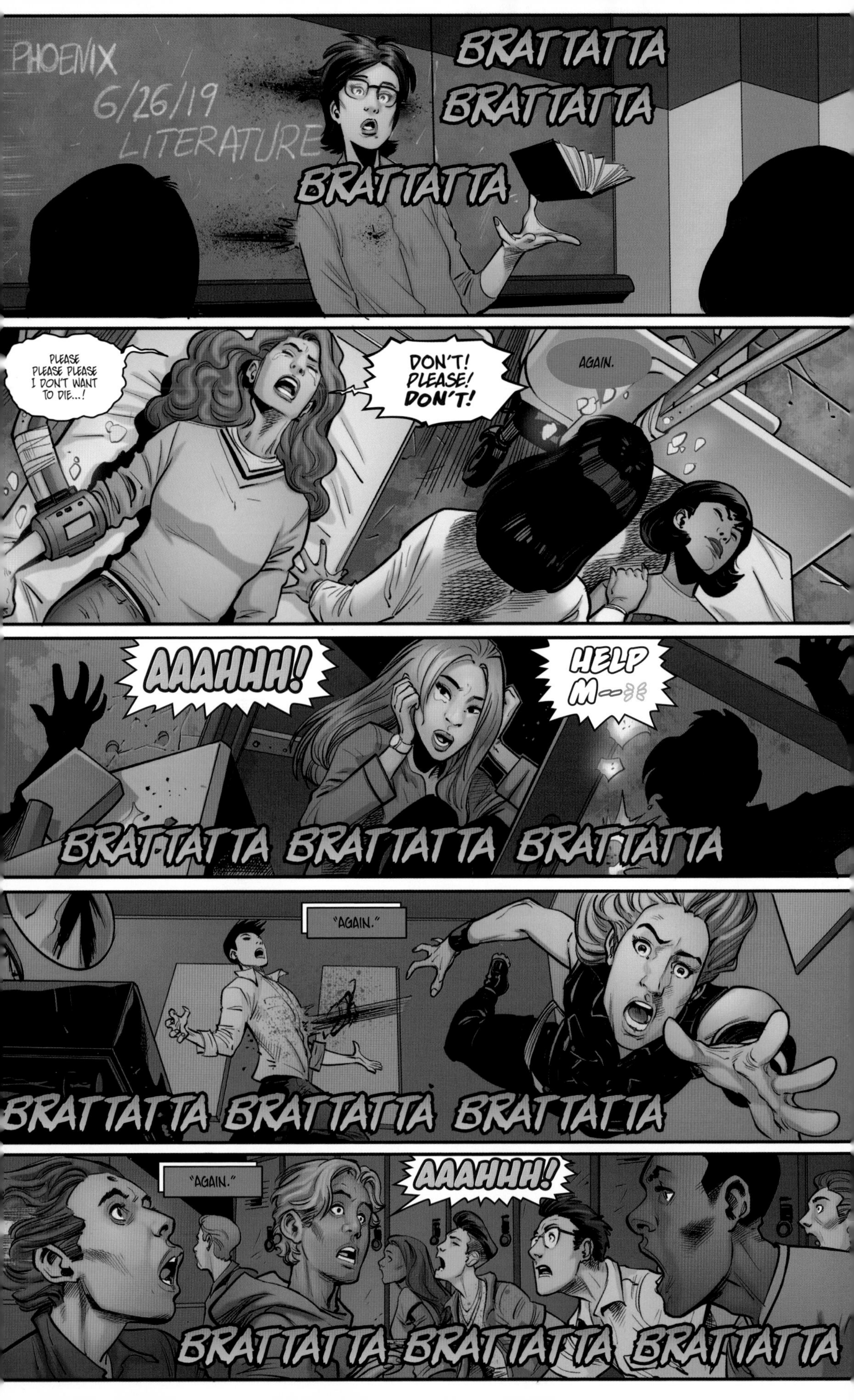
PHOENIX
6/26/19
LITERATURE
BRATTATTA
BRATTATTA
BRATTATTA
PLEASE PLEASE PLEASE I DON'T WANT TO DIE...!
DON'T! PLEASE! DON'T!
AGAIN.
AAAHHH!
HELP M--
BRATTATTA BRATTATTA BRATTATTA
"AGAIN."
BRATTATTA BRATTATTA BRATTATTA
"AGAIN."
AAAHHH!
BRATTATTA BRATTATTA BRATTATTA

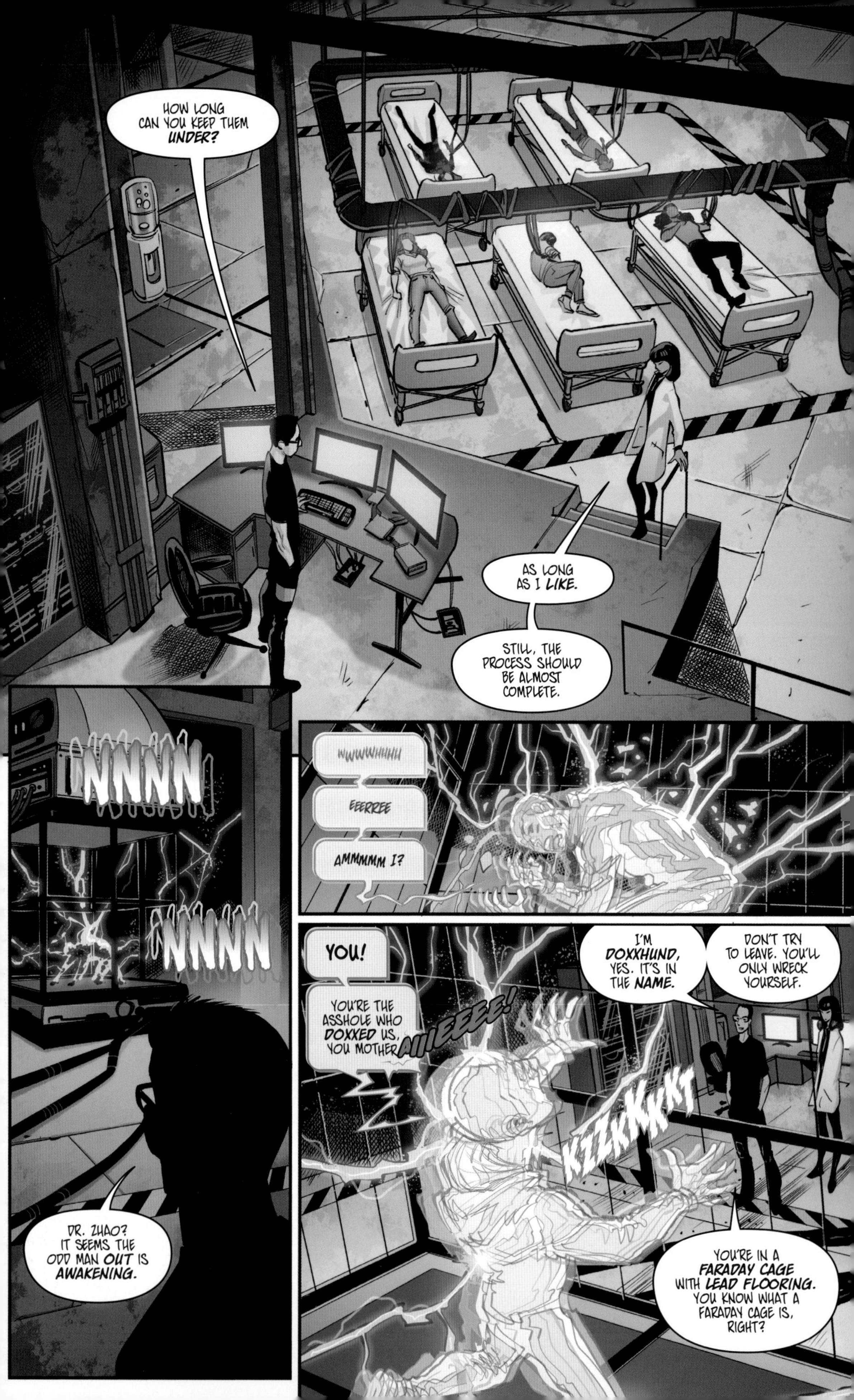
HOW LONG CAN YOU KEEP THEM UNDER?
AS LONG AS I LIKE.
STILL, THE PROCESS SHOULD BE ALMOST COMPLETE.
NNNN
NNNNN
DR. ZHAO? IT SEEMS THE ODD MAN OUT IS AWAKENING.
WWWWHHHH
EEERREE
AMMMMM I?
YOU!
YOU'RE THE ASSHOLE WHO DOXXED US, YOU MOTHERAIIIEEEEE!
KZZKKKKT
I'M DOXXHUND, YES. IT'S IN THE NAME.
DON'T TRY TO LEAVE. YOU'LL ONLY WRECK YOURSELF.
YOU'RE IN A FARADAY CAGE WITH LEAD FLOORING. YOU KNOW WHAT A FARADAY CAGE IS, RIGHT?

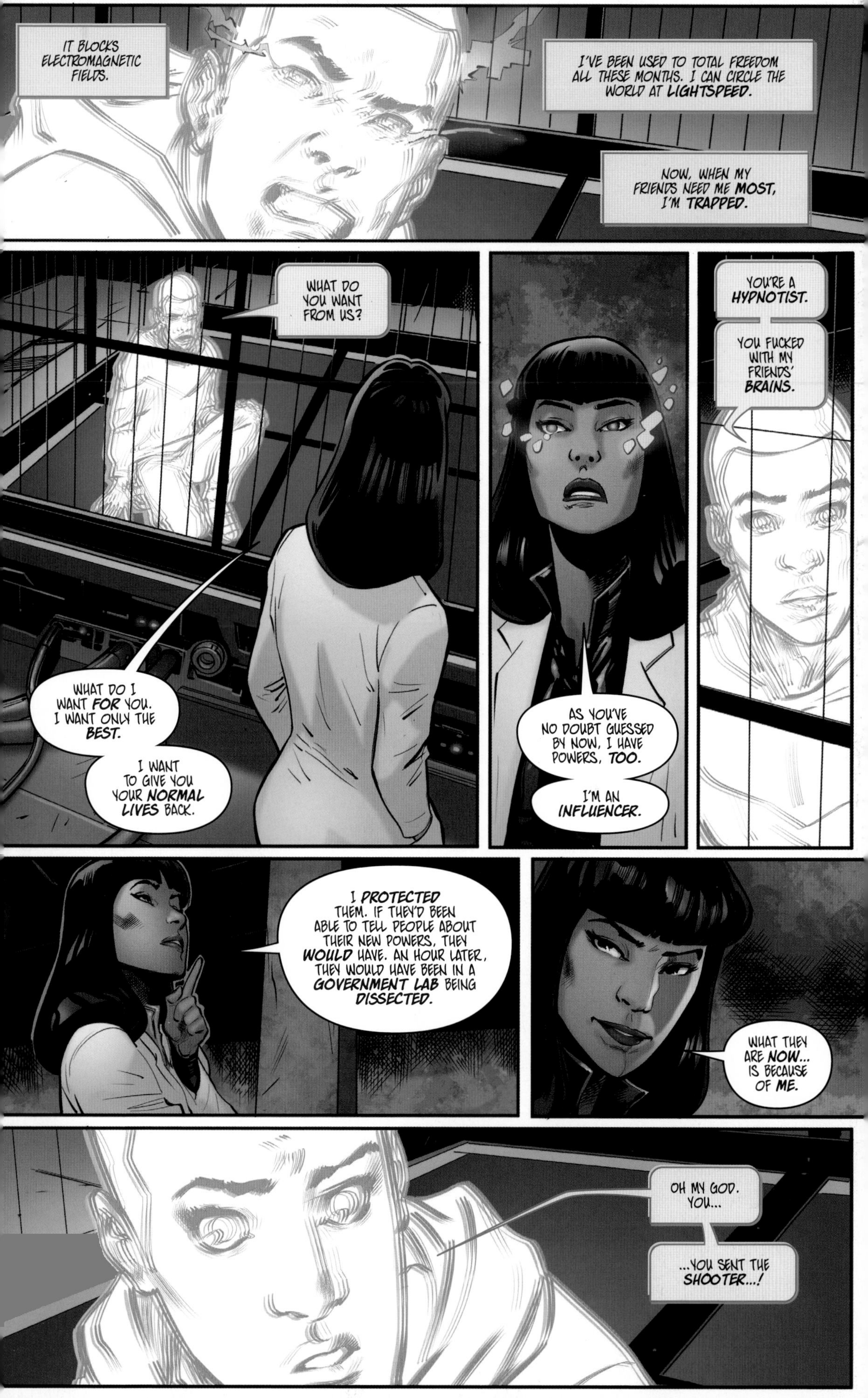
IT BLOCKS ELECTROMAGNETIC FIELDS.
I'VE BEEN USED TO TOTAL FREEDOM ALL THESE MONTHS. I CAN CIRCLE THE WORLD AT LIGHTSPEED.
NOW, WHEN MY FRIENDS NEED ME MOST, I'M TRAPPED.
WHAT DO YOU WANT FROM US?
WHAT DO I WANT FOR YOU. I WANT ONLY THE BEST.
I WANT TO GIVE YOU YOUR NORMAL LIVES BACK.
AS YOU'VE NO DOUBT GUESSED BY NOW, I HAVE POWERS, TOO.
I'M AN INFLUENCER.
YOU'RE A HYPNOTIST.
YOU FUCKED WITH MY FRIENDS' BRAINS.
I PROTECTED THEM. IF THEY'D BEEN ABLE TO TELL PEOPLE ABOUT THEIR NEW POWERS, THEY WOULD HAVE. AN HOUR LATER, THEY WOULD HAVE BEEN IN A GOVERNMENT LAB BEING DISSECTED.
WHAT THEY ARE NOW... IS BECAUSE OF ME.
OH MY GOD. YOU...
...YOU SENT THE SHOOTER...!

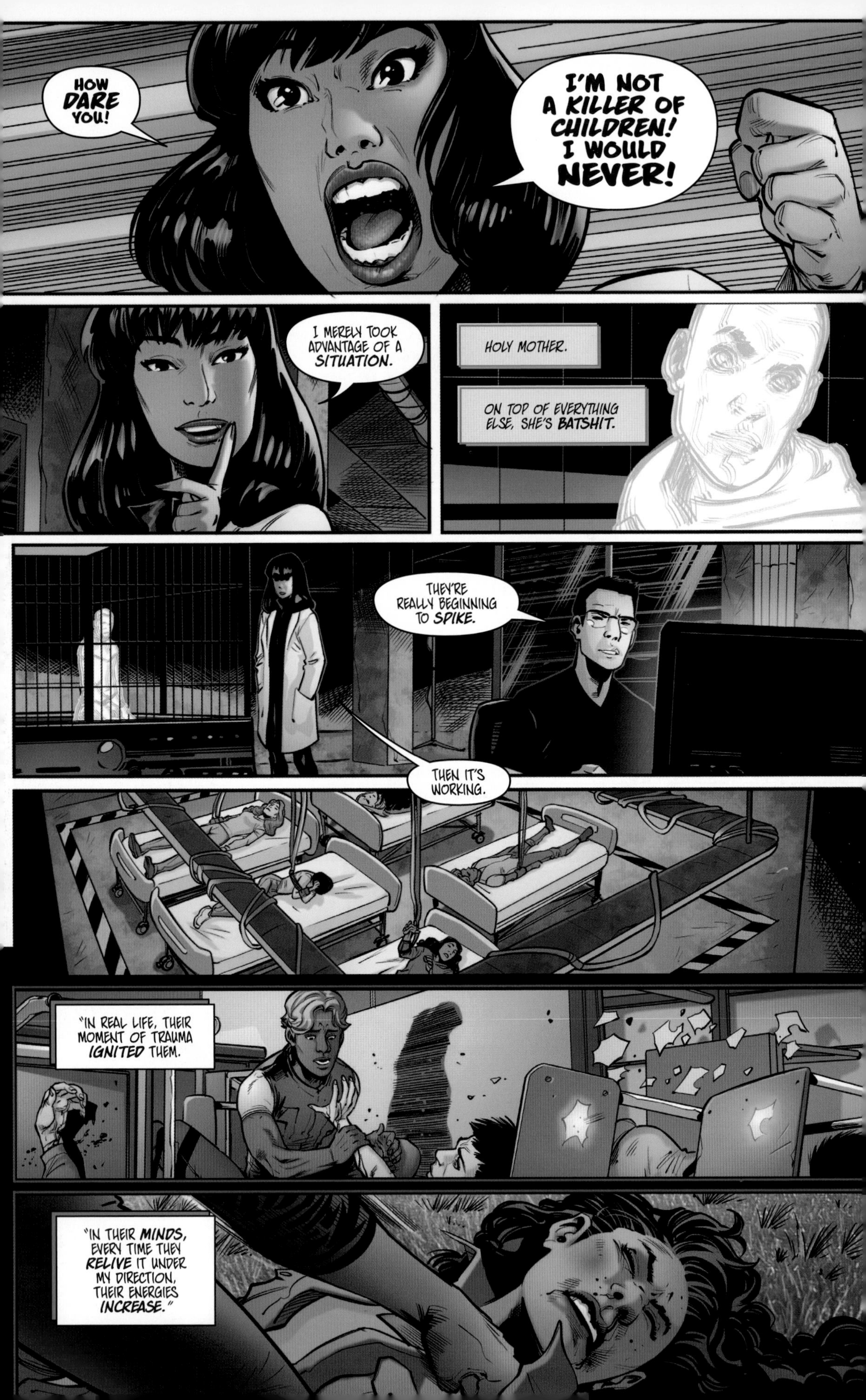
HOW DARE YOU!
I'M NOT A KILLER OF CHILDREN! I WOULD NEVER!
I MERELY TOOK ADVANTAGE OF A SITUATION.
HOLY MOTHER.
ON TOP OF EVERYTHING ELSE, SHE'S BATSHIT.
THEY'RE REALLY BEGINNING TO SPIKE.
THEN IT'S WORKING.
"IN REAL LIFE, THEIR MOMENT OF TRAUMA IGNITED THEM.
"IN THEIR MINDS, EVERY TIME THEY RELIVE IT UNDER MY DIRECTION, THEIR ENERGIES INCREASE."

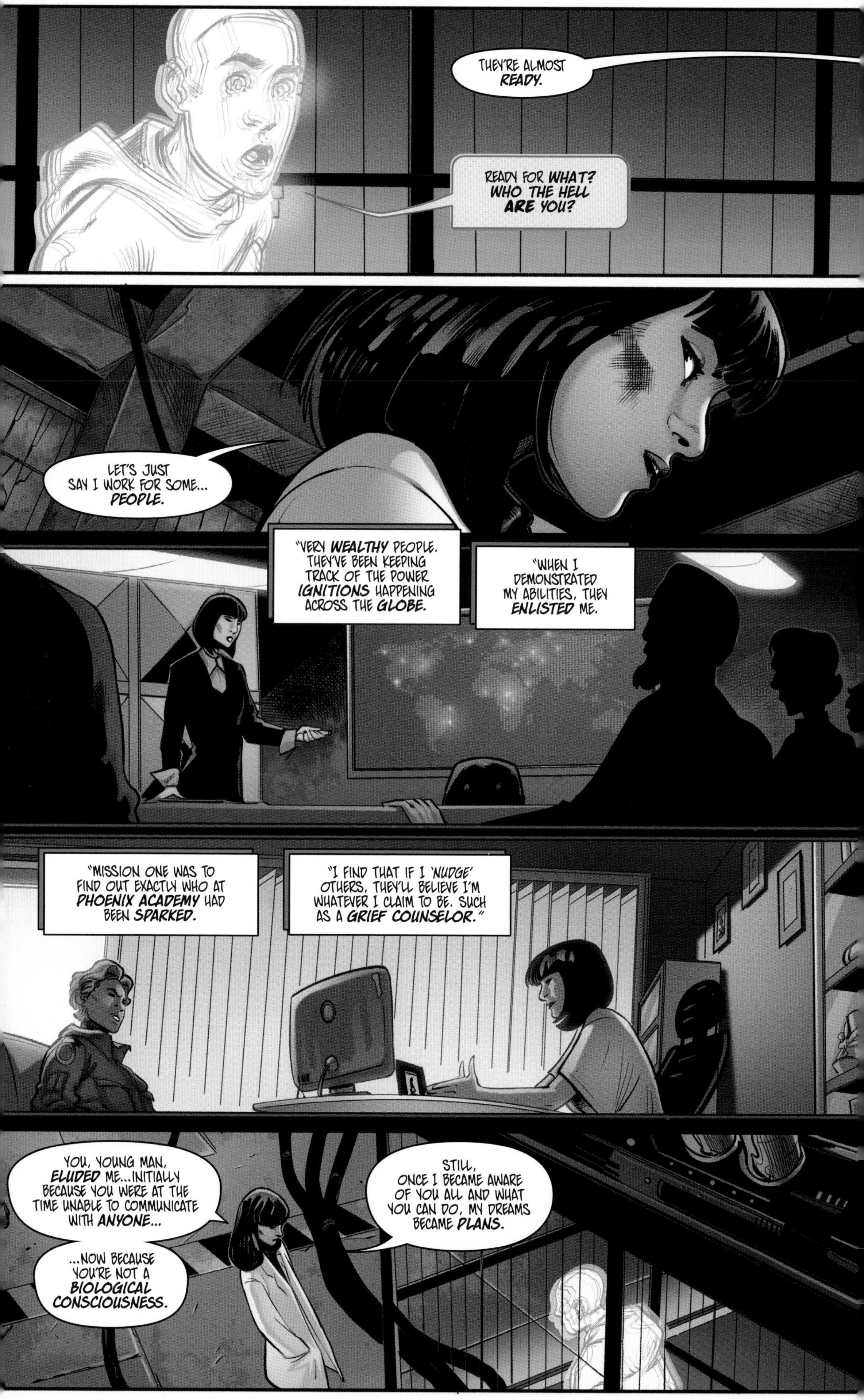
THEY'RE ALMOST READY.
READY FOR WHAT? WHO THE HELL ARE YOU?
LET'S JUST SAY I WORK FOR SOME... PEOPLE.
"VERY WEALTHY PEOPLE. THEY'VE BEEN KEEPING TRACK OF THE POWER IGNITIONS HAPPENING ACROSS THE GLOBE.
"WHEN I DEMONSTRATED MY ABILITIES, THEY ENLISTED ME.
"MISSION ONE WAS TO FIND OUT EXACTLY WHO AT PHOENIX ACADEMY HAD BEEN SPARKED.
"I FIND THAT IF I 'NUDGE' OTHERS, THEY'LL BELIEVE I'M WHATEVER I CLAIM TO BE. SUCH AS A GRIEF COUNSELOR."
YOU, YOUNG MAN, ELUDED ME...INITIALLY BECAUSE YOU WERE AT THE TIME UNABLE TO COMMUNICATE WITH ANYONE...
...NOW BECAUSE YOU'RE NOT A BIOLOGICAL CONSCIOUSNESS.
STILL, ONCE I BECAME AWARE OF YOU ALL AND WHAT YOU CAN DO, MY DREAMS BECAME PLANS.

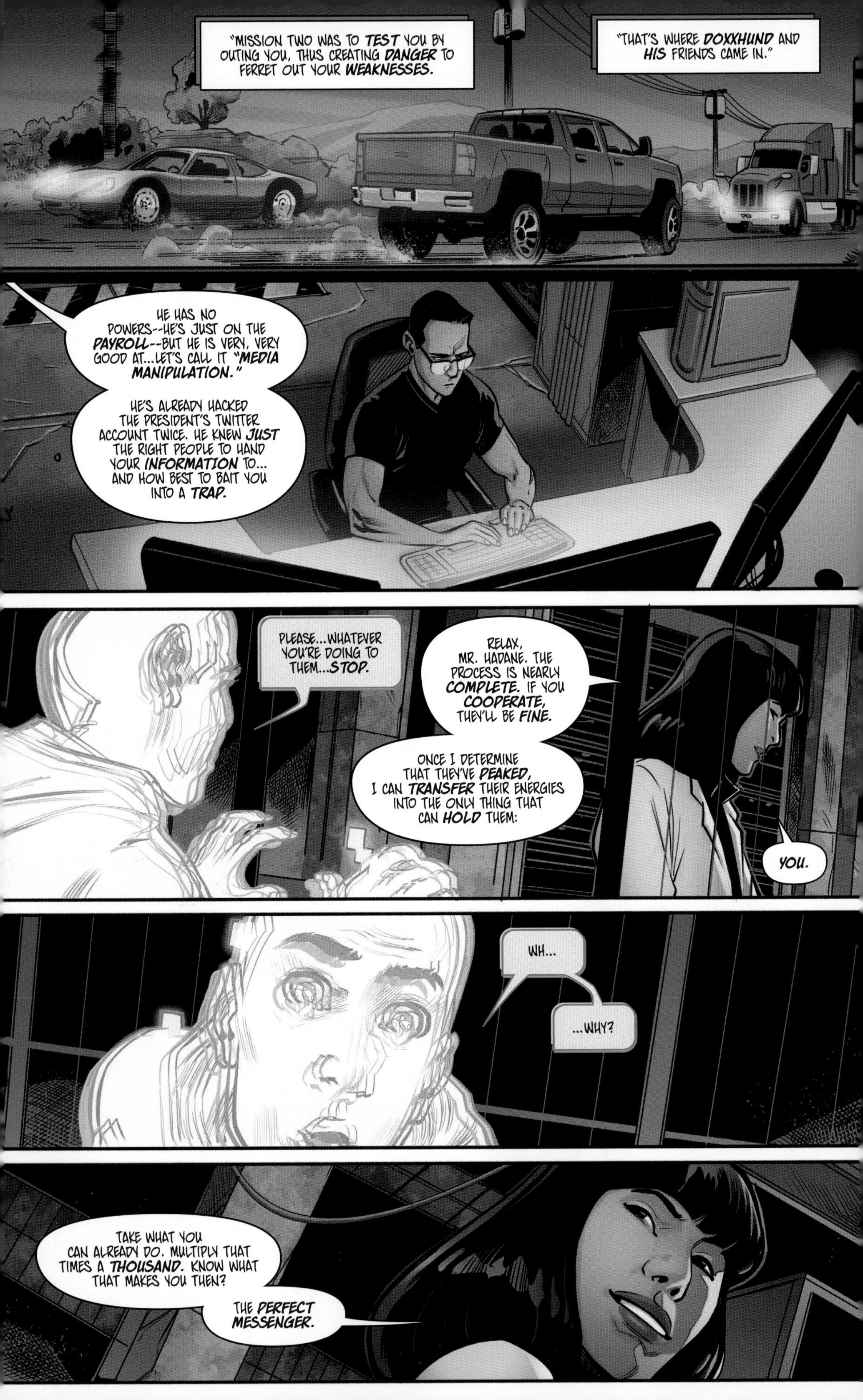
"MISSION TWO WAS TO TEST YOU BY OUTING YOU, THUS CREATING DANGER TO FERRET OUT YOUR WEAKNESSES.
"THAT'S WHERE DOXXHUND AND HIS FRIENDS CAME IN."
HE HAS NO POWERS--HE'S JUST ON THE PAYROLL--BUT HE IS VERY, VERY GOOD AT...LET'S CALL IT "MEDIA MANIPULATION."
HE'S ALREADY HACKED THE PRESIDENT'S TWITTER ACCOUNT TWICE. HE KNEW JUST THE RIGHT PEOPLE TO HAND YOUR INFORMATION TO... AND HOW BEST TO BAIT YOU INTO A TRAP.
PLEASE...WHATEVER YOU'RE DOING TO THEM...STOP.
RELAX, MR. HADANE. THE PROCESS IS NEARLY COMPLETE. IF YOU COOPERATE, THEY'LL BE FINE.
ONCE I DETERMINE THAT THEY'VE PEAKED, I CAN TRANSFER THEIR ENERGIES INTO THE ONLY THING THAT CAN HOLD THEM:
YOU.
WH...
...WHY?
TAKE WHAT YOU CAN ALREADY DO. MULTIPLY THAT TIMES A THOUSAND. KNOW WHAT THAT MAKES YOU THEN?
THE PERFECT MESSENGER.

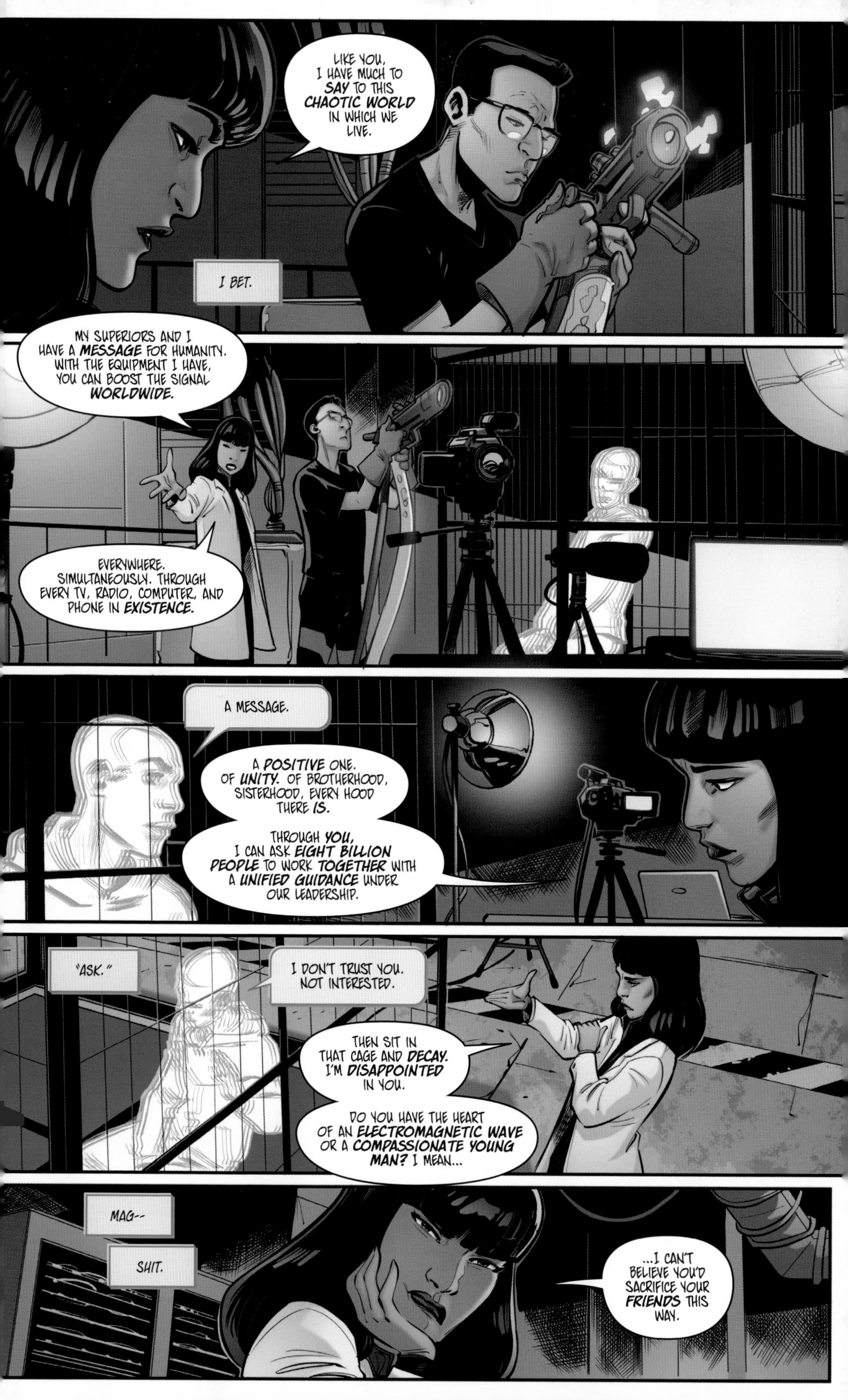
LIKE YOU, I HAVE MUCH TO SAY TO THIS CHAOTIC WORLD IN WHICH WE LIVE.
I BET.
MY SUPERIORS AND I HAVE A MESSAGE FOR HUMANITY. WITH THE EQUIPMENT I HAVE, YOU CAN BOOST THE SIGNAL WORLDWIDE.
EVERYWHERE. SIMULTANEOUSLY. THROUGH EVERY TV, RADIO, COMPUTER, AND PHONE IN EXISTENCE.
A MESSAGE.
A POSITIVE ONE. OF UNITY. OF BROTHERHOOD, SISTERHOOD, EVERY HOOD THERE IS.
THROUGH YOU, I CAN ASK EIGHT BILLION PEOPLE TO WORK TOGETHER WITH A UNIFIED GUIDANCE UNDER OUR LEADERSHIP.
"ASK."
I DON'T TRUST YOU. NOT INTERESTED.
THEN SIT IN THAT CAGE AND DECAY. I'M DISAPPOINTED IN YOU.
DO YOU HAVE THE HEART OF AN ELECTROMAGNETIC WAVE OR A COMPASSIONATE YOUNG MAN? I MEAN...
MAG--
SHIT.
...I CAN'T BELIEVE YOU'D SACRIFICE YOUR FRIENDS THIS WAY.

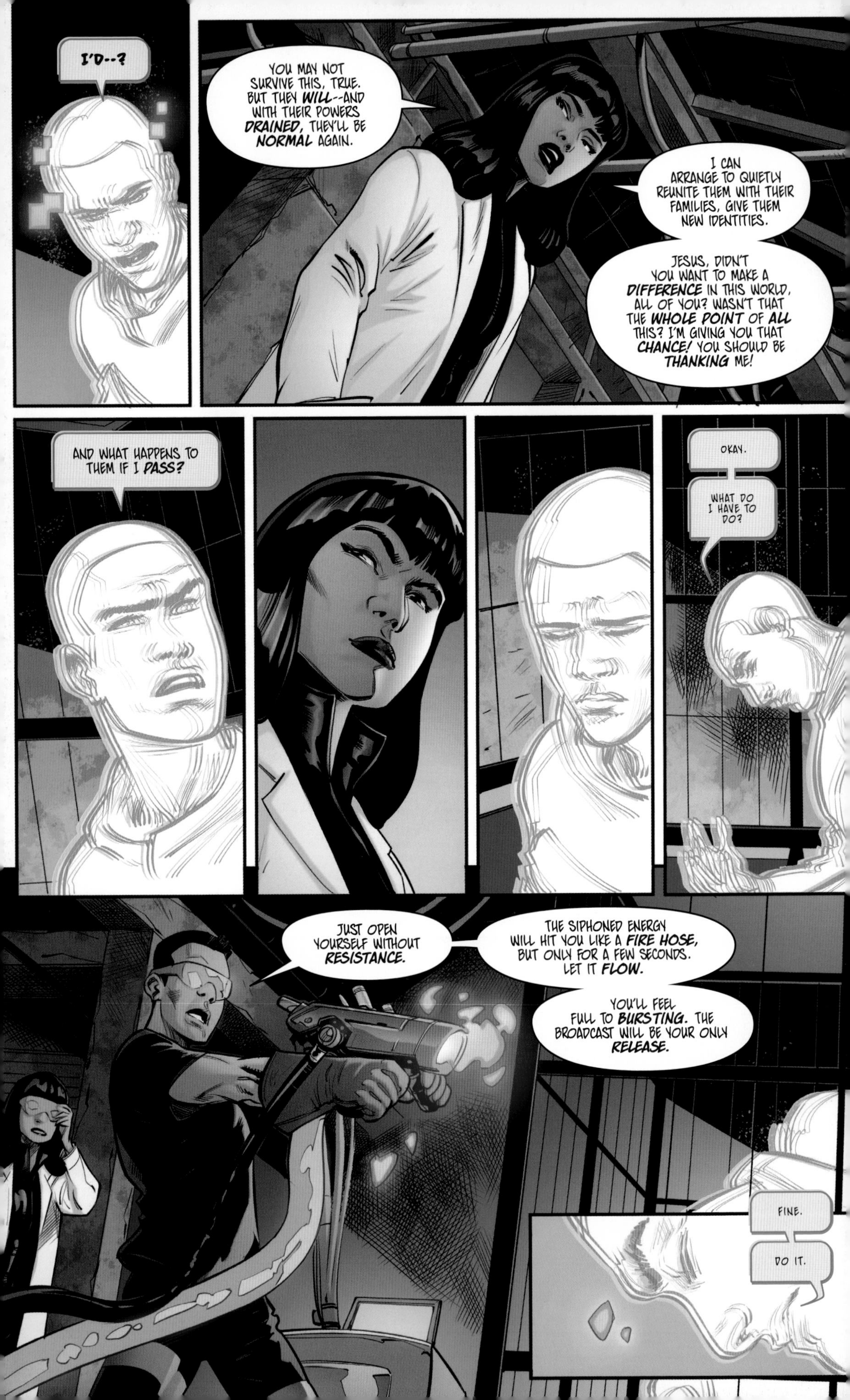
I'D--?
YOU MAY NOT SURVIVE THIS, TRUE. BUT THEY WILL--AND WITH THEIR POWERS DRAINED, THEY'LL BE NORMAL AGAIN.
I CAN ARRANGE TO QUIETLY REUNITE THEM WITH THEIR FAMILIES, GIVE THEM NEW IDENTITIES.
JESUS, DIDN'T YOU WANT TO MAKE A DIFFERENCE IN THIS WORLD, ALL OF YOU? WASN'T THAT THE WHOLE POINT OF ALL THIS? I'M GIVING YOU THAT CHANCE! YOU SHOULD BE THANKING ME!
AND WHAT HAPPENS TO THEM IF I PASS?
OKAY.
WHAT DO I HAVE TO DO?
JUST OPEN YOURSELF WITHOUT RESISTANCE.
THE SIPHONED ENERGY WILL HIT YOU LIKE A FIRE HOSE, BUT ONLY FOR A FEW SECONDS. LET IT FLOW.
YOU'LL FEEL FULL TO BURSTING. THE BROADCAST WILL BE YOUR ONLY RELEASE.
FINE.
DO IT.

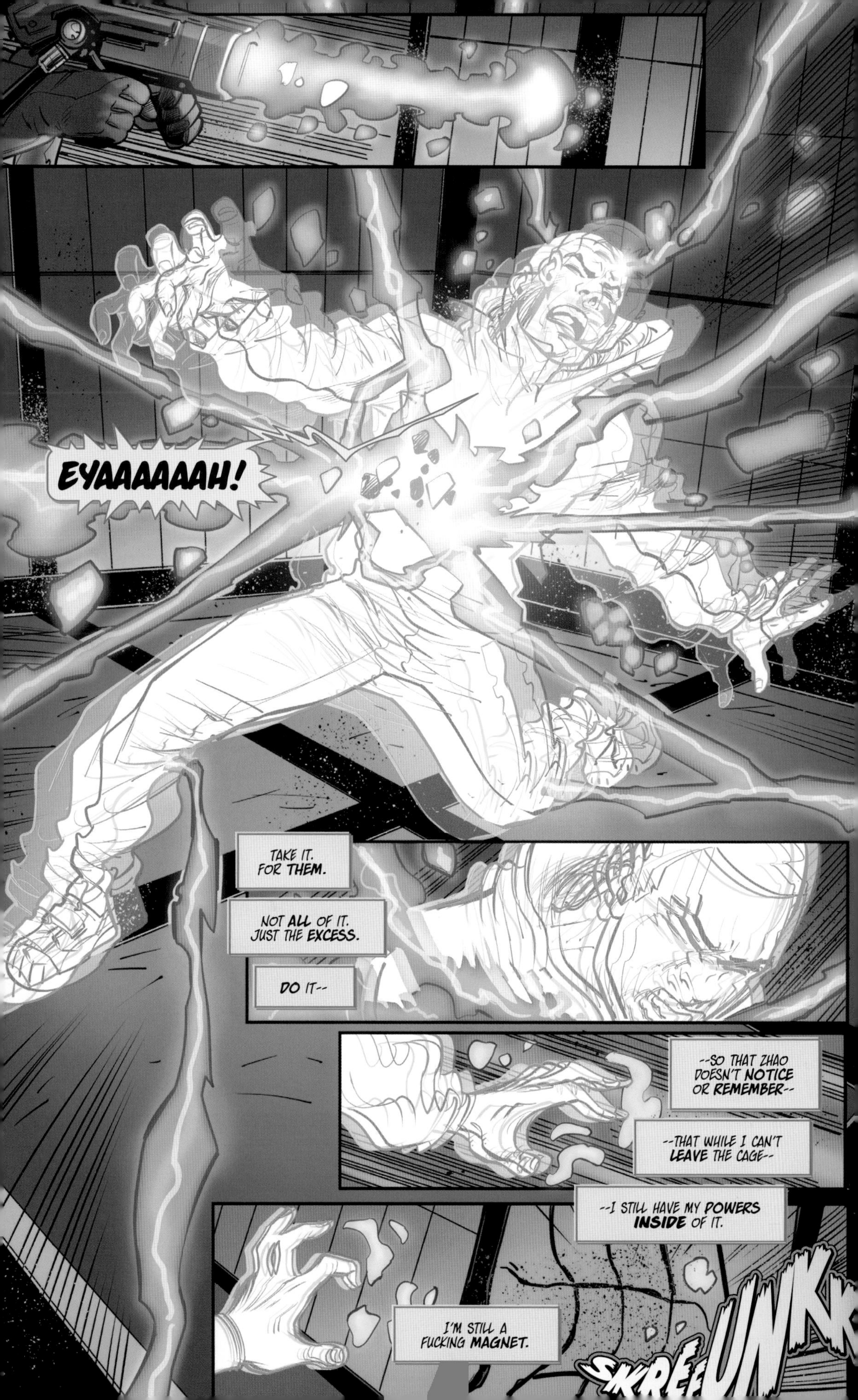
EYAAAAAAH!
TAKE IT. FOR THEM.
NOT ALL OF IT. JUST THE EXCESS.
DO IT--
--SO THAT ZHAO DOESN'T NOTICE OR REMEMBER--
--THAT WHILE I CAN'T LEAVE THE CAGE--
--I STILL HAVE MY POWERS INSIDE OF IT.
I'M STILL A FUCKING MAGNET.
SKREEUNK

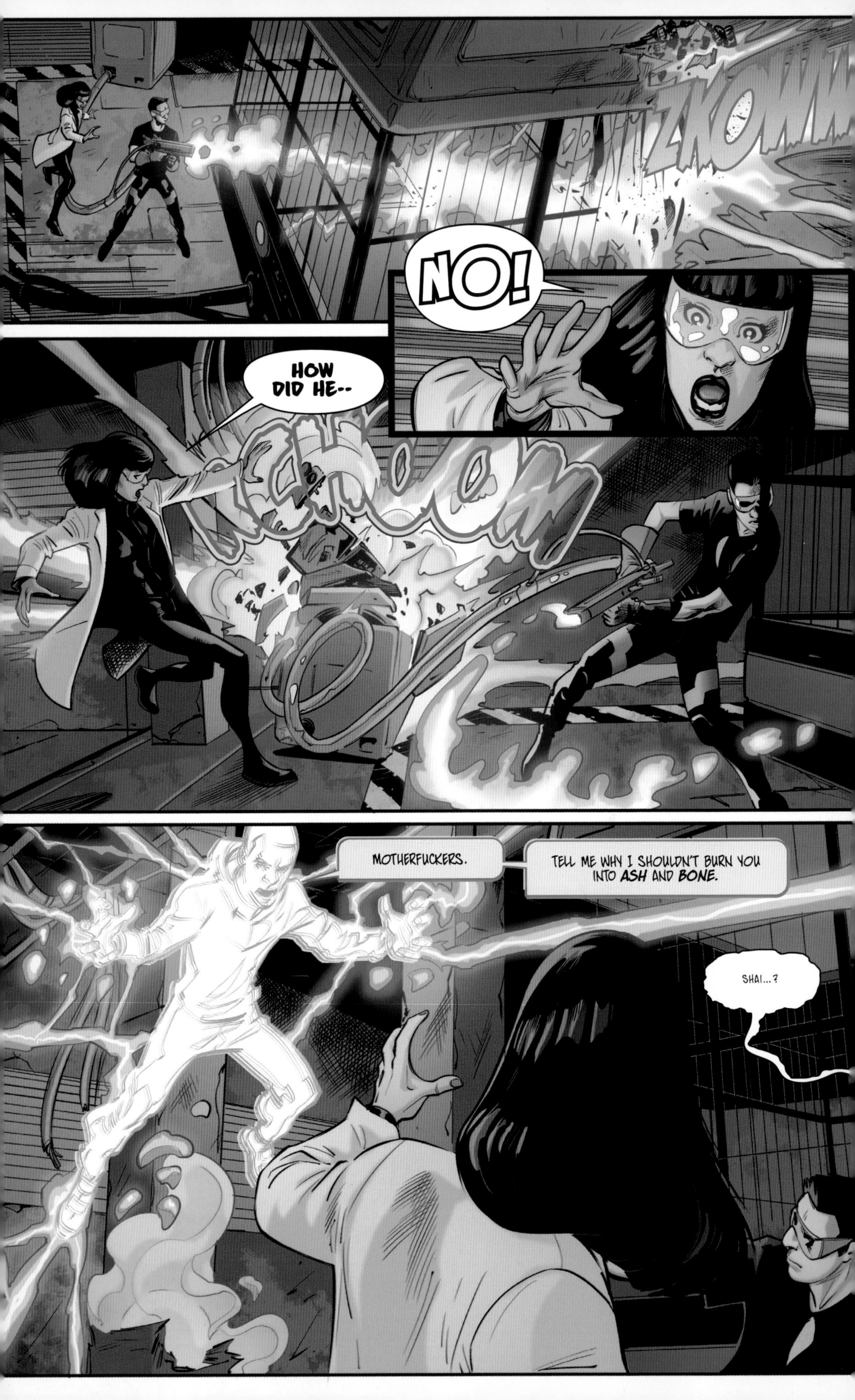
ZKOWW
NO!
HOW DID HE--
MOTHERFUCKERS.
TELL ME WHY I SHOULDN'T BURN YOU INTO ASH AND BONE.
SHAI...?

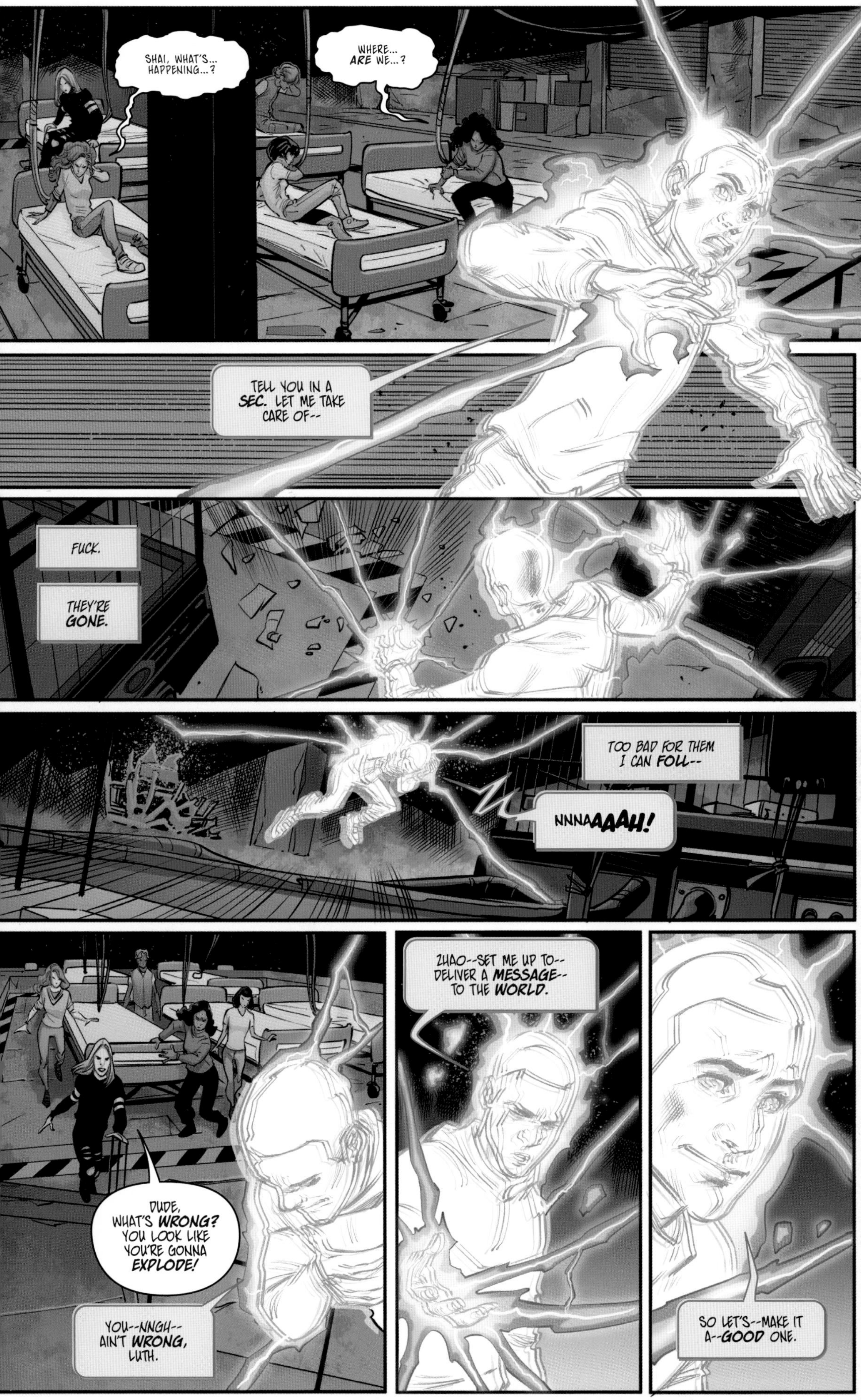
SHAI, WHAT'S... HAPPENING...?
WHERE... ARE WE...?
TELL YOU IN A SEC. LET ME TAKE CARE OF--
FUCK.
THEY'RE GONE.
TOO BAD FOR THEM I CAN FOLL--
NNNAAAAH!
DUDE, WHAT'S WRONG? YOU LOOK LIKE YOU'RE GONNA EXPLODE!
YOU--NNGH--AIN'T WRONG, LUTH.
ZHAO--SET ME UP TO--DELIVER A MESSAGE--TO THE WORLD.
SO LET'S--MAKE IT A--GOOD ONE.

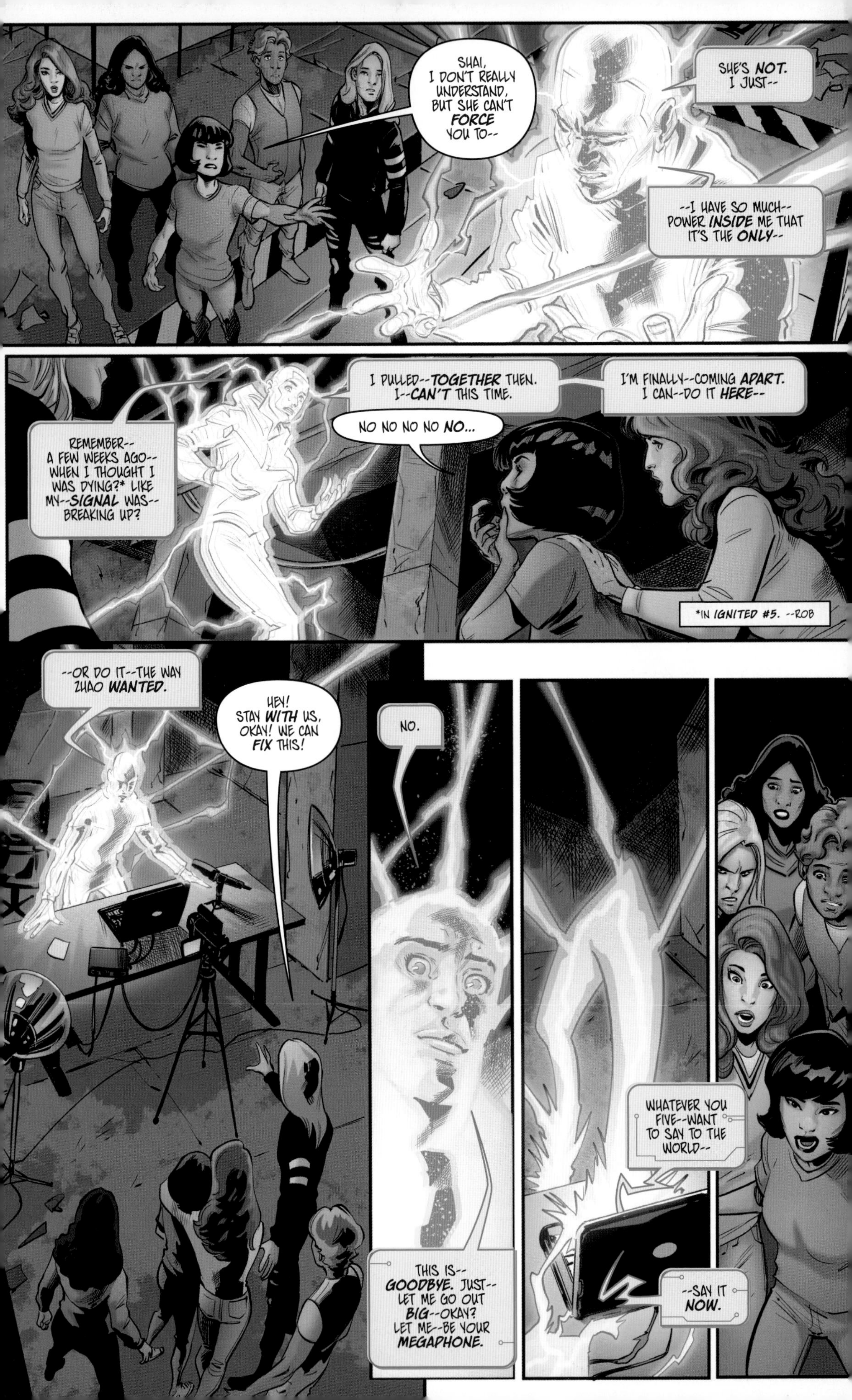
SHAI, I DON'T REALLY UNDERSTAND, BUT SHE CAN'T FORCE YOU TO--
SHE'S NOT. I JUST--
--I HAVE SO MUCH-- POWER INSIDE ME THAT IT'S THE ONLY--
REMEMBER-- A FEW WEEKS AGO-- WHEN I THOUGHT I WAS DYING?* LIKE MY--SIGNAL WAS-- BREAKING UP?
I PULLED--TOGETHER THEN. I--CAN'T THIS TIME.
I'M FINALLY--COMING APART. I CAN--DO IT HERE--
NO NO NO NO NO...
*IN IGNITED #5. --ROB
--OR DO IT--THE WAY ZHAO WANTED.
HEY! STAY WITH US, OKAY! WE CAN FIX THIS!
NO.
THIS IS-- GOODBYE. JUST-- LET ME GO OUT BIG--OKAY? LET ME--BE YOUR MEGAPHONE.
WHATEVER YOU FIVE--WANT TO SAY TO THE WORLD--
--SAY IT NOW.

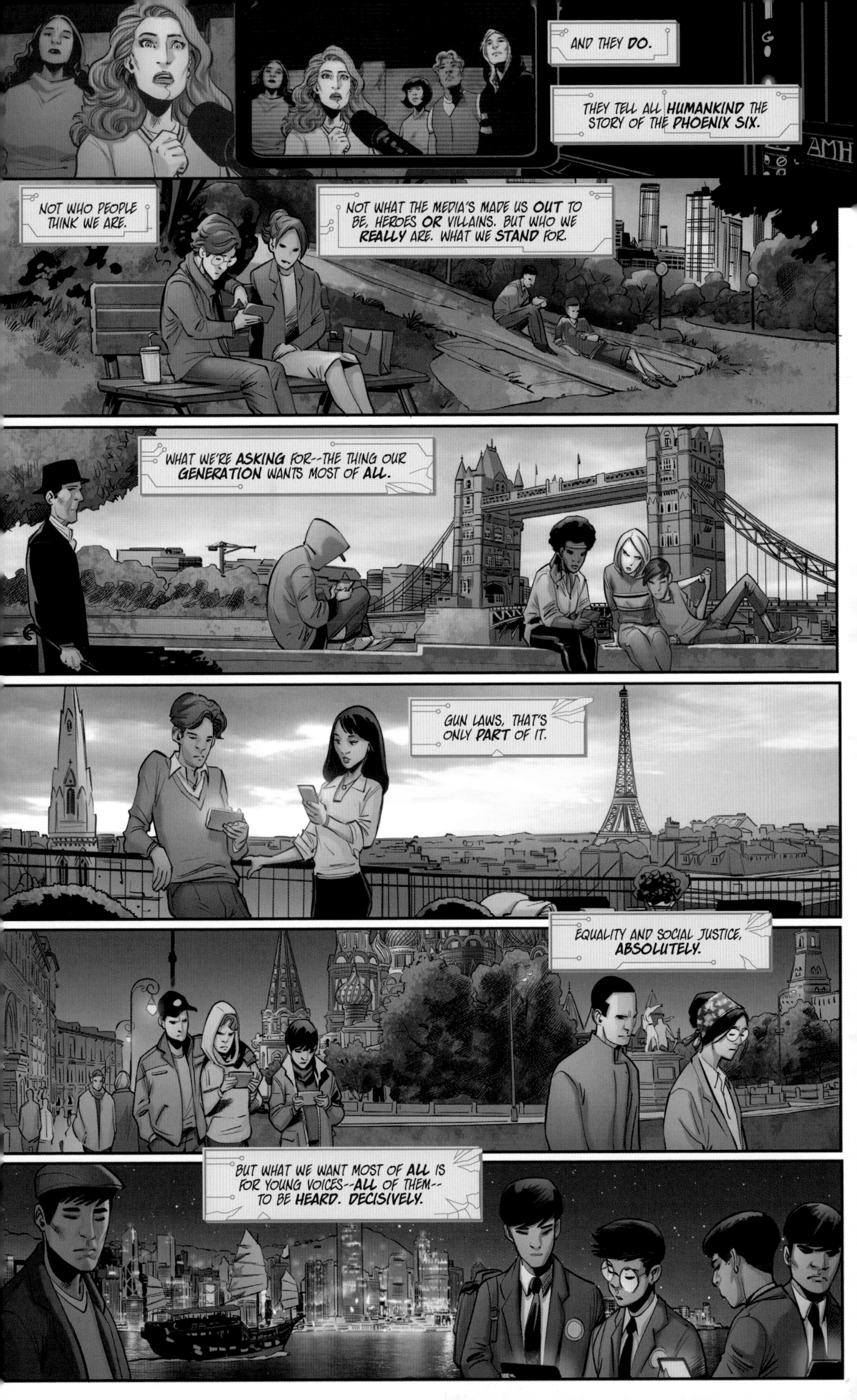
AND THEY DO.
THEY TELL ALL HUMANKIND THE STORY OF THE PHOENIX SIX.
NOT WHO PEOPLE THINK WE ARE.
NOT WHAT THE MEDIA'S MADE US OUT TO BE, HEROES OR VILLAINS. BUT WHO WE REALLY ARE. WHAT WE STAND FOR.
WHAT WE'RE ASKING FOR--THE THING OUR GENERATION WANTS MOST OF ALL.
GUN LAWS, THAT'S ONLY PART OF IT.
EQUALITY AND SOCIAL JUSTICE, ABSOLUTELY.
BUT WHAT WE WANT MOST OF ALL IS FOR YOUNG VOICES--ALL OF THEM-- TO BE HEARD. DECISIVELY.

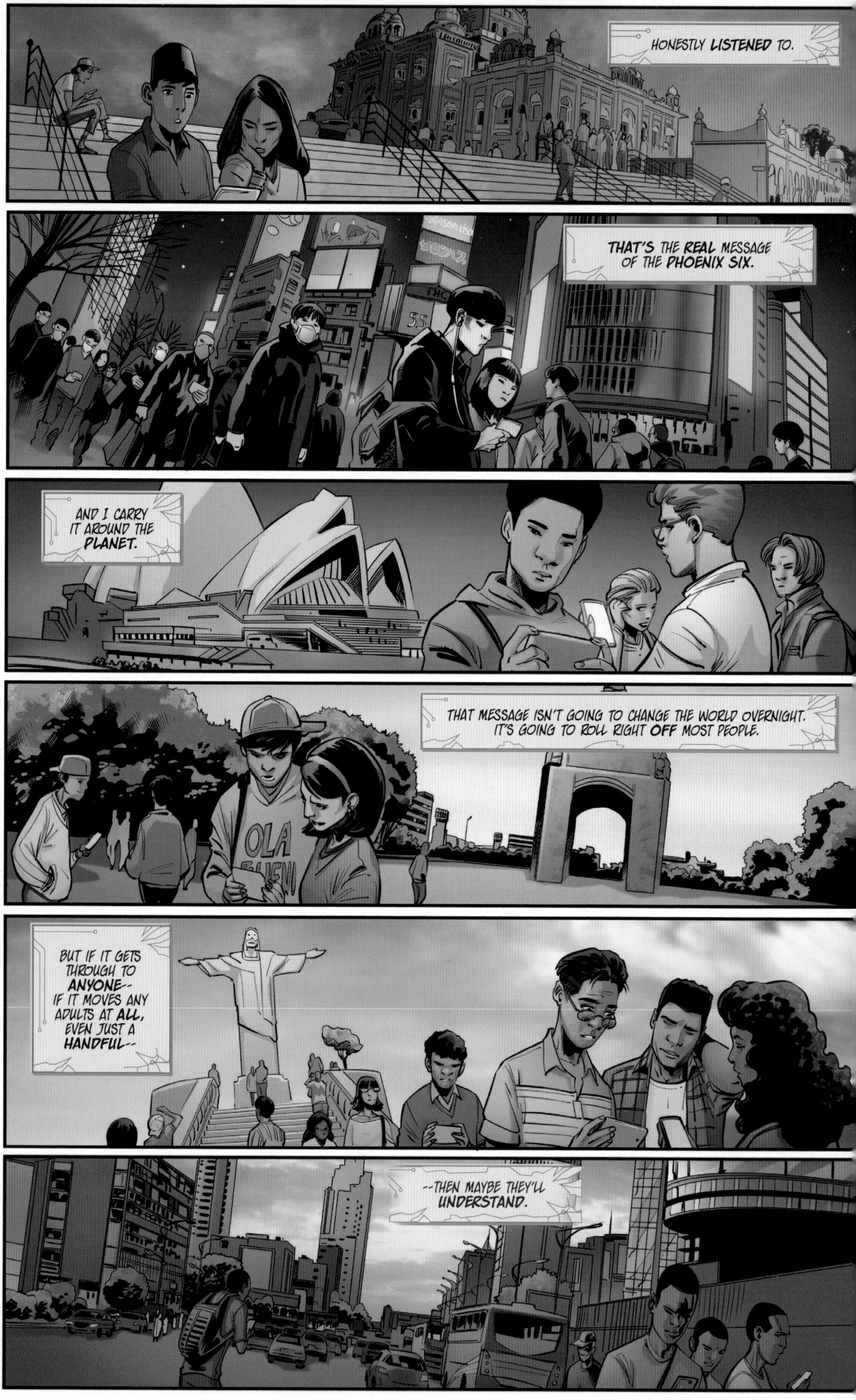
HONESTLY LISTENED TO.
THAT'S THE REAL MESSAGE OF THE PHOENIX SIX.
AND I CARRY IT AROUND THE PLANET.
THAT MESSAGE ISN'T GOING TO CHANGE THE WORLD OVERNIGHT. IT'S GOING TO ROLL RIGHT OFF MOST PEOPLE.
BUT IF IT GETS THROUGH TO ANYONE-- IF IT MOVES ANY ADULTS AT ALL, EVEN JUST A HANDFUL--
--THEN MAYBE THEY'LL UNDERSTAND.

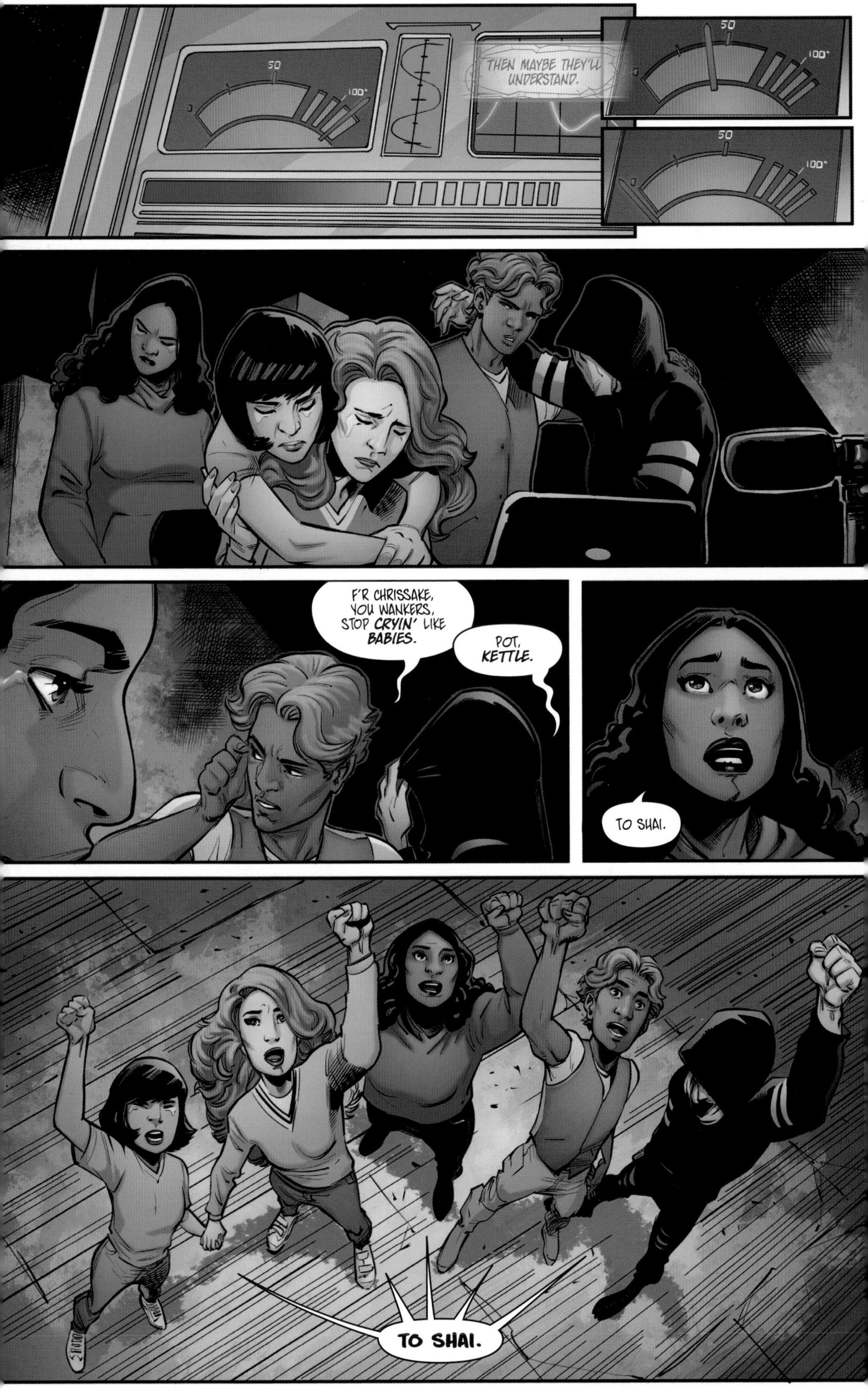
50
100°
THEN MAYBE THEY'LL UNDERSTAND.
50
100°
50
100°
F'R CHRISSAKE, YOU WANKERS, STOP CRYIN' LIKE BABIES.
POT, KETTLE.
TO SHAI.
TO SHAI.

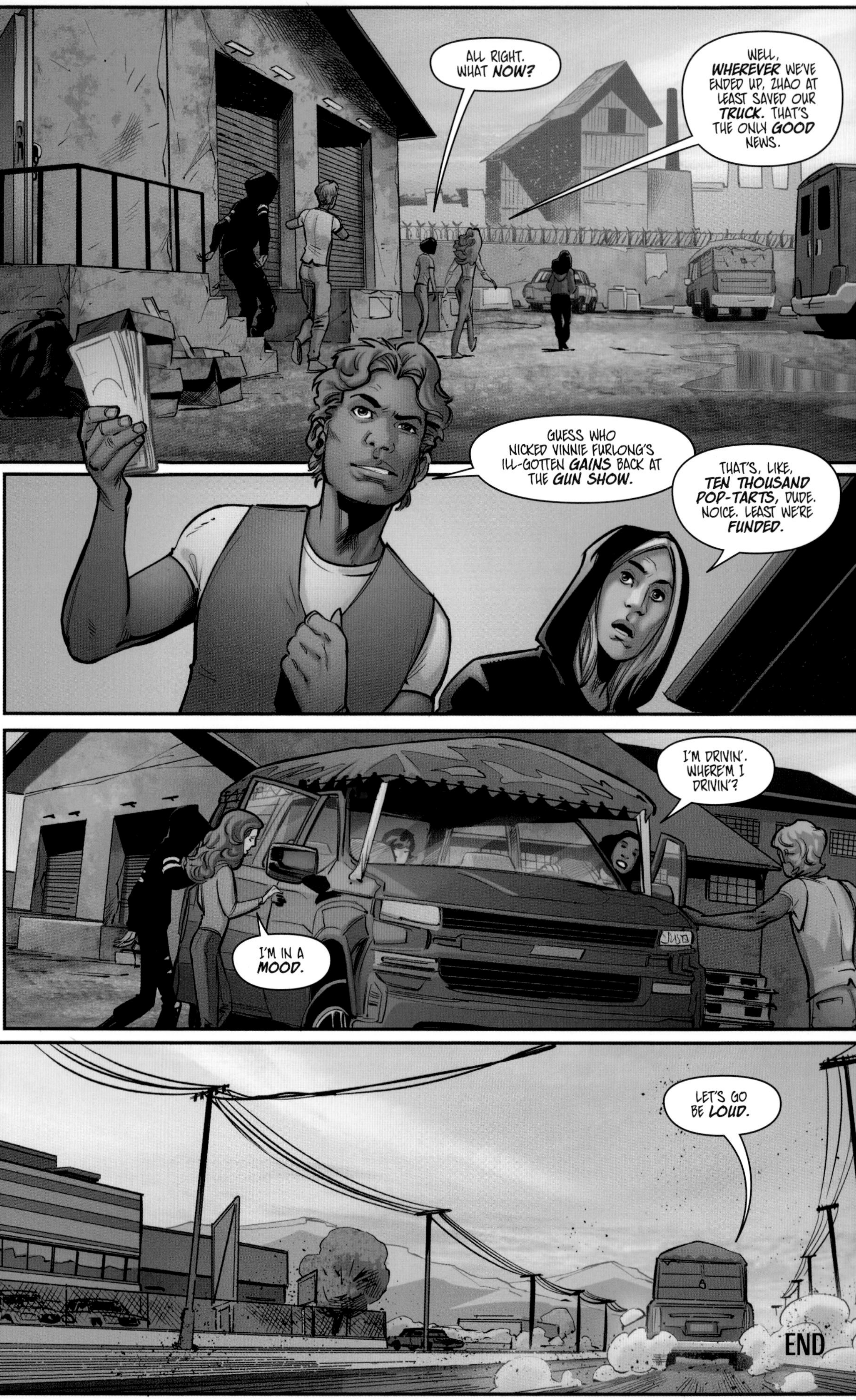
ALL RIGHT. WHAT **NOW?**
WELL, **WHEREVER** WE'VE ENDED UP, ZHAO AT LEAST SAVED OUR **TRUCK.** THAT'S THE ONLY **GOOD** NEWS.
GUESS WHO NICKED VINNIE FURLONG'S ILL-GOTTEN **GAINS** BACK AT THE **GUN SHOW.**
THAT'S, LIKE, **TEN THOUSAND POP-TARTS**, DUDE. NOICE. LEAST WE'RE **FUNDED.**
I'M DRIVIN'. WHERE'M I DRIVIN'?
I'M IN A **MOOD.**
LET'S GO BE **LOUD.**
END

HUMANITY FIRST

School shootings like the one that inspired our story happen in real life in this country with despicable frequency. We've reached out to various students who have survived these shootings and have invited them to speak their minds openly in the pages of **IGNITED**, saying whatever they feel needs saying.

04.20.99

Jessie Jones is a survivor of the Columbine attack that claimed the lives of fourteen students in one of the most infamous shootings in modern history.

I was a freshmen at Columbine High School in 1999, and things in society have only gotten worse as far as mass shooting and hate. I watched a YouTube video presented by a man who said we can blame it on video games, we can blame it on mental illness, etc., etc...but the fact is, it's everything!

It's the way society has conformed us as human beings. During my healing journey, after years of therapy, substance abuse, hospitalizations, self-harm, countless medications and suicide attempts, and being on social security disability, I have found that spirituality and spiritual practices such as mindfulness and meditation have gotten me to where I am today.

I am now a caregiver at an assisted living community for residents with dementia. During my time helping others, I've realized we are now more divided as a human race than ever before, and until we all figure out the ONEness we all share, learn to empathize and sympathize with others, connect with and love one another and become united as a whole, we will never know how strong we truly are in order to make the changes needed to stop all this the.

—**Jessie Jones**
August 2019

06.12.16

Brian Alvear's sister was killed in the infamous 2016 Pulse nightclub shooting. In all, the gunman took the lives of 53 people and wounded 49 more. Here's what Brian has to say about domestic terrorism:

Regarding gun violence, it is now no longer a matter of if you will lose someone you know or love in a mass shooting, but when. Do not let it get to that!

At the time it happened, the Orlando Pulse massacre was the largest mass shooting in U.S. history. Less than a year later, that cruel record was surpassed. And there are two things that stick out to me about the response to them: empathy and apathy. The empathy my family received from the city of Orlando, the LGBT community, and from strangers all over the world was an amazing thing. My mother had already lost a son to cancer a decade earlier and now had lost her youngest daughter, found in her best friend's arms. My sister became "the face" of the shooting because she happened to be Snapchatting at the time. The amount of love shown to us was incredible.

It wasn't long, however, before we noticed the apathy. The people in charge did nothing to stop this from happening again. We noticed the short-term memory of the media and general public as each new shooting surpassed the last, sometimes in the number of victims, sometimes in media coverage.

Let us please do what we can to ensure we are taking all the necessary steps to stop this, whether passing legislature to make it difficult or impossible for people to get the kinds of weapons that can cause so much destruction, or increasing conversations about mental health to help those who would ever dream of opening fire on innocents. I do not want to have an extended family whose only connection is that we lost someone in this horrendous way. #hugsnothate

—**Brian Alvear**
October 2019

IGNITED

COVER GALLERY

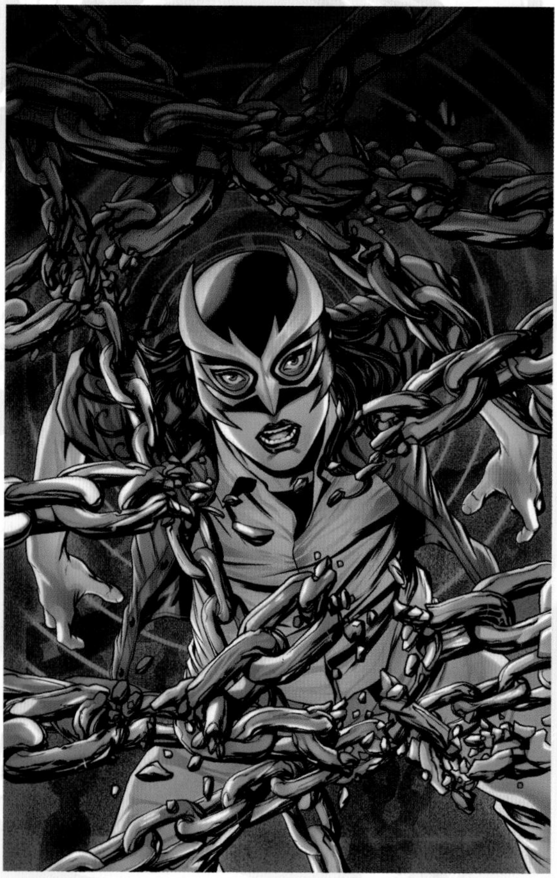

IGNITED #5 cover by Mike McKone & Ednane Ziane

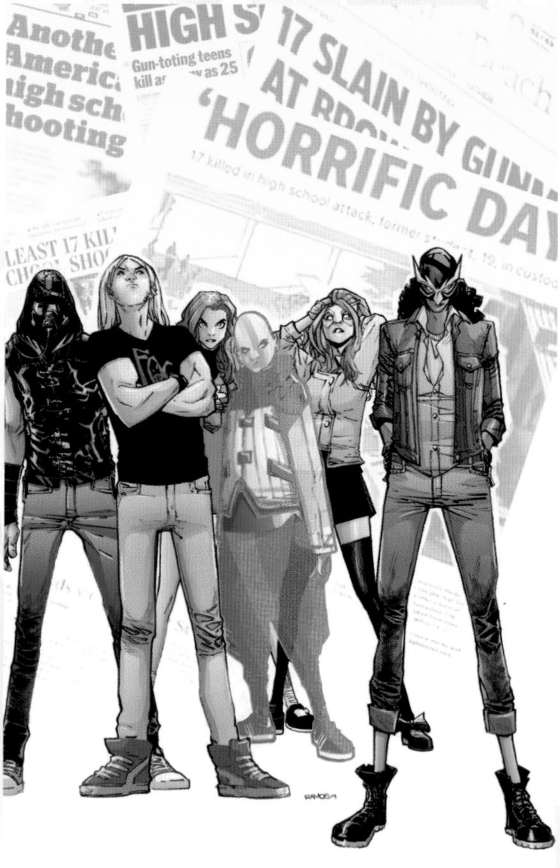
Gun-toting teens
'HORRIFIC DAY

IGNITED #6 cover by Humberto Ramos & Lee Loughridge

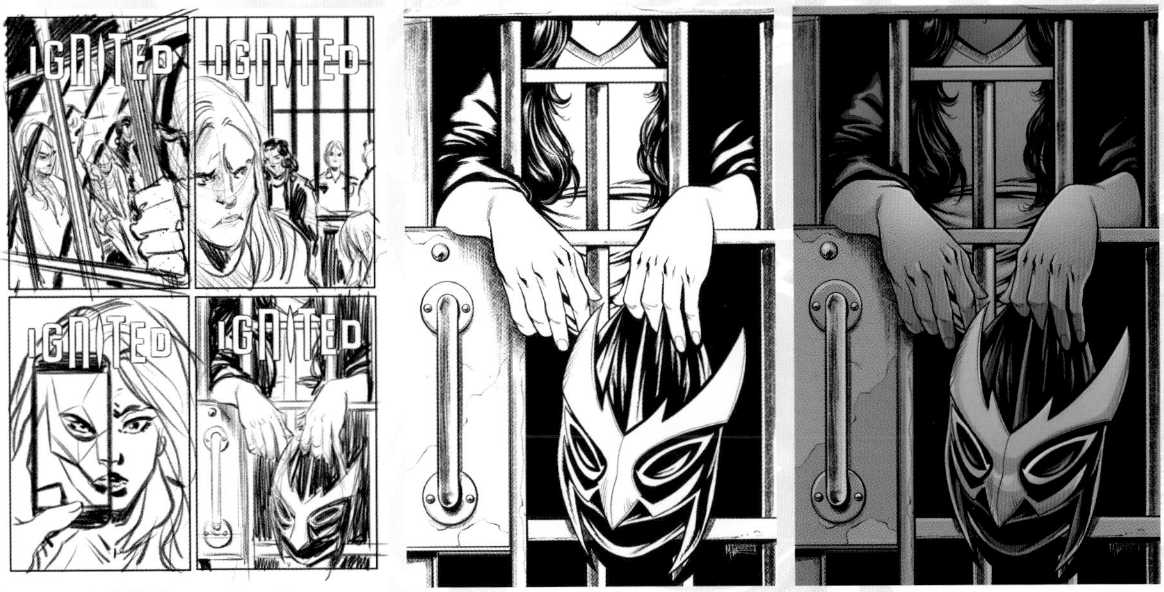
IGNITED
IGNITED
IGNITED
IGNITED

IGNITED #7 cover by Mike Norton & Lee Loughridge.
Sketches and Inks by Norton.

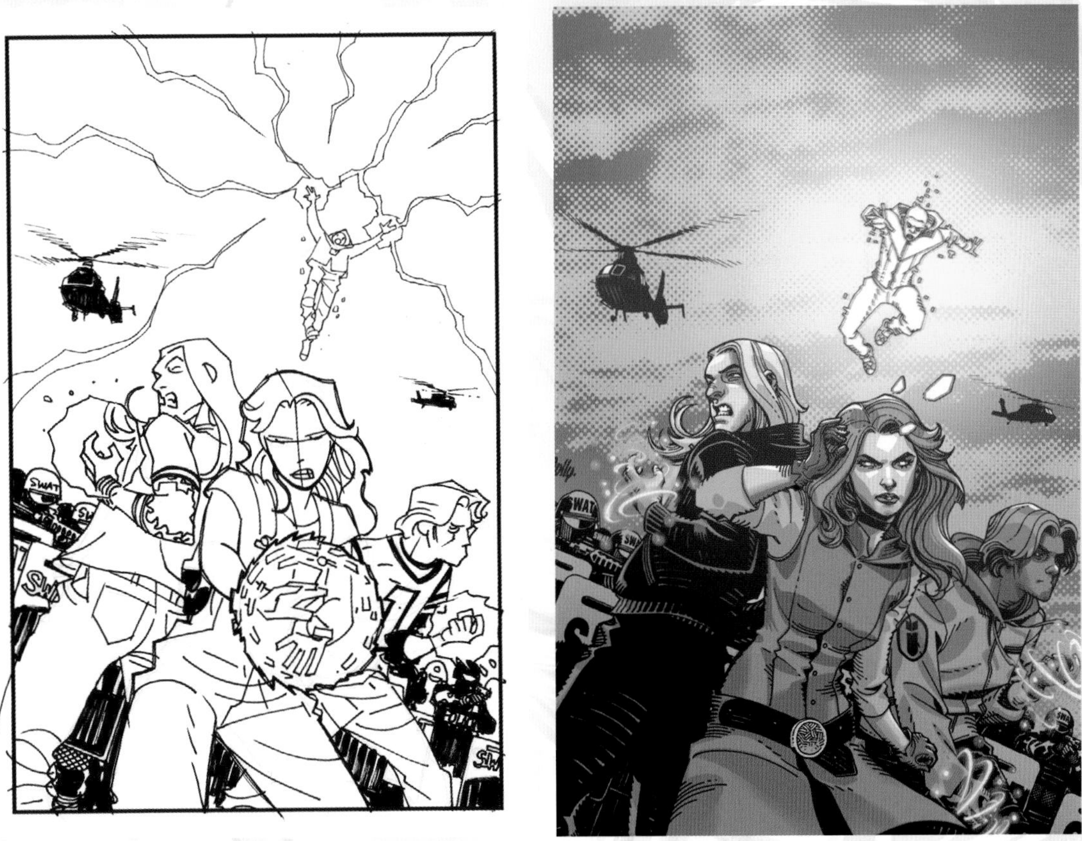
SWAT

IGNITED #8 cover and sketch by Cully Hamner.

IGNITED

COVER GALLERY

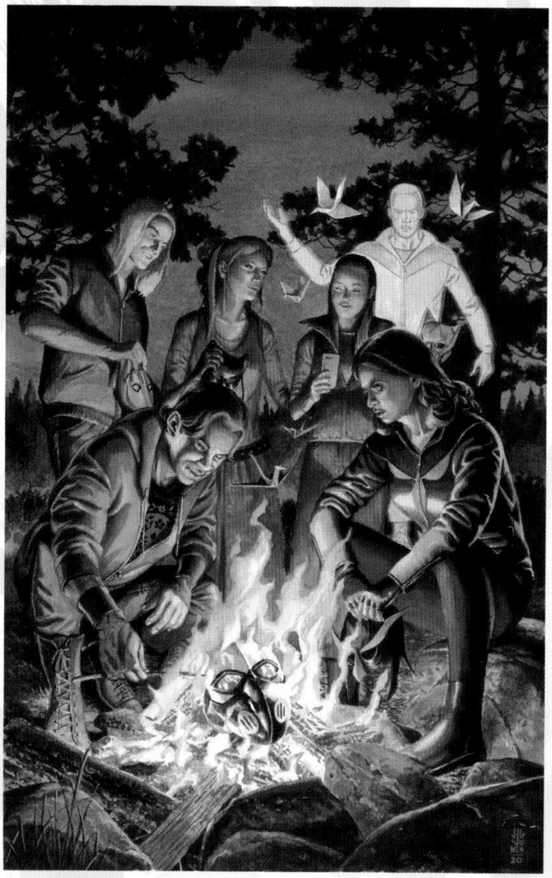

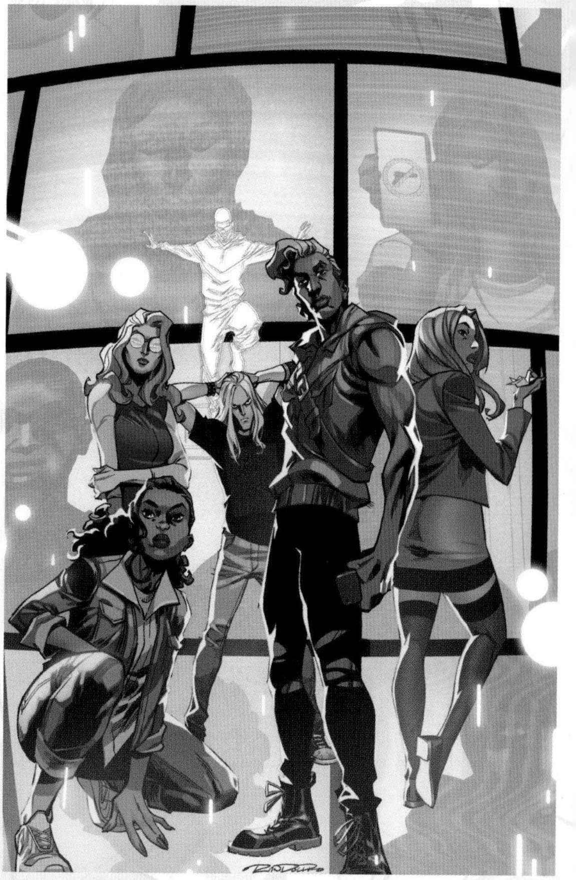

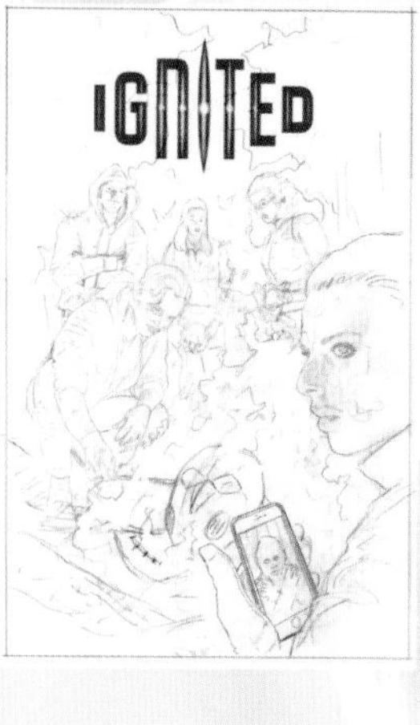

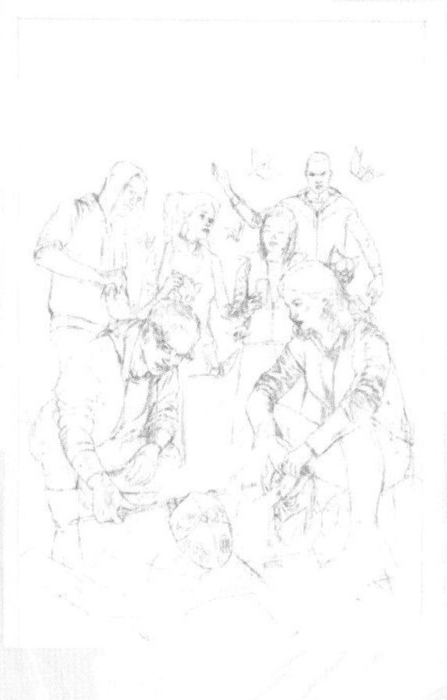

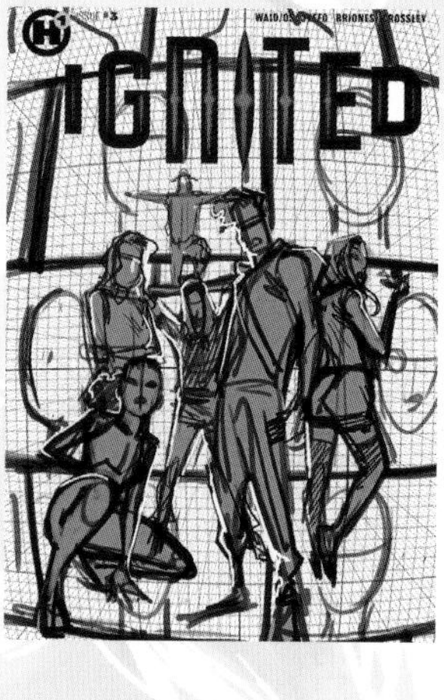

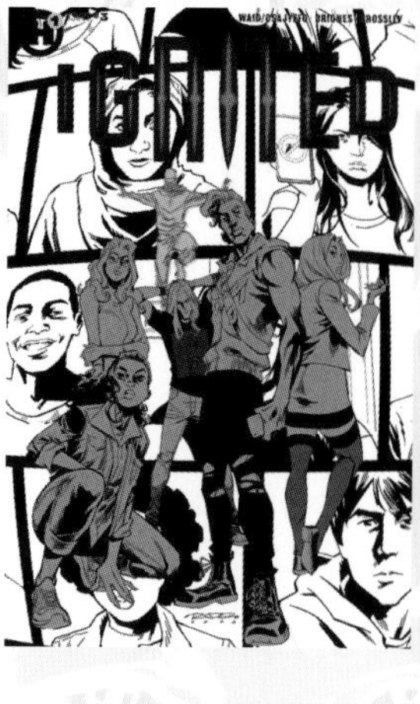

IGNITED #9 Cover and sketches by J.G. Jones.

IGNITED #10 cover by Khary Randolph & Mohammed Agbadi.
Sketches and Inks by Randolph.

BEHIND THE SCENES OF IGNITED

Mark Waid's script for IGNITED #10, pages 17-18, gave artist Phil Briones complete freedom over both the layout and location for these two pages. Phil's layouts are annotated to let everyone know where in the world each panel takes place. While coloring the pages, Jeromy Cox made his own notes to ensure time of day was accurate in each location.

IGNITED #10/Script/Ms. Page 19 — **MARK WAID**

PAGES SEVENTEEN and EIGHTEEN

PANEL ONE: THE KIDS, TEARY-EYED, GATHERED AROUND THE MIC AND STARING INTO THE CAMERAS, ANOUK SPEAKING.

SHAI CAPTION: And they DO.

SHAI CAPTION: They tell all HUMANKIND the story of the PHOENIX SIX.

PANELS: PHIL--FOR THE REST OF THESE TWO PAGES, WE NEED A BUNCH OF QUICK CUTS TO PEOPLE ALL AROUND THE WORLD LISTENING TO THE BROADCAST AND SEEING IMAGES OF THE VARIOUS KIDS AS THEY SPEAK. EVERYWHERE FROM REMOTE INDIA TO CALIFORNIA TO CONGRESSIONAL REPRESENTATIVES AND ANYWHERE IN BETWEEN, THE MORE VARIED, THE BETTER.

SHAI CAPTION: Not who people think we are. Not what the media's made us OUT to be, heroes OR villains. But who we REALLY are. What we STAND for.

SHAI CAPTION: What we're ASKING for--the thing our GENERATION wants most of ALL.

SHAI CAPTION: Gun laws, that's only PART of it.

SHAI CAPTION: Equality and social justice, ABSOLUTELY.

SHAI CAPTION: No.

SHAI CAPTION: But what we want most of ALL is for young voices--ALL of them--to be HEARD. DECISIVELY.

SHAI CAPTION: Honestly LISTENED to.

SHAI CAPTION: THAT'S the REAL message of the PHOENIX SIX.

SHAI CAPTION: And I carry it around the PLANET.

SHAI CAPTION: That message isn't going to change the world overnight. It's going to roll right OFF most people.

SHAI CAPTION: But if it gets through to ANYONE--if it moves any adults at ALL, even just a HANDFUL--

SHAI CAPTION/starts to break into static, but still fully legible: --then maybe they'll UNDERSTAND.

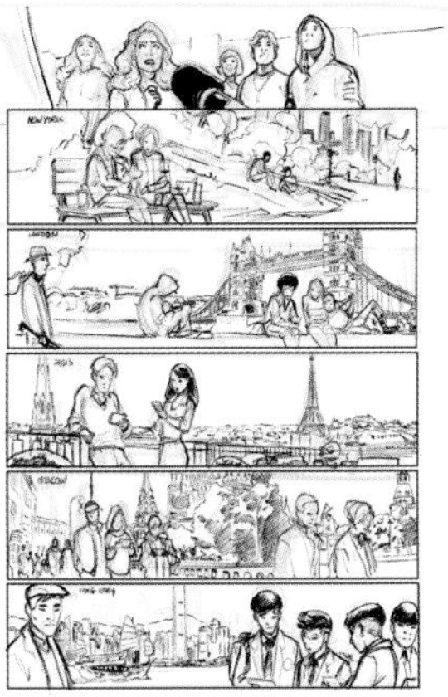

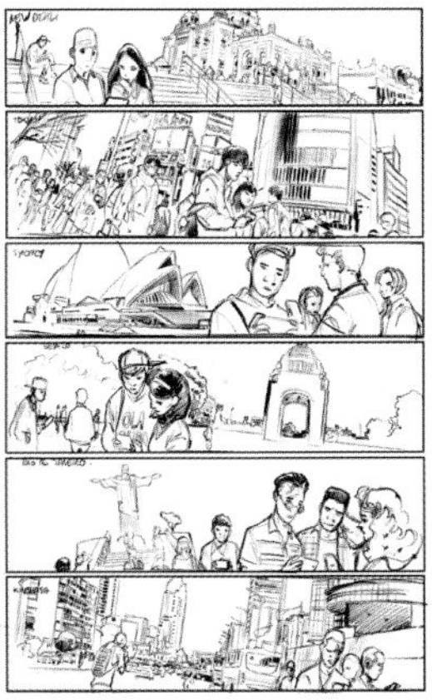

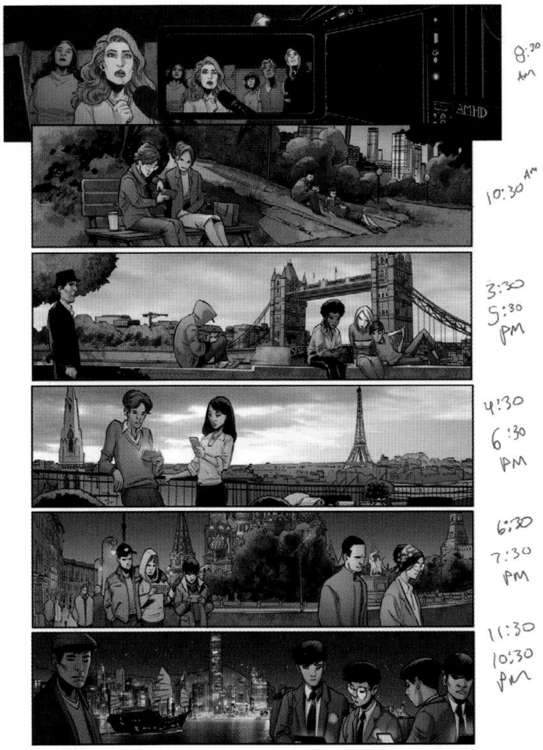
8:30 AM
10:30 AM
3:30 5:30 PM
4:30 6:30 PM
6:30 7:30 PM
11:30 10:30 PM

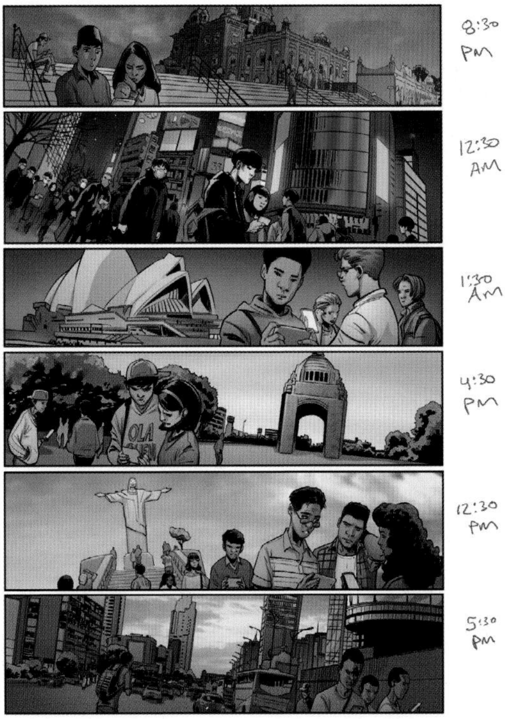
8:30 PM
12:30 AM
1:30 AM
4:30 PM
12:30 PM
5:30 PM